U-BOAT
ACE

Wolfgang Lüth

U-BOAT ACE

the story of WOLFGANG LÜTH

Jordan Vause

BLUEJACKET BOOKS

Naval Institute Press
Annapolis, Maryland

Naval Institute Press
291 Wood Road
Annapolis, MD 21402

First Bluejacket Books printing, 2001
ISBN 13: 978-1-55750-863-8

Library of Congress Cataloging-in-Publication Data

Vause, Jordan.
　　U-boat ace : the story of Wolfgang Lüth / Jordan Vause.
　　　　p.　　cm.
　　Originally published: Annapolis : Naval Institute Press, c1990.
　　Includes bibliographical references and index.
　　ISBN 1-55750-863-1 (alk. paper)
　　1. Lüth, Wolfgang. 2. World War, 1939–1945—Naval operations, Submarine.
3. World War, 1939–1945—Naval operations, German. 4. World War, 1939–1945—
Campaigns—North Atlantic Ocean. 5. Germany. Kriegsmarine—Biography.
6. Sailors—Germany—Biography. I. Title.

D784.G3 V38 2001
940.54′51—dc21   2001044541

Printed in the United States of America on acid-free paper ∞
10   9 8 7 6 5

CONTENTS

To Carmel

List of Equivalent Ranks (World War II)

Germany	United States
Obersteuermann	Chief helmsman, a senior enlisted rank of some importance*
Seekadett	Naval cadet*
Fähnrich zur See	Midshipman
Oberfähnrich zur See	Senior midshipman*
Leutnant zur See	Ensign
Oberleutnant zur See	Lieutenant (junior grade)
Kapitänleutnant ("Kaleu")	Lieutenant
Korvettenkapitän	Lieutenant commander
Fregattenkapitän	Commander
Kapitän zur See	Captain
Kommodore	Commodore (used only by a Kapitän zur See holding a flag officer's position)
Konteradmiral	Rear admiral
Vizeadmiral	Vice admiral
Admiral	Admiral
Generaladmiral	Navy equivalent of the German Army colonel general*
Grossadmiral	Fleet admiral

*No equivalent rank exists in the U.S. Navy.

FOREWORD

We of Lüth's generation were given two lives. In our first life we were hard-charging and reckless; in our second life, after a fall like that of Icarus, we became introverted, restrained, confused. We survived the fall, but we must bear responsibility for it. We are still trying to understand why it happened.

Wolfgang Lüth plunged into the darkness with us. I can see him during a last conversation shortly before his death, "with hollow cheeks and sunken eyes" like one of the figures in Rodin's "Burgesses of Calais," exhausted after years of siege, a rope already at his neck, delivered unconditionally into the hands of a merciless victor.

Lüth, like the knight Parsifal, died a young man, but his conduct and his achievements had won for him the respect of his men and the recognition of the world. Like Parsifal, he lived in harmony with the values, the norms, the rules of behavior dictated by his social and political environment. Loyalty, courage, honor, and country were the pillars of his life. Myths have grown up around these words, from the *Iliad* through the *Nibelungenlied* to Rilke's "Cornet"; the words are personified in the hero who stands up for them at the risk of his life, who errs, who suffers, yet who passes on his beliefs. Parsifal, the knight, the hero.

Lüth was not the knight of Dürer, accompanied by Death and Satan. He did not see the evil of the political state for which he lived and staked his life — the extent of its hubris, its perversion of values and virtues. He did not see that many of his traditional values were already gone, destroyed. He did not perceive the ambiguity of the state's skewed perspective, nor that of his own.

In the same way, many of the ideas that he presented and published, particularly those on leadership and personnel management, were shaped by circumstances and the spirit of the times.

Lüth's style of leadership was formed primarily by events far out of the ordinary in the U-boat war: long voyages to distant waters that lasted anywhere from two to seven months; a monotonous onboard routine; great but relatively easy success. His experience contrasted with that of others engaged in the terrible operations in the North Atlantic, where a man's life expectancy was about four months.

This style, which Lüth set forth in the lecture "Problems of Leadership," harmonized with his political surroundings. Thus the lecture attained the status of an ideological manual, the weight, almost, of an honor code at the German Naval Academy, whose commandant he became.

Once we know their limitations, we have to ask ourselves if his words can be accepted now as they were spoken then. It is as though one were looking into a kaleidoscope, glimpsing many-colored stones in a shifting mosaic. The stones represent the cardinal virtues, Lüth's virtues, of intelligence, moderation, courage, and justice. But when the kaleidoscope turns, another picture takes shape. The stones are the same, their effect different; they have been changed by their surroundings in some way.

Mankind has always had to live with the prospect of the apocalypse, the Götterdämmerung. The many-headed beasts from land and sea were always there, and the harnessing of nuclear power brings them that much closer. In place of a Parsifal, the ideal knight, therefore, we have the logician, the clear thinker who can lead his men with steady nerves, discrimination, and intelligent self-control.

From my acquaintance with Wolfgang Lüth, by tradition a Balt and a Prussian, and therefore combative but disciplined, I am sure he would have pursued this path had fate allowed him to survive.

*Erich Topp
Konteradmiral a.D.*

ERICH TOPP
KONTERADMIRAL A.D.

PREFACE

Most writers claim to have too many people to thank and too little space to do so. I am no exception to this unfortunate rule.

Information on the early part of Wolfgang Lüth's life is sketchy. Herr Franz Hahn, former director of the WGAZ, the museum of the Marineschule-Mürwik, and Lüth's niece, Dr. Vera Lüth Brown, were both helpful in filling the gaps. Wolfgang Lüth himself gave us a few biographical facts when his own book, *Boot Greift Wieder An,* was published during the war. His career from the time he entered the Reichsmarine until the beginning of the war is documented by records at the Deutsche Dienststelle in Berlin, which is fortunate, since his Marineschule and Reichsmarine records seem to have been lost for good.

The deck logs of Lüth's four boats, U-9, U-138, U-43, and U-181, are all available on microfilm at the National Archives in

Washington, D.C. They were of inestimable value, not because anything of Lüth himself can be read from them, but because they are the only record of his actions besides *Boot Greift Wieder An*. The book itself is surprisingly accurate. Covering a period of almost two years (through January 1942), it contradicts neither Lüth's deck logs nor Admiralty records, and men who served in his boats can verify many of the specific episodes he describes.

Lüth's crewmen are the primary source of information about him. At least a dozen contributed to this research, five of whom were interviewed in their homes. One or two men wanted nothing to do with this book, but most were helpful. I am deeply grateful to one officer in particular, Fregattenkapitän Theodor Petersen, for his patience and generosity over the years. Most of the photographs in the book were given me by crewmen. Both Petersen and Josef Dick surrendered their equator crossing certificates, and Dick provided a stack of U-181's old newspapers.

Wolfgang Lüth's lecture, "Problems of Leadership in a Submarine," can be found in German and English. Many books about the Battle of the Atlantic or about U-boats contain excerpts. I worked from an English version given me by Mr. Gus Britton of HMS *Dolphin*, but the translation (by the U.S. Navy Office of Intelligence) was not a good one and some passages had to be taken directly from the German original. Several source books deserve mention. *The Naval War Against Hitler* by Donald McIntyre and *War in the Southern Oceans* by L. C. F. Turner et al. were especially useful. Peter Padfield's *Dönitz: The Last Führer*, though controversial among members of the surviving U-boat community, was also good. Dönitz's autobiography, *Ten Years and Twenty Days*, is factual but self-serving and dull.

I would like to thank Dr. Jürgen Rohwer, who took the time to read and comment on the manuscript, and Admiral Erich Topp, who was good enough to write the forward to it. Special thanks go to Dr. Jack Sweetman and Mr. Dwight Messimer for their encouragement, and to my German teacher Mrs. Virginia Hunewill, wherever she is.

As for others who provided assistance, I regret that in many cases I was unable to find out the name behind the title or see the face behind the signature. The following individuals and organizations have my sincerest thanks: Frau Ilse Lüth, Kapitän zur See Ernst Bauer, Herr Jürgen Bialuch, Lieutenant-Commander Donald Crawford, RN, Flottillenadmiral Otto Kretschmer, Baron von Müllenheim-Rechberg, Korvettenkapitän Jürgen Oesten, Konteradmiral Karl Peter, and the staffs of the National Archives, the Public Records Office, the British Ministry of Defence, the Royal Navy Submarine Museum, the Deutsche Dienststelle, the Bibliothek für Zeitgeschichte, the Stiftung Traditionsarchiv Unterseeboote, the Marine Offizier Vereinigung, the Verband Deutscher U-Bootfahrer, the Danish Meteorological Office, the Berlin Document Center, and Schaltung-Küste.

INTRODUCTION

The Battle of the Atlantic — the series of conflicts between Allied navies and German U-boats fought primarily in the convoy lanes of the Atlantic Ocean — proceeded without quarter from the first day of World War II to the last. On 3 September 1939 Fritz-Julius Lemp, commanding U-30, sank the British passenger liner *Athenia*. On 7 May 1945 an RAF bomber dispatched U-320 off the west coast of Norway. Between those dates, according to most sources, U-boats sank some 2,800 Allied merchant ships of 14 million tons.

"Until [the Germans] were beaten" wrote Nicholas Monsarrat at one time, "they were total enthusiasts for world domination, wholehearted agents of a hideous tyranny which, if not finally checked, would have brought the curtain down on human freedom for generations to come . . . and among the worst of these willing servants of world enslavement were the men serving in German U-boats."[1] Half the world agreed.

But the U-Bootwaffe was not that simple, and it is no surprise that opinions about U-boats and the men who sailed in them are still divided today. Some people look upon U-boat sailors as heroes. Others consider them to have been no more than modern-day pirates. Today, almost fifty years after the last U-boat sank the last ship, the general view seems to be that the U-boat sailor had a dirty job to do and he did it very well. As Captain Richard Compton-Hall, RN, writes: "All war is murderous: that is its nature; and submariners were particularly skilled at dealing destruction and with it, necessarily, death. The Germans, as losers in both wars, saw their (very few) U-boat contraventions of the seaman's code proclaimed and punished whilst the Allies, as winners, were not arraigned. But any belief that there was some kind of clear-cut division between U-boat men and Allied submariners in their conduct is arguably untenable and invidious."[2]

The most successful and probably best-known U-boat ace of World War II was a man named Otto Kretschmer, who accounted for over a quarter million tons of enemy shipping in the space of eighteen months. Second only to him was Kapitän zur See Wolfgang Lüth. Lüth achieved the distinction of sinking 230,000 tons of shipping, almost fifty ships. He completed sixteen war patrols in four U-boats, and on his last patrol he was at sea a record 203 days. He was the first of two officers in the Kriegsmarine to receive the Reich's highest award for valor, the Knight's Cross with Diamonds, and when he became commandant of the German Naval Academy in August 1944 he was thirty years old — the youngest full captain on the books.

Wolfgang Lüth did a dirty job well. More correctly, he did his job well most of the time, badly some of the time. For behind the glitter and impressive numbers there moved an intriguing, elusive, contradictory figure, a man whose combination of strengths and imperfections seemed to encapsulate the paradox of the careers led by so many U-boat commanders, men spawned by the Nazi regime they served and yet not entirely of it.

I will warn you now: You may not like what you read about Lüth. He was a Nazi. He advertised it, loudly and often. He could be prudish and petty, cruel sometimes. His best friend in the Kriegsmarine went so far as to say that Lüth had no idea of the misery he so often inflicted on the crews of sunken ships, nor did he care.

Lüth did have one remarkable virtue. Not bravery so much, not brilliance, but this: He cared for his men. He watched over them like a stern but well-intentioned German father, and his concern did not stop at the brow of his boat. From the day a sailor reported aboard to the last day of the war, wherever he was, whatever he did, however he sinned, that sailor was the valued ward of Kapitän zur See Wolfgang Lüth.

The result is an odd imbalance of achievement and notoriety that the following pages are unlikely to change. History could not make up its mind about Wolfgang Lüth—whether he was good or bad, whether he was a hero or a villain, whether he was worth mentioning at all.

I think he was. You must decide for yourself.

U-BOAT
ACE

1

PREPARATION

An early spring day in the North Atlantic, nothing in sight except the sea and the clouds. The sea was black and quietly speckled with moonlight, and the gray clouds only half concealed the stars in the sky. It was cold, very cold.

U-43 was four days out of port. The lookouts, four of them, yawned as they scanned the horizon in every direction. They were tired and they were wet, but still they stood and watched. They watched the water not for its beauty but for ships, the clouds not for birds but for bombers. The North Atlantic in 1941 was a killing ground. They were the hunters; they were the quarry.

"Ship!" called one of them suddenly. "Red Six O." He pointed and the three beside him turned and looked. "I see it," said another with a quiet whistle of amazement. Not a tanker, this one, not a tired old tramp; she was a fully rigged sailing ship, a big three-masted schooner. He called down the alarm.

Almost at once another man emerged. He had a dirty white cap on his head and a cigar in his mouth. "Good," he shouted, clapping his hand on the lookout's back, eyes following the boy's outstretched arm. "What do you have for me?"

The boy grinned proudly. "A sailing ship, *Herr Kaleu.*" Wolfgang Lüth raised his binoculars. From the distant darkness the ship approached him soundlessly, a spirit of the sea. "About a mile," he said through his cigar. "Very pretty."

Two officers had followed Lüth up to the bridge. Hans-Joachim Schwantke, his second watch officer, had a look. "She is a pretty ship," he agreed. The second man, a *Konfirmand*, a commander in training along only for the one patrol, asked if they were going to sink her.

"Of course," replied Lüth impatiently. "But she isn't worth a torpedo. Schwantke, call away the gun crews. All of them. Get Becker up here. Let's give him something to shoot at."

The word was passed. A mad invisible scramble ensued belowdecks, then the gunners came up. They climbed down and out to the guns, putting on their lifejackets and buckling themselves into their lifelines. Boxes of ammunition were taken from the magazines and placed in the control room. The men formed a human chain from the control room to the bridge and from there to the gun mounts, ferrying up the boxes hand to hand. The bridge watch was doubled. Gunnery Officer Richard Becker and *Obersteuermann* Theodor Petersen appeared, Becker with glasses so that he could spot, Petersen with a megaphone so that he could relay Becker's commands to the gun crews.

The sailing ship waited serenely; she and U-43 were now only 500 meters apart. "Watch," said Lüth to the Konfirmand at his elbow. "I'm going to give the order to fire and when I do there'll be hell on that ship." Lüth stared at the sailing ship completely absorbed as the ammunition boxes were passed up around his legs.

"Clear for firing!" called Becker from the weather deck.

Lüth kept his eyes on the ship. He hesitated briefly, then cried, "Open fire!"

With a roar and a flash, the 105-mm cannon forward of the tower opened up on the sailing ship. The first shot was short; the second misfired. "Damn!" hissed Becker. The 20-mm machine gun in the bridge wouldn't fire either. "Wet ammunition," someone remarked laconically.

The silence resumed as U-43 moved closer to her target. A new box of 20-mm shells came up the chain. In flagrant disregard of established procedure the faulty shell was extracted from the cannon, carried hot across the deck, and tossed overboard. A new one was loaded.

"Clear for firing," called Becker, this time not so loudly.

The cannon roared again, then a bang and a stutter heralded the two after guns, a machine gun in the bridge and a 37-mm gun on the main deck aft. The gun crews in U-43 were stale but they had no trouble finding their range. The schooner was almost on top of them and the first shot from the cannon hit her pilot house. It collapsed in a puff of smoke.

Now the besieged ship came alive, men pouring from her smoking interior. "Look" shouted someone in the bridge, "they're trying to launch their boats." The third shot started a fire on the schooner's decks. It spread quickly up the masts and into the rigging, burning hard and roaring higher with each additional shell until the entire ship was aflame.

No effort was made to save her. Two lifeboats got away safely, floating in a sea made orange by ashes and embers raining down from the sky. A column of smoke rose above the burning deck and into the clouds. "The foremast is going," called a voice after several minutes. "The mizzenmast . . ."

"Like the Flying Dutchman," the Konfirmand said nervously, but Lüth didn't hear him. At that moment a freak wave swept up and over the U-43's tower. As it subsided, so did the deafening sound of the U-boat's three guns. Turning toward the 105-mm cannon, Lüth saw that it was unmanned. The wave had washed one of its crew straight over the side. He was hanging by his lifeline and the rest were struggling to pull him in.

"What the hell are you doing?" Lüth screamed into the spray, jabbing a finger at the bonfire in the distance. "Keep shooting and let that bastard swim!"

"One of ours, Herr Kaleu," Schwantke told him quickly.
The gunners hauled their shipmate back on board and scamp-
ered to their posts. The gun resumed firing, one round every
minute with a high explosive followed by an incendiary. Meanwhile the two after guns continued with their driving barrage.
And they continued for almost an hour. The gun crews were
soaked with sweat. Their backs hurt, their arms ached. The
sailing ship was burning at the waterline, smoke billowing
from her shattered hull. She was dying. After a while she
rolled gently on her side. And still Lüth's guns fired into the
tangled wreckage, round after round, as she burned and he
watched and all the men labored.[1]

What happened in the last six years of Wolfgang Lüth's life,
the war years, is as clear as the image of that ship he set burning one night in May 1941. The war itself has seen to it. His
first twenty years are more obscure: "I was born on 15 October
1913, in Riga (Russia), the son of August Lüth. During the
war I lived with my mother and my four brothers and sisters
in Breslau, while my father was interned in Siberia. In 1921 we
returned to Riga. I was educated there and completed my *Abi-
tur* [exams] at a German high school, and I entered the German Navy in early 1933. in late 1936 I was promoted to
Leutnant zur See, and in 1937 I entered the *U-Bootwaffe* as a
watch officer. . . ."[2] This single, sparse paragraph was written
in 1942; it is what Lüth himself thought worth mentioning
about his life. A few details can be added. Lüth was the fourth
son and youngest child of August and Elfriede Lüth. His
father operated a small business in Riga, a factory that produced fine knitwear. His grandfather Friedrich, for whom the
business was named, had started it after moving east from
Lübeck in the mid-nineteenth century. Among August Lüth's
customers was the Imperial Russian Army; Russian soldiers
may have been wearing Friedrich Lüth's clothing when World
War I began in 1914. Nevertheless, August Lüth was interned
in Siberia and his family evacuated to Breslau for seven years.
From the day they returned in 1921 until the day Wolfgang
Lüth entered the navy in 1933, he lived in Riga. He was edu-

cated at the local *Gymnasium* until 1927, getting his *Reifezeugnis,* the equivalent of a high-school diploma, in 1929, and entering the prestigious Gottfried Herder Institute in 1931 to study law.[3] His career seemed assured. Then, on 1 April 1933, only two months after Adolf Hitler became chancellor of Germany, Lüth left the institute to join the *Reichsmarine.*

He reported on that day to Stralsund, on the Baltic coast southeast of Denmark, and was assigned as a recruit to a small, scrubby island called Dänholm for basic infantry training. Stralsund was the first stage in the well-established, comprehensive training program for German naval officers; it was designed to ensure that only the best would make it to the second stage.

The three-month training at Stralsund was hard, conducted much like a modern-day boot camp. The recruits were treated as soldiers. They dressed in field gray, boots, and helmets, and they were issued rifles (all sailors, whether fresh recruits or not, were regarded primarily as soldiers in the *Wehrmacht*). They lived in barracks, drilled on parade fields, ran in formation, and scrambled through obstacle courses while drill instructors screamed at them. Not until they had successfully completed basic training were the new recruits even allowed to wear a naval uniform. Wolfgang Lüth completed the course.

After Stralsund came three months of training under sail, and for this Lüth was sent to the Reichsmarine training ship *Gorch Fock.* It would be interesting to know more about this stage of Lüth's life. The experience of sailing on a tall ship is something a man never forgets, and it certainly has a formative effect on his career. Unfortunately there is no record of Lüth's performance in the *Gorch Fock,* or at Stralsund for that matter. Everything was lost or destroyed in the war.

To imagine him as a young seaman, one must draw on information from more informal sources. Lüth probably looked much as he did in later photographs. He was of medium height, slender, with blue eyes and a rather large nose. Perhaps he had more hair in his youth; during the war he was bald except for a band of hair around his head that made him look like a tonsured monk. His smile revealed a wide gap between his two front teeth. When he let his beard go during long war patrols, it grew from the jawline and left his cheeks bare. He was distinctive rather than handsome—once at a lecture on racial theory he was told he had the typical elongated head and facial features of the Bavarian nobility. This amused him to no end.[4]

Several members of Crew 33 remembered Lüth as a young man. Jürgen Oesten, also a successful U-boat commander, thought him quiet, almost introverted. He was not a cheerful person, but he did not lack for humor. "Lüth was a Balt," wrote Oesten without elaboration, as if this simple fact of his birth explained everything about him.[5] Perhaps it did.

Riga was a major Baltic port and a primary outlet for products like Russian lumber and furs. Merchant ships left its docks every day for Western Europe and beyond. The Germans had lived in Riga since the days of the Teutonic knights; they were responsible for its position as a trading center since the days of the Hanseatic League, four centuries later. By 1913 the German community represented a large section of Riga's population.

Riga was also the capital of Latvia, a small Baltic province of the vast and decaying Russian Empire. When Lüth was born in 1913, Russia was celebrating 300 years of Romanov rule, the last 50 years of which were a trying experience for the Baltic states in general and for the German community of Riga in particular. Friedrich Lüth had arrived in Riga just at the inception of Tsar Alexander III's policies of "russification," that is, his systematic search for and destruction of all that was foreign to Russian culture and tradition. Although Latvia and the two other Baltic states, Lithuania and Estonia, were given their independence at the end of the war, repression did not end. The old policy of russification became the new one of "latvianization"—a more benign form of persecution, but similar in its ends.

A large number of Baltic Germans, including the Lüths, were nevertheless determined to stay. To live in Riga as a German, in a society within a society and continually under siege, was bound to have its effect upon a young man like Wolfgang

Lüth. Most people who knew him agree; and his Baltic roots are usually invoked when he is discussed. In particular, it may explain his wholesale embrace of National Socialism.

During Lüth's childhood the German nation had been transformed. The old empire was gone, swept away in World War I. Germany had been defeated in battle, humiliated by the terms of peace, and bankrupted by the awful reparations it was forced to pay. It had been divided physically, and without having moved a step many of its citizens now lived in foreign, often hostile, countries. The republican leaders of postwar Germany tried to restore their people's vanquished pride and national identity, but in this they failed. By the time Lüth entered law school, Germany was heading toward National Socialism. Both he and his country had been ready to accept it for some time.

National Socialism lifted the banner of a united German nation, the elusive Grossdeutschland in which all true Germans dwelt and from which all minorities, undesirables, and non-Germans were to be excluded. Presumably this nation would include the German-speaking regions of Eastern Europe. Those who had persecuted the German people within their own boundaries — including Latvia and certainly the Soviet Union — could expect to be punished. National Socialism offered a remedy to the shame of Versailles, an injustice that was never really in dispute and that grated on Germans outside as well as inside the fatherland's official boundaries.

Apparently, the new doctrine was accepted with various degrees of enthusiasm in the family of August Lüth.[6] Wolfgang himself wholeheartedly embraced National Socialism; this is evident in his later writings. It was probably no coincidence that he entered the service so soon after a National Socialist government was formed in Germany.

After his training in the *Gorch Fock,* Lüth was sent to the light cruiser *Karlsruhe,* a training ship in which cadets of the Reichsmarine became, for a while, ordinary seamen. That they should experience the "other side" of life in the navy and thus better understand those whom they would eventually have to command was considered necessary for officer candidates. Lüth embarked on 23 September 1933, newly promoted to *Seekadett*. Between October 1933 and June 1934, as he and his classmates toiled on her deck plates and in her engine rooms, the *Karlsruhe* sailed around the globe, from Germany, through the Straits of Gibraltar and the Mediterranean Sea, to Aden, Calcutta, Brisbane, Honolulu, and Boston.

The cruise aboard the *Karlsruhe* was probably the greatest learning experience of Wolfgang Lüth's life. During those eight months he walked the streets of port after port, where he came face to face with his future enemies—men who were friendly, men who had families like his, and men who were as prepared to die as he. An unpublished Kriegsmarine manuscript describing the training of a German naval officer had this to say about world cruises of German ships: "Of other nations and always outside the vision of one's own, the young seaman stands as a representative of his people. He knows that his country is judged as he is judged, and he therefore recognizes early on the importance of strict self-discipline and an increased sense of personal responsibility. The impressions he gets of other lands and other peoples, their circumstances, their opinions and peculiarities, teach him to look upon his own country with so much the greater love."[7]

The *Karlsruhe* returned to Germany on 6 June 1934 and soon thereafter an examination was given to Crew 33. Those who failed it were through; those who passed were promoted to midshipman and sent to the Marineschule for training as commissioned officers.

The Marineschule-Mürwik, where officer candidates of the Reichsmarine received their formal training, was an almost mystical place; the Red Castle by the Sea, they called it, or simply *Mutterhaus*. "It is the place where every military virtue is found in its purest form; where every military concept is used as a tool of education," wrote one German admiral during the war. "Her effect, her influence, in the German Navy is without bound, since she is the first and most important source of every officer's training and since every officer will pass on to those he will command, that which she has taught to him."[8]

The red-brick buildings and three-spired clock tower of the Marineschule-Mürwik overlook the approaches to Flensburg

The Marineschule-Mürwik (the German Naval Academy). Every officer candidate received his formal education here, and every officer carried something of it with him for the rest of his life. Lüth attended the Marineschule in 1934/35, and for him, more than most, it was hard to leave. (Courtesy Marineschule-Mürwik)

Harbor on the east side of the Jutland peninsula. The name Mürwik comes from a small suburb of Flensburg beyond the gates. It is a beautiful and historic place, founded in 1910 by the kaiser himself who, flighty and superficial as he was, saw clearly the need for a strong German navy and well-trained officer corps. The inside of the main building is like a museum, with glass-encased exhibits, busts, paintings, flags, banners, and life preservers from the glory days. There is a memorial hall where the heroes and the dead of German navies are honored. A general economy of ornament prevails; the whitewashed halls and rooms are as shipshape and spartan as the warships themselves in which the school's graduates served out their careers.

Wolfgang Lüth entered the Mutterhaus in June 1934. Before him lay ten months of education in strategy and tactics, seamanship and navigation, marine engineering, gunnery, and naval history. Along with these courses came training in riding, fencing, gymnastics, sailing, riflery, etiquette, and naval courtesy and tradition—in short, every subject required of a soldier, an officer, and a gentleman.

In April 1935, one month after Adolf Hitler formally repudiated the Treaty of Versailles, Lüth completed his course of study at the Marineschule and was administered the *Offiziershauptprüfung*, the comprehensive final examination that not only measured achievement but also established initial rank in the fleet. A series of service schools—torpedo, antisubmarine, and coast artillery—followed. Then his formal training ended, and he was posted to the fleet.

In December 1935, Lüth reported to the cruiser *Königsberg*. He was not yet commissioned. The officers of the ship to which he was assigned would decide among themselves after a suitable period of observation whether to commission him or not, and in fact he carried out all the normal duties of a junior officer in the *Königsberg* for ten months before being promoted to Leutnant zur See.

He was included by name in the manning report of November 1936 as one of the officers on board, but any specific duties he may have been assigned were not listed. According to Ernst Bauer, who served in the *Königsberg* with Lüth, he was a division officer and a *FLAK-Leiter*, an officer in charge of one or more of the *Königsberg*'s antiaircraft gun turrets. In light of later events, we may assume that this was a billet he very much liked.[9]

Bauer said nothing about how well Lüth performed that job. Again, records from this time are scarce, and any idea of a man's progress has to be either gathered secondhand or interpolated from available data. The first real measure we have of his performance, and it is only a relative measure, is the number he was assigned when commissioned in October 1936. At that time Lüth ranked 32 out of the 115 officers in Crew 33. This took into account a variety of factors—the results of examinations the new officers had to take, their performance at sea and in school, and evaluations by their seniors—and was used to determine rank and relative seniority. A man's number was a useful indicator of his past performance, not of his future potential.

Lüth was one of 123 men sworn in on the Dänholm in spring 1933. Eight had gone since then. Among those left were a few who would become famous in the war, most of them as U-boat aces: Ernst Bauer, Günther Heydemann, Hans Jenisch, Günther Krech, Jürgen Oesten, Reinhard Hardegen, and Herbert Wohlfahrt. A few would achieve a measure of renown because of some specific event they were involved in, for example, Gerd Suhren, the first chief engineer in the U-Bootwaffe to win the Knight's Cross. And a few others had names already well known: von Stulpnagel, von Trotha, Lüdde-Neurath.

They are the famous. But most of the names—March, Balser, Linder, Otten, Kasch, Klug—never were. Their short German surnames fill the roster like the proud recruits they once were. Now that roster serves only to remind us that fame is a fickle thing. Ninety percent of Crew 33 disappeared in the obscurity of time. March was ranked first in his class in 1936, Balser number two. Wolfgang Lüth, on the other hand, just barely hovered in the top third, and Ernst Bauer, probably the second most successful man in Crew 33, was ranked fifty-first.

When the *Karlsruhe* left Kiel Harbor on her world cruise in 1933, she created a minor sensation by flying a brand-new red, white, and black swastika ensign. Apparently, her captain had acted on his own in hoisting it.[10]

This was the banner that would become a universal symbol of evil, a harbinger of death, a piece of cloth looked on with a hatred perhaps unprecedented in the history of mankind. But in 1934 the ensign held no such connotation; it was a glorious thing, a symbol of victory. In hoisting the swastika, the *Karlsruhe* announced the rebirth of the German Navy.

The Reichsmarine Wolfgang Lüth entered in 1933 was small and insignificant compared with the fleets of Germany's old enemies. The proud Imperial Fleet that had battled the Royal Navy to a standoff at Jutland in 1916 was no more. It had died in Scapa Flow.* The navy of the Weimar Republic, the product of Versailles, was a humble and insufficient substitute. The terms of the treaty had allowed Germany to keep six battleships and six cruisers. These could be replaced only by newer, smaller ships. All naval aircraft were banned. A number of smaller craft could be retained, but no submarines — Germany's old policy of unrestricted submarine warfare against Great Britain and its allies had not sat well with them. These were material restrictions. In one respect they did not matter, because for many years after the war it was fiscally impossible for Germany to keep a navy even of this size. There was, however, the psychological factor. The Imperial Fleet had lived a short but glorious life; many episodes in the war at sea were a source of pride to World War I veterans. And so when that swastika was flown in 1933 from the decks of the *Karlsruhe*, it signaled the reappearance of the German Navy. Whatever it came to mean later, at this point in time it erased the ignominy of surrender and defeat.

In June 1935 Germany and Great Britain concluded the Anglo-German Naval Treaty, a tacit recognition by the two countries that the restrictions of Versailles could no longer be enforced. The treaty allowed the construction of a larger surface fleet, one that reflected more accurately the new position of Germany among nations. It also allowed Germany for the first time to build submarines.

The submarines had actually been built already; they had only to be assembled. Almost immediately after the treaty was signed, the first German U-boat flotilla of the postwar period was created with six small units. Admiral Erich Raeder, commander in chief of the newly rechristened Kriegsmarine, selected Karl Dönitz, former captain of the cruiser *Emden,* to be its commanding officer. By the end of the year twenty-two submarines

---

*At the end of World War I, the ships of the German Fleet were scuttled by their crews in Scapa Flow as the only honorable alternative to surrendering them. Reaction in Great Britain was understandably negative at first, but gradually people came to see it as "the right thing to do" under the circumstances, and probably something the Royal Navy itself would have done.

Grossadmiral Karl Dönitz, Commander-in-Chief, U-boats. Dönitz was given command of Germany's first postwar U-boat squadrons in 1935. For the next ten years he directed German U-boat operations: after 1943 as Commander-in-Chief of the German Navy, and after Adolf Hitler's death in 1945 as Führer. Karl Dönitz was charged at Nuremberg with war crimes, almost certainly because of his military success. Fairly or not, he was convicted and served ten years in Spandau prison. (Courtesy Roger Bender)

had been commissioned, and Dönitz was in command of them all. His title in 1935 was Führer der U-Boote (leader, U-boats). In 1939 he would become Befehlshaber der U-Boote (commander in chief, U-boats), or more simply, BdU, a title used for both his position and his office.

The formation of Dönitz's new command was the event that finally determined Lüth's career and his life, for in February 1937 he left the *Königsberg* to enter the new U-Bootwaffe. No one can say why he made the move. Perhaps Dönitz asked him; Dönitz often did ask young officers point-blank to come join his new service, and there was no refusing him. Perhaps Lüth succumbed to the allure of the U-Bootwaffe; it was an exciting place to be in those days, the posters depicting dashing officers on gleaming new boats beneath streaming pennants, aircraft flying overhead in formation. Maybe he didn't care for the *Königsberg* or the surface navy in general. Maybe he made his move in response to a dare.

Whatever the reason, it meant another seventeen months of training. Lüth first had to attend the submarine school in Neustadt/Holstein for nine months, from April 1937 to January 1938, then torpedo school again until May. He was promoted to *Oberleutnant* on 1 June 1938, and in July — five years after entering the Reichsmarine, three years after joining the fleet, and two years after being commissioned — Wolfgang Lüth reported to U-27 as a second watch officer.

U-27 was a type VII oceangoing submarine of 500 tons. Over 600 VIIs were eventually built, making it the most ubiquitous boat of the war. No doubt Lüth quickly adjusted to life on board — the close quarters; the constant noise; the smells of diesel oil, moldy food, sweat, and chlorine gas; and the grinding ritual of standing watch, eating, sleeping as best you could, then standing watch again. It was a life described by many on the outside as awful, even hellish, but as Dönitz himself once wrote, "Every submariner felt himself to be as rich as a king and would trade places with no man."[11]

The men Lüth worked with were a separate breed, different from their counterparts in surface ships. U-boat sailors took fierce pride in their work, in the hazards and discomforts it entailed. They believed they were the best men in the Kriegsmarine. Their loyalties were more likely to lie with their boat and her officers — if these officers deserved it — rather than with the nation, the navy, or the Reich. At the end of the day, they could make or break a new Leutnant zur See like Wolfgang Lüth.

Lüth made two patrols in U-27, both of them in the summer and early fall of 1938, and both of them for the most part along the coast of Spain. Since Spain was still in the throes of a bloody civil war (a war in which Germany participated), this patrol was not far removed from combat duty, and in fact Lüth won his first medal, a bronze Spanish Cross, while serving in U-27.

During the second patrol, U-27 almost found herself in a real war. In September Adolf Hitler demanded that Germany be permitted to occupy German-speaking portions of western Czechoslovakia. It was the start of the Sudetenland Crisis, and U-27, along with the rest of the German fleet, was put on full war alert.

Hitler's demand sent a shudder through the German High Command; no one believed that Great Britain and France would stand idly by, even less that they would back down. It smelled of war, one Germany could not win and should not fight. Of course members of the High Command expressed these concerns to Hitler, so that when his demand was met, the Sudetenland given to him, it only lessened their prestige in his eyes and confirmed his own low regard for their opinions. In a roundabout way, however, the events of September 1938 were beneficial for the Kriegsmarine, especially the U-Bootwaffe.

Before the Sudetenland Crisis, Hitler had chosen not to regard Great Britain as a potential enemy. He observed the terms of the Anglo-German Naval Treaty and, in fact, did not even build to treaty limits; the size of the Kriegsmarine remained small in relation both to the Royal Navy and to the rapidly expanding German Army and *Luftwaffe*.* But after the crisis was resolved, Hitler told Raeder to expect war with Britain, sometime in the future, no sooner than 1944.

In January 1939, therefore, an ambitious new naval construction program, the Z Plan, was submitted and approved. The Z Plan would build a fleet which, although still not equal to Great Britain's, would stand Germany in good stead if a conflict broke out. Expansion was projected across the board, and the U-Bootwaffe fared especially well: Dönitz was promised almost 250 U-boats by 1948.

*In fact, before 1939 German yards were incapable of building more ships than the treaty allowed.

But 1948 was ten years away. Clearly, the Z Plan was a long-term undertaking; it ruled out the prospect of general war for at least five years. Of course, if war were to break out sooner than that the outlook for the navy was grim, not to mention the prospects for the nation; *"finis Germaniae,"* Dönitz wrote. But Hitler vowed to Raeder that such a thing would never happen.

This was a false promise. As the year 1939 rolled on it became increasingly clear that something, sooner or later, *would* happen. Hitler, lulled by his perception of the West as complacent and weak, made one rash move after another. Germany occupied western Czechoslovakia in March. This violated the agreement the Führer himself had made only six months before and prompted Great Britain and France to issue a guarantee to Poland, the country most likely next on Hitler's list, that if it were invaded, they would declare war on Germany.

In April Hitler unilaterally renounced the Anglo-German Naval Treaty. In August, Germany and the Soviet Union made a shocking announcement: The two countries had signed a mutual nonaggression pact.

Now it was only a matter of time. War was in the air and most people knew it. Fewer people knew that war would break out in a matter of days, even hours, or that the forces of the Reich were assembling even as the German leaders paraded the prospect of a lasting peace.

Wolfgang Lüth was not one of those privileged few who knew the day and the hour. Whether he desired war, or even suspected that it was imminent, is an open question. Surely he did not know that the coming war would make him a hero. And surely he did not know that while he would live to see the end of the war, the war would kill him along with Germany.

ALL BEGINNINGS
ARE DIFFICULT

Tuesday, 22 September 1914. Europe was at war.

It was for the most part a land war. There had been skirmishes at sea, the clash of warships Victorian style, the odd sinking now and again. But the huge fleets kept apart for fear of being sunk or courting undue risk. The North Sea, the water that separated the warring nations, lapped quietly on its shores.

Three large warships of the Royal Navy were in the North Sea that September day, sailing off the Dutch coast through the choppy gray waters of the Broad Fourteens. They proceeded slowly, deliberately, in a line as straight as a ruler's edge. Though on patrol, they looked like nothing so much as three huge and mindless dinosaurs plodding through the mists of a primeval swamp, oblivious to the forces that would soon sweep them into extinction.

HMS *Aboukir, Cressy,* and *Hogue* had indeed been made old by the world's new navies. Destined for the breakers, they were serving out their last days as patrol vessels in the North Sea — well out of harm's way, so far out in fact that they carried crews of old men, Royal Navy reservists, and cadets from Osborne. The war, the enemy, and the threat of attack seemed remote. It was morning, and most of the men were thinking about breakfast. When the unthinkable happened, they had time only to be surprised.

At about 0600, the bridge watch in the *Aboukir* heard an explosion and felt their ship lurch to one side. Soon the old warship was settling, and as she ground to an awkward stop in the water a cacophony of voices filtered up from below. "A mine," someone said, "we've been hit by a mine!" "A boiler has exploded!" "A magazine's blown, we're taking on water!"

In fact, it was a torpedo from the German submarine U-9, which lay just below the surface to the north. Her captain, a young Kapitänleutnant named Otto Weddigen, watched the sinking ship through his periscope. This was Weddigen's first patrol in U-9. He had taken her out to sea the day after his marriage, eager "for any undertaking that promised to do for the imperial navy what our brothers in the army were so gloriously accomplishing."[1] He had been waiting for just this opportunity.

The *Hogue* and the *Cressy* approached the stricken *Aboukir.* Her crew was abandoning ship, hundreds of them already flailing about in the water waiting for boats to pick them up. Weddigen could not believe it. The English, he wrote later, were playing his game, and he would not even have to leave his position. He began another run, this time on the *Hogue.*

The tragedy for the three ships was that war was a game, an age-old game played by age-old rules, one of them being that you did not fire on a combatant engaged in rescue operations. The *Aboukir* was sinking, whether from a mine or a torpedo her crew did not know. A fair hit, but now the game had ended. There was a winner and a loser. The *Hogue* and the *Cressy* were off-limits.

But then the *Hogue* was hit twice, starboard amidships. She leapt right out of the water at the force of the blow, to the men of the *Cressy* looking like a horse that had been viciously spurred, or a steel spring that had been held at one end and struck at the other. She hung there for several minutes, then rolled over and smashed her port lifeboat, killing hundreds. Black smoke poured from a giant hole in her hull.

By now the *Aboukir* had also turned turtle and naked crewmen were scrambling desperately up her sunlit, red copper bottom. It was clear to everyone that a torpedo attack was under way, and yet the *Cressy* stood dead in the water, her boats lingering to pull men from the sea.

Her crew readied for a hit. All hatches were secured, all watertight doors closed. Tables and chairs were cast overboard so that men in the water could cling to them. The crew, as was the practice then, began to take their clothes off. In their minds they could see periscopes everywhere. The gunners among them opened fire on the water. A piece of wreckage was hit, dead on, and the men on the railings cheered loudly. Then someone spotted another periscope in the opposite direction. There were at least three distinct sightings reported afterwards and at least one sinking. But U-9 was neither seen nor sunk, and as the men cried and clapped Weddigen began his first run on their ship.

Her starboard bow was hit twice. She rolled over in less than ten minutes, and for a brief moment all three ships were flashing red copper to the sun. Then slowly, one after the other, they went under. Before breakfast in London, the sea was rid of them—three old cruisers carrying almost 1,500 men and boys.[2]

Weddigen returned to Kiel unseen and unscathed. He was given the sort of reception usually reserved for royalty. The kaiser awarded him the Iron Cross, and U-9's crew painted another, larger cross on her conning tower.

Weddigen died at sea only six months later. He soon became a legend, a paladin in sepia. When a second U-9 was commissioned in 1935 and then a third in 1967, the Iron Cross of Otto Weddigen was prominent on both of their conning towers.

Weddigen's action in U-9 heralded the age of modern submarine warfare. The sinking of those three old cruisers in 1914 changed the nature of war—not in degree, but in kind. Before

Otto Weddigen — the ideal. In 1914 Weddigen sank three British armored cruisers in one hour as captain of the first U-9. For this he was awarded the Iron Cross by Kaiser Wilhelm II, and his crew promptly painted a much larger cross on the conning tower of his boat. Weddigen died at sea in March 1915, a hero and a legend that nobody, not even Wolfgang Lüth, could hope to recreate. (Courtesy Horst Bredow)

his patrol, the U-boat was viewed as an evil toy and submarine warfare a frivolous sideshow; afterwards, it was feared as the most dangerous weapon of the war. It could have been *the* decisive weapon of World War I if its true potential had been recognized early on.

Weddigen was also the first U-boat ace. The U-boat ace would be as celebrated in his own circles as the air ace was in his — not as flashy perhaps, and certainly more hated, but celebrated nonetheless. As the war went on Weddigen was followed by a stream of other names, among them Otto Hersing, Walther Forstmann, Max Valentiner, Otto Steinbrinck, Walther Schwieger (the man who sank the *Lusitania*), and Lothar von Arnauld de la Perière (the man who accounted for more tonnage than anyone in history to this day). The list grew considerably during World War II as dozens of new aces were created. Kapitänleutnant Heinrich Liebe, the captain of U-38, was one of them.

Wolfgang Lüth reported to U-38 on 24 October 1938. This duty would last eleven months, during which time the war broke out. He had been assigned as her first watch officer. It was a promotion, an increase in responsibility, an unspoken sign that he was considered worthy of command, and that, if he didn't fail miserably, he would eventually get his own U-boat. The position of first watch officer, comparable to that of executive officer or first officer in other navies, was a significant one, suggesting that even in 1938 Lüth was being groomed for a command of his own. He was expected by this time to have mastered all the necessary skills. Although it was not likely in peacetime, more than once during the war an officer in his position would have to take command after the loss or disability of the captain. The first watch officer was also the navigator and torpedo officer, and often Lüth found himself immersed in routine affairs that the captain himself did not want to administer.

U-38 was larger than U-27, a type IXA oceangoing boat of 750 official "treaty" tons. She lay lower in the water than U-27. Her lines were cleaner and sleeker, and she was equipped with eleven more torpedoes and an extra gun. She had the capacity, at least in theory, to steam 8,000 nautical miles and back again without refueling, and she carried a crew of fifty.

Her commanding officer was the only man to whom Lüth would be subordinate. Heinrich Liebe was one of the best, or so he would be after all the numbers were added up. By the end of the war he would have sunk thirty ships, won both the Knight's Cross and the less common Oak Leaves, and survived.

Nevertheless, Liebe was a fawn-eyed, jug-eared pedant who possessed neither the charisma nor the dash to be a media hero like many less successful men. He was an "ass," in the words of Wolfgang Lüth. The two did not get along. It may have been a clash of egos, not uncommon in the U-Bootwaffe, or it may have started with some unpleasant incident that was left to fester. According to one of Lüth's officers, the problem was simply that Liebe was a stickler for detail, and Lüth, even at that stage in his career, tended to overlook details in order to concentrate on results.[3]

Aside from the log of U-38, only one other document tells us about the boat and Lüth's experiences on board. Much later in his career, after he had been assigned permanently to shore in 1943, Lüth published *Boot Greift Wieder An* ("The Boat Attacks Again," a title that loses most of its zing in the translation). He collaborated on it with Kapitänleutnant Claus Korth and at least one ghost writer from the Reich propaganda office. It is a simple recounting of the more memorable events in Lüth's and Korth's wartime careers.

Boot Greift Wieder An was supposed to be propaganda, but neither the manner in which it was written nor the events Lüth wrote about seem particularly biased. Most of them can be verified easily against Allied and German sources, and much of the anecdotal material is confirmed by ex-crew members today. The book ends in early 1942; the first two chapters cover the actions of U-38 during September 1939.

The account begins immediately after U-38 received the signal from BdU to commence hostilities. She had been at sea since 19 August 1939, in an assigned sector of the eastern Atlantic, due west of Portugal. "I was watch officer in one of the most modern German submarines," Lüth wrote. "The captain was Kapitänleutnant Liebe, who later won the Oak Leaves." He never mentioned U-38's number, nor, for reasons of security, did he identify any other boats mentioned. "We were already at sea and had succeeded in avoiding every warship and merchant we had sighted. . . . Reports about the Polish situation became increasingly serious, and we were wondering now what England would do." Not just Lüth or Liebe, either. On 1 September German air and ground forces invaded Poland; the entire Reich was waiting, wondering whether Adolf Hitler had made another brilliant bluff or whether the Western powers would finally react to him.[4]

Hitler lost; his enemies reacted. Great Britain, obligated by treaty to defend Poland and having received no response from Berlin to the demand that the operation cease and Germany withdraw its forces, declared war two days later. On 3 September 1939 U-38 received this message: "England has declared war. Submarines attack! Commerce war according to Prize Regulations." About the same time another signal was sent out — by the Admiralty to all units of the Royal Navy. Being uncoded, many German ships intercepted it. Perhaps U-38 did. "Total Germany," it said. That was all, but it was everything.

Dönitz heard it, and Raeder; they were shattered. The worst had happened: the war that Hitler had guaranteed would not begin before 1944 had just begun, and the Kriegsmarine was not ready. The U-boat admiral had less than sixty serviceable boats; he was heard to remark glumly that it was going to be a long war and that Germany would not win. Raeder was even glummer when he said that the best the Kriegsmarine could be expected to do was die with dignity.[5]

Only a short time after U-38 was directed to commence hostilities, an enemy warship was sighted and identified by Lüth as the French minelayer *Pluton* of 1,300 tons, this following a feverish search through the fleet guide. Unfortunately for Liebe, France had not yet followed the lead of Britain in declaring war. It remained, for the moment, neutral, and he was forced to let the *Pluton* sail. Both Liebe and Lüth were disappointed, but "one week later we heard on the radio: French minelayer *Pluton* exploded in harbor by mines . . . nobody took the news better than our little submarine [and] we didn't feel so bad about our bad luck anymore."*

Eight days later U-38 stopped the British steamer *Manaar*, according to the rules, by a shot across her bow. Instead of

---

*The French minelaying cruiser *Pluton* (4,800 tons, commissioned 1931) had been renamed *La Tour d'Auvergne* in early 1939. She was sunk in Casablanca Harbor on 13 September by a mine.

sending the ship's papers over as he should have done, her master began to shoot back. That was against the rules. A lengthy artillery duel ensued in which U-38 finally submerged to fire a single torpedo into the *Manaar*'s bow—not a pretty attack. It is representative of the major problems BdU and his boats were having with Prize Regulations.

In a protocol known as Prize Regulations, signed in 1935, Great Britain and Germany had agreed to follow a set of rules relating to the sinking or capture of merchant vessels by warships in the event of hostilities. It was extremely difficult for these rules to be followed by submarines. Prize Regulations, for example, said that before they could be sunk all merchant ships had to be stopped, their papers inspected, and their crews removed. If crew members could not easily make it to shore, the attacking vessel had to take them. For a submarine, with barely enough room for her own crew, this was ludicrous.

During the entire operation the submarine had to remain on the surface, exposed and vulnerable; a single shell could render her helpless. The merchant ship was prohibited by Prize Regulations from "engaging in any warlike act," but Great Britain had been arming her merchant fleet since the beginning of the war, and of course the ships had no qualms about firing. As far as Dönitz was concerned, this was unfair, and he made his opinion known. But in September and October he followed Prize Regulations anyway.

On 22 September U-38 sank the British tanker *Inverliffey* in a sea of burning oil. Liebe and Lüth were wondering what to do with the stranded crew, who did not have a means of landing themselves safely, when, according to Lüth, an American tanker steamed into view.

> She had left England before the war began and was not carrying oil. We stopped her with a shot across the bow (nobody could see our signal flags) and steamed towards her at top speed, in order to pass our tanker crew over. Suddenly [the tanker crew] became restless. The American was still some distance away, and they were all gesturing with their hands in the direction of the horizon.
>
> "Destroyer, sir!" shouted the captain to us in the bridge. We had seen the small cloud of smoke as well, but we hoped that it was

only a cloud. We tried to reach the American even faster; with luck we would do it. If the destroyer came up too fast, we would have to dive and the crew of our tanker would have to swim for it. The captain was the only one without a life preserver and we gave him one of ours. He was so upset that he kept saying "Please dive quickly so that nothing happens; we would rather swim!"

But we didn't have to dive; the smoke turned out to be clouds after all. Now came the next problem; we signalled the American to send a boat over, but they lay stopped, doing nothing. Her entire crew was standing at the rails in their life preservers waiting for their ship to be sunk as well. Finally our tanker crew lined up on the weather deck, waved their caps and shouted "Send a boat! Send a boat!" That helped and a boat was sent over to pick them up.

They looked up at us in thanks and two Irishmen secretly made the *Deutschen Gruss*. . . .[6]

Of course, these gentlemanly encounters could not continue. As the months passed, the restrictions laid upon German submarines by Prize Regulations were lifted one after the other. First the regulations were bent, then they were broken, and finally they were ignored. By the end of November any unmarked merchant ship—enemy or neutral—within a declared zone around the British Isles could expect to be sunk without warning.

Because there were so few boats, and because Karl Dönitz had been trying to adhere as best he could to Prize Regulations, U-Bootwaffe operations in the early months of the war resembled less a tonnage war and more a series of isolated, dramatic events. On 3 September, for example, the British passenger liner *Athenia* was sunk by U-30, commanded by Fritz-Julius Lemp, in complete disregard of Prize Regulations. Dönitz went into predictable contortions over Lemp's error and, in an apparently unique bit of backfilling, had U-30's deck log altered to erase the evidence of it. The Reich propaganda office blamed the sinking on the personal intrigues of Winston Churchill, newly appointed First Lord of the Admiralty.

Two weeks later U-29, commanded by Otto Schuhart, sank the aircraft carrier *Courageous*. On 14 October, in what is considered the single most daring submarine operation of the war, a

Günther Prien. Prien, first of the great World War II U-boat aces, was a brilliant tactician and an avid Nazi, hated by those who had to serve under him, but Karl Dönitz's favorite until the day he was lost at sea in 1941. (Courtesy U.S. Naval Institute)

U-boat commanded by Günther Prien sank the battleship *Royal Oak* in Scapa Flow.

Penetrating the Royal Navy's anchorage at Scapa Flow had been an unrealized dream since World War I. It was attempted twice during that conflict by U-boats, both times unsuccessfully. As Dönitz knew, victory at Scapa Flow would be a coup of inestimable value for both Germany and the U-Bootwaffe. To carry out the operation, he chose the self-assured, politically safe young captain of U-47, Kapitänleutnant Günther Prien.

Early in the morning of 14 October, after sneaking into Scapa Flow past the blockships guarding Kirk Sound, U-47 approached the *Royal Oak*, a 25-year-old veteran of World War

Prien upon his return from Scapa Flow. When Prien sank *Royal Oak* in October 1939 he accomplished what was probably the most daring and dangerous U-boat operation of the war. After the sinking he became a reluctant media sensation. "I am a submarine captain," he complained, "not a movie star." (Courtesy U.S. Naval Institute)

I, and fired one torpedo at her bow. It missed. The U-boat undetected, made a second run and fired three more torpedoes. Within minutes, the *Royal Oak* turned turtle and went to the shallow bottom of Scapa Flow with 833 of her 1,200 men.

When U-47 returned to Wilhelmshaven, Prien and his entire crew were greeted at the pier by Dönitz and his staff, then flown to Berlin, where Prien was given the Knight's Cross by Adolf Hitler and feted to the point of declaring, "I am a submarine captain, not a movie star." He was christened The Bull of Scapa Flow, and his crew painted a huge white bull with steam coming out of its nostrils on the conning tower of U-47.

As for Lüth, U-38 was only the beginning. Until 1939 his progress in the U-Bootwaffe had been no different than that of any other junior officer. He had risen to second in command of a U-boat, which was good, but he had not yet been given command. There was every opportunity for him to fail in U-

38, none to succeed; a knight cannot win glory for himself on another knight's horse. There was every opportunity for work and death, but none for fame or fortune until he could take that last step up to a command of his own. But in December 1939 Lüth took that step. He was given his opportunity, his mount, and in an odd twist of fate—or, if you like, a whim of the detailer's pen—it turned out to be the Iron Cross Boat, the second U-9.

The assignment of Lüth to U-9 was significant, but not overly so; she was not a "prize." Just because she carried a cross on her tower did not mean she was better protected—or treated—than the average U-boat. In fact, she suffered a rather ignominious end. The two U-9s were not even similar. Weddigen's was one of the first U-boats ever built, in 1910. Lüth's boat, built in 1935, benefited from a quarter-century of research, development, and wartime experience. Weddigen's boat was much larger than Lüth's, marginally faster, but boxy and wet and prone to mechanical failure. The newer one, with rounded hull and raked bow, resembled less an underwater tramp and more an encapsulated corvette—a modern boat in every respect.

Modern, but after only four years of service, obsolete. A type IIA coastal U-boat, a "canoe," she was too small and too restricted in range to be of any use beyond the North Sea and the European coast. The type IIA was on its way to being replaced by the larger type VIIs like U-27 and the type IXs like U-38. In the first year of the war canoes were employed out of necessity, and they were successful. As the war went on, however, they were either retired, moved to less hazardous theaters, or used as training boats.

Nor were there many similarities between Otto Weddigen and Wolfgang Lüth themselves. Lüth was not the man that Weddigen was. He would be taking over a boat that came imbued with tradition, and there was always for him the burden, whether actual or imaginary, of living in Weddigen's shadow.*

---

*An interesting aspect of this perception was the cross itself. Lüth did not like the unofficial insignia of his fellow captains, Prien's snorting bull,

When Weddigen sailed in 1914 he accomplished something unique in the history of naval warfare. Lüth could never have hoped to do the same when U-9 departed Kiel for Brunsbüttel by way of the Kaiser Wilhelm Canal on 16 January 1940.* It was raining, and the seas were high, not unusual for January in the North Sea. A U-boat was unpleasant under these conditions, most of all for the bridge watch—the watch officer and his lookouts—who had to stand for hours in full rain gear as they scanned the horizon continuously for aircraft, enemy warships, and targets. The waves continued to swell, and finally they were high enough to crash directly over the bridge and down the open bridge hatch into the control room. The next morning a smoke float stored in the tower got wet and ignited after an emergency dive. Immediately, thick black smoke began billowing through the spaces of the U-boat. The float, which could not be extinguished, was tossed back up into the tower and sealed off. It was not an auspicious beginning.

At 2030 that same day U-9's lookout sighted a ship sailing south at ten knots, unescorted, with no zigzag. She was the Swedish merchant *Flandria*. Her lights were on. U-9 was sailing west at eight knots. It was dark, but visibility was excellent and so the tactical situation seemed straightforward. Lüth would simply have to fire his torpedoes ahead of the ship at an angle which would ensure a hit.

Kretschmer's horseshoe, Mohr's edelweiss, and hundreds more. "*Sein, nicht scheinen*," he often said. "Actions speak louder than words." But he dared not remove the Iron Cross of Weddigen from U-9 (Petersen, letter to author, 12 December 1983).

*Data in the text relating to the positions, movements, or physical condition of Wolfgang Lüth's boats are taken from his *Kriegstagebücher* (war diaries or deck logs):

1. Deck log of U-9, microfilm publication T-1022, file PG 30006, roll 2928, National Archives, Washington, DC.
2. Deck log of U-138, file PG 30128, roll 2883.
3. Deck log of U-43, file PG 30040, roll 2929.
4. Deck log of U-181, file PG 30168, roll 2885.

Passages from the deck logs will not be referenced individually.

The Iron Cross Boat. U-9, commissioned in August 1935, was the second of three boats to bear the number. Weddigen's iron cross can be seen at the side of her tower, the only distinguishing mark on any of Wolfgang Lüth's four U-boats. U-9 was already obsolete when Lüth took command of her in 1939, but since there were so few boats available then, she remained at sea in a variety of roles until 1944. (Courtesy Horst Bredow)

For a target with constant course and speed, this angle, called the director angle, was calculated easily on paper; most good commanders could do the simple geometry in their heads. Of course, the boat would have to be brought about to aim the torpedo tubes, and if the target changed course or speed during the run, the solution would be ruined. These were unavoidable considerations; otherwise the *Flandria* was a textbook target in U-boat tactics.

But Wolfgang Lüth was distracted from his calculations. He was distracted because squeezed into the tiny bridge of U-9, with him and his first watch officer and the lookouts, was most of the rest of the crew. He had invited his men to watch him sink his first ship and up they came like hungry guests to a banquet. It was an unwise move. What, he wrote later, would have happened if the boat had had to dive quickly? What if U-9 itself—dead in the water and unable to dive—were attacked?

The bridge was packed with eager spectators. Slowly the boat swung into firing position. The forward torpedo tubes were made ready to fire. Lüth hesitated, unsure of himself, waiting for better position. At this point he happened to turn around during the run and see his men—more than he had expected—staring awestruck at the ship. Amid the predictable jostling and shuffling, the coughs and the whispers, Lüth miscalculated the director angle. His first torpedo, fired at 2223, traveled wide.

A collective groan rose up behind him as he began to maneuver the boat into position for a second shot. He could feel his crewmen at his back, restless now and wet. Suggestions were called out. He waited for U-9 to come about, regretting the attention he had attracted. At 2240 the boat fired on its target again, and again missed. Another collective groan.

During this second run on the *Flandria* one of the lookouts sighted another ship, the *Patria,* also Swedish, approaching from the south. Lüth was forced to decide almost instantly between the two ships. If he wasted any more time on the *Flandria,* the *Patria* might escape and then he would lose both ships. But if he broke off his attack on the *Flandria,* even at once, he might not be able to catch up with the *Patria.* And the longer he thought about it, the better the chance that one ship or the other would see U-9.

Lüth did not know either ship was Swedish: the *Flandria* was illuminated, but not her flag, and the *Patria* was too far away. If either were armed, U-9, with most of her crew jammed into the bridge, was a sitting duck. In any case, the Swedes would have radios and signal flares—a quick call in the night might alert a nearby warship.

Lüth decided to continue the attack on the *Flandria.* His pride was at stake. What would Weddigen have thought?

After another hour of careful maneuvering, a third torpedo was fired at 2330. The men on the bridge waited out the ensuing seconds anxiously, hands on each other's shoulders, necks craned for a better look. And then it happened, Lüth's first victory. The torpedo struck the *Flandria* amidships. A column of black smoke rose in the moonlight and a loud explosion rang out over the water. She sank in twenty seconds to ragged cheers.

Surprisingly, nobody on the *Patria* seemed to see this. She continued on her original course and speed as if U-9 was not there, and Lüth, who had made all of his mistakes, began a much more professional torpedo run on her.

He aimed for the gap between the *Patria's* foremast and her bridge. At 0145 a single torpedo struck her amidships with such force that it tore her stern completely off. Her forward section remained afloat for some time. The deck lights came on so that lifeboats could be launched. Through his binoculars Lüth watched the *Patria's* crewmen struggle to save themselves. Under the glare of the lights one man ran wildly aft, expecting to reach the fantail, and fell headlong into the sea.

Neither the *Flandria* nor the *Patria* was a big vessel, each about 1,200 tons. Lüth, however, being young, inexperienced, and prone to exaggeration, recorded that his first kill had been 4,000 tons and his second 8,000 tons. Eventually he would overestimate his total tonnage in U-9 by 80 percent. This tendency was to be tempered by the end of his career. Then, his reported tonnage exceeded his actual tonnage by just 12 percent (on the whole, the tonnage figures reported by BdU were not unrealistic; they compare favorably with the wildly optimistic estimates of the U.S. Navy in the Pacific).[7]

U-9 returned triumphant to Wilhelmshaven on 22 January after a patrol of six days. "The spell had been broken," wrote Lüth, "and a trust established between captain and crew." Trust was priceless, something every commander needed. It had not been handed to him on a plate; it had been earned. "If an officer is successful," Lüth wrote later, "his men will like him even if he is a fool."[8] His words could not have been more apt. During that attack on the *Flandria* he had put his entire crew in jeopardy. But the fact that two ships sank made it acceptable. And the fact that he invited his crew along to watch them sink demonstrated early on the quality that would make him an exceptional commander. What better gift could he have given his crew than to let them share in the moment of his first kill?

If the sinkings were inspirational, Lüth's next mission was decidedly not. In early February he received orders to lay mines in Moray Firth on the west coast of Scotland, an operation called Albatros in German. Technically it was a good idea. The submarine was better at minelaying than both the surface minelayer and the airplane because of its maneuverability and low profile. But the ratio of risk to reward was uncomfortably high, and U-boat sailors hated it. "A thankless task," Lüth explained in his book. "The minelayer hasn't even the pleasure of seeing firsthand the success of his weapon." That was the worst part of it; the torpedo was an instrument of instant gratification, whereas it might be weeks, even months, before a ship struck a mine.

U-9 sailed on the afternoon of 6 February. She was well on her way across the North Sea before someone discovered that her operational orders had been left behind in port. A frantic hunt through piles of paperwork yielded nothing, and Lüth gathered his officers to talk. The obvious move was to return to port for new orders. But that would have made Lüth look utterly ridiculous ("Sorry, I forgot something"), and he could not bring himself to do it. What would Weddigen have said?

The only alternative was to continue without orders, which was equally bad. They spelled out Operation Albatros's course, the times for laying mines, which were based on the tide and current data for Moray Firth, and most important, the precise locations for those mines. A mine laid in the wrong place could be disastrous; never mind the ships, U-boats had to cross minefields too.

Lüth and his officers—the first watch officer, the chief engineer, and the helmsman—sat and stared glumly at one another for some time, not knowing what to do. Then they stumbled on a solution. Each, it turned out, had committed parts of the orders to memory; together they might be able to reassemble them. Of course there were gaps, but at this point Lüth was almost cocky. As he wrote later, to fill them in "we would have to rely . . . on common sense"—a statement, if heard back home, that would have sent the BdU staff into screaming fits. Never mind; Lüth was *not* going to be embarrassed again in front if his crew.

The sky was continuously overcast. U-9 sailed blindly across the North Sea and reached Scotland by dead reckoning, quite a feat of navigation. The boat's exact position was obtained at dawn on 9 February when the radio operator in U-9 managed to obtain a line of bearing on the transmitter station at Burghead.

After that Lüth was able to find his way easily with the help of lights burning brightly around Moray Firth. Nine mines were laid, more or less where the orders had specified, in a line west-southwest from Tarbet Ness light in Cromarty Firth. U-9 departed the Firth, sneaked back across the North Sea, and en route even managed to sink the ancient Estonian freighter *Linda* off the north coast of the Scottish peninsula. On 12 February, U-9 arrived in Wilhelmshaven as though nothing had happened.

Aller Anfang ist schwer. All beginnings are difficult.

3

THE IRON CROSS BOAT

In his book *The Sea Wolves,* Edwin Hoyt includes a full-length photograph of Wolfgang Lüth and his wife. At the time of the photograph Lüth was a relatively famous man and much decorated. Hoyt's captions reads, "One of Dönitz's boys with his bride."[1] When Karl Dönitz wrote his memoirs he mentioned Lüth exactly twice,[2] and when Peter Padfield wrote his exhaustive biography of Dönitz, no mention was made of Lüth at all.[3]

These are significant omissions, and not the only ones. Wolfgang Lüth is not a man for the history books. And yet he is important for several reasons. First and most obvious, he sank a large number of ships. Second, he won numerous combat decorations, including the highest award in the Wehrmacht. So what? one might argue — tonnage tallies and medals are tawdry measures of a man. But a third reason compels us to recognize Lüth as a figure of some prominence in the war at sea. The war was a global affair. The Battle of the Atlantic stretched from the North Atlantic to the Indian Ocean, from Norway to Cape Hatteras to Madagascar to the Straits of Malacca. A single soldier could hardly have hoped to be everywhere in such a grand theater, and yet Lüth was, or almost. Perhaps no other man took part in so many of the famous campaigns in the war at sea; perhaps no other man operated in so many far-flung fields of battle. Lüth seemed to be wherever the shooting was, something professional fighting men pray for but seldom achieve.*

In the spring of 1940, for example, German submarines participated in two major campaigns of the early war: the invasion of Norway and the invasion of the West. They did not play a large part in either case, and the small number of U-boats at sea ensured that only a few men in the U-Bootwaffe would participate. Lüth was a veteran of both campaigns.

On 1 April Adolf Hitler signed the orders for Operation Weserübung, the invasion and occupation of Norway and Denmark. The entire German fleet was involved, and all U-boats, including U-9, were recalled from sea to participate. The invasion had the potential of being a stunning victory for Dönitz, a vindication of every theory of submarine warfare he had put forth so stridently and proof of the need he had expressed for more boats.

Weserübung had been contemplated in one form or another by Raeder and his staff since the beginning of the war. Norway was a vital strategic link, since Germany had been obtaining much-needed iron ore from Swedish ports and shipping it down the coast in Norwegian territorial waters. Great Britain, well aware of this, made a decision in March to mine the coast of Norway and to land troops at several points, forcing German transports into the North Sea. The Royal Navy had

---

*The U-boat commander who ranged the farthest in actual miles was not Lüth but Kapitänleutnant Heinrich Timm. Timm took U-251 to the Kara Sea and U-862 to the approaches to Sydney Harbor. However, he didn't accomplish anything out of the ordinary in between.

already laid some of these mines when Weserübung began. The German invasion would have the effect of forestalling a British invasion.

The naval side of the German operation has been called audacious, in other words, tactically unsound. For success it depended more on surprise than on proven principles of naval warfare. The German fleet was divided into six groups, each assigned to support troop landings at different points on the Norwegian coast. U-9 would be in Group III, bound for Bergen with the light cruisers *Köln* and *Königsberg.* The U-boats were assigned several missions. They were to protect German forces from seaward during the landings; they were to prevent enemy landings during and after the operation; and they were to keep the lanes of communications open between the fatherland and the invasion force. Commerce war was not contemplated; for this and several other reasons, Dönitz had his doubts about the invasion, but he described himself on the whole as "fairly confident of success."[4]

The U-boats participating in Operation Weserübung left early. U-9 cast off her lines before dawn on 6 April, pulling out of Wilhelmshaven Harbor. At 0755 she passed the last buoy, and at 1030 she left Heligoland to port. Nobody on board, not even Lüth himself, knew then where he was going or why. The orders, written on water-soluble paper, were sealed in an envelope on Lüth's desk; he was not allowed to open the envelope until U-9 had received a signal, prearranged, from BdU.

It came at 2030 that same evening, the codeword Hartmut. The pre-invasion phase of Weserübung had begun. U-9, waiting at sea some 100 miles southwest of Stavanger, proceeded to the waters west of Utvar light at the mouth of Sogne Fjord. Simultaneously, the large surface units of Groups I and II— *Scharnhorst, Gneisenau, Hipper*—together with fourteen destroyers, eased out of Wilhelmshaven for Narvik and Trondheim. Other groups would sail at intervals, depending on the distance to their invasion positions.

The element of surprise deemed so vital to German success was lost almost at once when Groups I and II were sighted approaching southern Norway. But no actions were taken by the Royal Navy until the evening of 7 April. At that time the Home Fleet, led by the British battleship *Rodney*, left Scapa Flow.

The movements of the fleet were tentative; the Admiralty, half expecting a breakout by German capital ships toward the west, kept it away from the Norwegian coast. The battleships *Scharnhorst* and *Gneisenau* did eventually turn to the northwest, distracting several destroyers and the British battle cruiser *Renown* from the approaches to Narvik. But British hesitancy in general allowed the German invasion groups to proceed freely to their stations. A completely one-sided attack by the destroyer *Glowworm* on the German *Hipper* was the only action before the invasion itself.

The invasion of Norway began at 0500 on 9 April. It succeeded, probably beyond the dreams of planners in Berlin. Every objective, whether by ruse, by treachery, or by sheer force of arms, was taken that day. Losses on land were light. The Kriegsmarine had a worse time of it; the new heavy cruiser *Blücher* was sunk in a fierce attack by shore artillery and torpedoes in the approaches to Oslo. But the U-boats, particularly U-9, seemed to miss the invasion altogether.

U-9 remained in her assigned operational area throughout the day, well away from the action. "Many loud detonations heard," Lüth noted that evening in the boat's log, "most likely German air attacks on a part of the English fleet at Bergen. . . . Surfaced for a better look." But there were no units of the British fleet at Bergen. The landings took place virtually unopposed.

Lüth cruised up and down the coast for three days, waiting, then had to refuel at Bergen. His lookouts never sighted so much as a mast of the Royal Navy during this time, even though the battle was warming: A fierce counterattack was being mounted against German forces in the Vestfjord; enemy bombers had attacked and sunk the *Königsberg* at her berth in Bergen; and a British submarine had torpedoed the *Karlsruhe*, which eventually had to be scuttled off Kristiansand.

U-9's only battles were fought against boredom and the miserable weather of the North Sea. Her assigned task was impracticable, Lüth reported afterward; with such low visibility he could achieve nothing. As Dönitz was always trying to impress, unsuccessfully, on his superiors, a U-boat was best suited for the offense, otherwise it was wasted.

U-boats thus had little effect on the outcome of Operation Weserübung. It was not just because of inactivity or misuse; unlike U-9, many of them were on the offensive, and many of them were given the opportunity to succeed. It was worse than that.

On 11 April U-48, a unit of Group V, fired torpedoes at two enemy cruisers and missed both of them. U-47, commanded by Günther Prien, attacked a harbor full of British warships at Harstad without success and barely escaped after temporarily running aground. On 19 April U-47 fired a spread of torpedoes at the battleship *Warspite,* all of which failed to meet their target. On 13 April, following similar failure, aircraft sank U-64 in Herjangsfjord; her crew escaped through the bridge hatch and twenty fathoms of icy water. U-49 was sunk on 15 April and U-1 on the sixteenth.

At noon on 20 April, after Lüth had left Norwegian waters for home, U-9 was submerged at a point about fifty miles northeast of the Shetlands when the boat's listening apparatus detected propellers. A couple of enemy destroyers were sighted, and at 1248 Lüth fired two new torpedoes at one of them. U-9 dived after firing, and forty-eight seconds later an explosion was heard, "followed instantly by a second larger explosion, like a boiler blowing up." Now U-9 detected only one set of propellers. "I am sure that this destroyer was sunk," wrote Lüth in a post-mission report. BdU concurred: "The sinking of a destroyer is most probable." But there is no record of any Allied warship being lost at that time or place.*

Altogether, German submarines launched forty-three attacks on British warships (four on the *Warspite* alone) that month. None succeeded, and four U-boats were lost. It was not a good ratio. In fact, it was no ratio at all. Captains were

---

*Lüth did not identify the ship he had attacked. It may have been the Polish *Grom*, but more probably her sister ship *Blyskawica*.

depressed, crews dispirited. Prien, who knew his own ability, was bitter and disconsolate. "How can I be expected to fight with a wooden rifle?" he demanded, echoing the general suspicion that there was something wrong with U-boat torpedoes.[5]

There was indeed a problem with the torpedoes. As is often the case, the men who had to use the weapons knew it long before anyone else. The new G7e electric torpedo, which had just been released to the U-Bootwaffe after extensive testing, did not work as it was designed to. Its mechanisms were too delicate: The depth-control device was affected by air pressure within the boat and the temperature of the water; the proximity fuse in the torpedo, designed to detect the magnetic field of a warship's hull, was frustrated by magnetic countermeasures; the steering gear did not steer properly. In fact, it was such an inferior weapon that the manufacturers were brought before a military court. It was a phenomenon that would occur later in the U.S. Navy.

An angry and disappointed Dönitz released his U-boats from Weserübung at the end of April. He visited each of them afterward, in person, to revive flagging morale. He also went back to the old torpedoes.

Toward the end of April a decision was made to send U-9 to the First U-Flotilla in Gotenhafen as a training boat. She was almost five years old and in questionable shape. With the war at sea lagging in the wake of the Norwegian debacle, the little canoes were no longer critical. The decision to retire her, entirely logical, was reversed with no explanation on 4 May, and the next day Lüth began preparing his boat for another patrol. The tone of the signal was so urgent that he felt compelled to issue a recall of his crew from liberty.

The reason for the change was Germany's invasion of France and the Low Countries. This was perhaps Adolf Hitler's greatest gamble. If it did not pay off, he would be out of power within weeks.

The invasion, *Fall Gelb* (Case Yellow), was an immense undertaking; it involved 135 divisions of the Germany Army and most of the Luftwaffe. But the Kriegsmarine, its strength

A rather scruffy Lüth in 1940, standing under U-9's port running light. The elements have stripped the paint from Weddigen's cross, but the metal lining is still there. (The running lights were never used; in this case they were a holdover from peacetime.) (Courtesy Horst Bredow)

seriously depleted during the invasion of Norway, did not participate. The harassing tactics of smaller German surface units aside, the Royal Navy was able to operate with impunity in the lower North Sea and the Straits of Dover during the invasion and subsequent evacuation of troops.

The decision to send U-boats into the area was made almost as an afterthought. A number of factors—mine fields, the tricky tides and shallow depths of the straits, the weather, and a superior enemy force—frustrated the effort, and as in Norway, the effect of U-boats on the outcome of the invasion was minimal.

U-9 departed Brunsbüttel at midnight on 6 May, again with sealed orders. She cruised west and then south, traveling on the surface by night and resting by day on the bottom of the North Sea to avoid detection by fishing boats in the area.

Franz Gramitzki, the new first watch officer, was scanning the lights of these fishing boats on the evening of 8 May when he saw one that appeared to be blinking. As he and Lüth stared, the light turned into a shadow, then a shape, then the dimly recognizable form of an enemy submarine. Neither man could identify the silhouette. They decided she was British, perhaps one of the *Grampus* class. In fact, she was the French boat *Doris,* newer and larger than U-9, steaming insouciantly on patrol.

Lüth began to track the *Doris* at 2350. U-9 was at a disadvantage, for even at that hour she had a bright horizon behind her. But the *Doris* took no action other than to make an erratic, half-hearted zigzag.

U-9 approached to about 700 meters without being seen, then Lüth fired two torpedoes from the stern tubes. One was a new G7e electric torpedo, the other the more reliable G7a, driven by compressed air. The latter struck the *Doris* just aft of the conning tower. The initial blast, small, blossomed seconds later into a huge orange ball of fire as the French boat's own torpedoes were set off. A column of smoke and water rose twenty-five meters into the night sky, white at the base, red at the top, sending debris raining down on U-9 as the *Doris,* in the center of a huge oil slick, slipped below the water's surface.

She was the only warship Lüth ever sank. There were no survivors.

The operational area assigned to Lüth for the invasion was a square twelve miles across; the eastern side faced the Schelde estuary and the southeastern corner pointed toward Ostend. He reached it at 2230 on 9 May, ninety minutes before the receipt of the signal to commence Fall Gelb and five hours before the start of land operations in the west.

The treacherous tides and currents off the Belgian coast plagued Lüth. His depth-sounding apparatus had broken down during the night, forcing him to bump along the seabed like a sick shark. U-9 ran aground at least once on her own, and destroyers forced her under the surface for four hours on the evening of 10 May.

When U-9 surfaced again and Lüth climbed to the bridge, he saw lights in the distance, the searchlights and flashes of the antiaircraft guns in Dunkirk and Ostend. He also saw the Estonian freighter *Viiu,* a black shadow against the eerie, flickering horizon. U-9 sank the *Viiu* at midnight on 11 May, and she went down accompanied by the mournful wail of her siren. "We were kind of disappointed that [she] had not burned," Lüth wrote afterward in an oddly prescient moment, "but then we weren't at the theater."

Soon thereafter they sighted the masts of an armed merchant. As U-9 was being brought around to attack a minesweeper was spotted in the distance. She being a more important target, U-9 turned toward her and while the U-boat readied herself once again for firing a surfaced submarine was seen trailing the minesweeper. This was even better—an embarrassment of riches. They would take the submarine instead.

But the submarine, it turned out, was damaged and under tow. They would have to target the minesweeper after all. U-9 swung back around to readjust for firing, only to be caught in the current and swept away. And so Lüth lost all three ships.

He did sink the British merchant *Tringa* later that day, but immediately afterward one of her escorts drove U-9 to the shallow bottom. The crew of U-9 huddled in silence for almost nine hours, waiting for the angry warship to ram her periscopes just beneath the surface. Nothing happened.

Lüth was force to leave the area after only a week at sea, his fuel and torpedoes exhausted, his crew exuberant but jittery.

At 0900 on 15 May enemy aircraft were sighted off Borkum; Lüth stopped his engines until the threat had passed. No sooner had he started them again when a torpedo, fired from an unseen but presumably British platform, passed a few meters before his bow. Had U-9 not been detained by the aircraft she would have been lost. In *Boot Greift Wieder An,* Lüth thanked Churchill for his cooperation.*

U-9 pulled into Wilhelmshaven late that night where, like a Grand Prix driver, his eye on the watch, his foot on the pedal, Lüth took on fuel, torpedoes, and provisions. He pulled out at dawn the next day, tires burning, for battle again.

The situation in Belgium and France had changed dramatically in the few days he was absent from the front (in the U-Bootwaffe a boat was at the front whenever she was on operational patrol). General Heinz Guderian entered France with his panzer divisions on 13 May. He was driving hard, and almost unchecked, toward the French coast. The entire British Expeditionary Force, some thirty divisions, and most of the French and Belgian forces were caught between Guderian's panzers to the south and Field Marshal Fedor von Bock's infantry divisions to the northeast, in Belgium and the Netherlands.

Lüth picked up a German propaganda broadcast on 17 May: "A U-boat has sunk a tanker and a large armed merchant. It shows that we will soon have this vital area [the Schelde] all to ourselves." "This kind of nonsense is only making our job harder and will cost us some success," Lüth wrote tersely. But it was not just the radio that was making his job difficult. His operational area was now swarming with enemy warships, and he spent the next three days battling tricky tides and avoiding destroyers. Antwerp fell to Bock's infantry forces

---

*There were French submarines in the area as well, but apparently Lüth didn't know that.

THE IRON CROSS BOAT ◆ 45

on 20 May, stemming the flight of merchants from the Scheldt and leaving few targets. Mechanical problems continued to plague U-9, and her diesel engines failed repeatedly.

On that same day Guderian reached the sea at Abbeville, cutting the Allied armies in two and trapping almost a million men in Flanders. They were forced to begin a painful retreat to the coast while Guderian wheeled north toward Boulogne and Bock pressed down from Antwerp. "Fires in the direction of Dunkirk," noted Lüth on the evening of 21 May. "Explosions and fire observed in the direction of Dunkirk," he observed next day.

At noon on 23 May lookouts sighted tugs escorting the Latvian ship *Sigurds Falbaums* in the direction of the English coast. She was moving slowly over the shallow water, secure with her escorts. Lüth decided to sink her. At 1230 he fired two torpedoes from a good distance. One of them struck the *Sigurds Faulbaums* amidships. She broke in two and sank quickly, her forward section settling vertically on the bottom, her bow protruding several meters above the water.

The crew was taken off, and after a prudent wait U-9 approached her through the wreckage. Several empty lifeboats floated on the surface. From one of them Gramitzki retrieved a pack of cigarettes, which he was promptly forced to share with his shipmates; in another Lüth found the papers of a Belgian soldier and thought that he had sunk a military transport. He later changed his mind. The *Sigurds Faulbaums,* as it happened, was a German ship sailing under Latvian registry. She had been captured by the British and was being taken back to Great Britain as a war prize when U-9 sank her. But sometime between this incident and the U-9's return to Wilhelmshaven Lüth got an entirely different notion into his head, who knows where. "We've just sunk a Jewish ship," he wrote in his log.

Back in Germany he began to brag publicly about sinking a ship owned and operated by the refuse of the Reich. Finally he was told that his Jewish ship belonged to an old and distinguished German shipping line in Riga, Max Faulbaums, that she most certainly was not Jewish, and that he would be well advised in the future to keep quiet.[6]

The humiliation seemed to have made an impression on Lüth. He was no quibbler when it came to politics—he was an unabashed Nazi—but the political remarks he made later in his career were not quite so rash.

The patrol continued. In the early morning of 24 May, U-9 was cruising on the surface toward the coast of Norfolk. At 0300 two shadows were sighted in the moonlight, small cruisers or large destroyers. Lüth decided to attack.

He came within 1,000 meters of one and gave the order to fire. Almost at once a call came back: "The tubes won't open!" The bow caps—the doors to the forward torpedo tubes—were jammed shut. "This is what comes from all that crawling around on the bottom," he later fumed in the log. "We tested the bow caps yesterday and now this!"

This and more. U-9 was sighted by her target. Lüth took the boat down seconds before the enemy steamed over his head and dropped five depth charges on top of him. "Too bad," he wrote laconically as he prepared for the inevitable barrage, "it was a good opportunity. . . ." The U-boat began to zigzag slowly below the surface in hopes of sneaking away, but by now the ships had her cold. The water was too shallow, the odds were long. Six more depth charges came down, then five more after that. It was as if, Lüth wrote, "an enraged man were standing on the fantail of [his] ship throwing beer barrels on top of us one after the other." U-9 was forced to the bottom. One piece of machinery broke down, then another, the electric motors rattled, the rudders came loose, the diving planes froze. The last thing Lüth saw before the lights went out was his own face in a mirror, "the face of an old man. . . ."

The boat could not move, not without a cacophony of rattles, squeaks, and knocks announcing their presence: "Here we are, kill us." So Lüth decided shortly after 0700 to play dead, to lie on the bottom in total silence until nightfall with all his onboard machinery turned off and all his crewmen in their bunks. The damage report was long: "[D]epth sounder, pit log, air compressor, tachometer, alarm system, magnetic compass oscillating; air search and attack periscopes broken; main bilge pump, friction clutch uncertain; emergency lighting;

everything fastened down in radio room now loose; mirrors, etc., broken."

Lüth did not know that by now there were four Royal Navy destroyers on the surface. Each was dropping depth charges at random, some nearer, some farther off. As it happened, they had lost the boat and were blanketing the area in order to score a lucky hit.

At 1100 he had chocolate and potash cartridge passed around, the chocolate for nourishment, the potash to filter the stale air. The boat was made ready for abandonment; scuttling charges were prepared and life jackets distributed. The boat was dark and getting colder.

> The crew wear only their socks, in order not to make any noise while walking. Water is leaking into the boat forward, so that we are becoming bow-heavy; everyone sits in the stern to compensate, very close together because there are no seats. Only the most important watchstanders forward. Everything is deathly still. Propeller noise! They come closer and closer. They are over the boat now.
>
> Any minute now. No? Still not? Now! Four, five, six bombs explode. The boat shudders. The compartments report damage. Two lamps are still working and they cast an eerie light in the boat. A terrible mess: the crew's boots are lying about, empty life preserver cases. Mattresses and blankets are laid out on the deck so that everyone can proceed quietly and so that watchstanders can lie down at their posts; we must save our air.[7]

Chief Engineer Wiebe and Machinist's Mate Altenburger were both aft trying as quietly as possible to patch the boat back together. The hydrophone operator continued to report in whispers what most could already hear through the hull: the sound of propellers, the rumble of exploding depth charges. Gramitzki, awakened after one charge knocked a box on his head, mumbled something about the troubled times they had to endure and promptly went back to sleep. Lüth crept from one bunk to the next, checking to see that snoring crewmen had not dropped the potash cartridges from their lips.

The depth-charge attack is a peculiarly modern form of naval warfare; these was nothing like it before World War I. The experience is unpleasant, to say the least, and it cannot be appreciated by someone who has not survived one.

Several vivid descriptions of this type of attack endure. Heinz Schaeffer, commander of U-977, compared the impact of a depth-charge exploding to a huge hammer smashing into the boat's hull. "This is war, all right," he wrote, "real war, not a film war with waving of flags and blaring music."[8] To Herbert Werner, author of *Iron Coffins,* waiting between explosions was the worst: It "made us lose any sense of time . . . any desire for food."[9] Lothar-Günther Buchheim, a war correspondent and author of *Das Boot,* described this awful anticipation as being physical, to the point that the hull of a boat under siege became like the skin of the man inside. "Even the smallest sound is painful, a touch on a raw wound. As if my nerves had escaped . . . and were now exposed."[10] Perhaps if there had been an opportunity to fight back it might not have been so bad. But waiting was all one could do. "So-called heroism," commented Peter Cremer after describing a particularly nasty attack on U-333 in 1943, "has not much to do with it."[11]

It was a test of endurance rather than a proper engagement. The U-boat could not fight back. She could lose but never win. And yet, paradoxically, it was the opportunity of a lifetime for her captain. "It is common knowledge," Lüth observed, "that when the depth charges start to explode everyone looks to the officers." Everything the officer did, every expression on his face, every motion of his eyes, his head, his hands, his feet, was watched closely. A captain had to be especially careful, for his attitude was all too quickly transferred to his men. If he looked worried, they would panic. If he looked confident, they would at least be quiet. And if he smiled through the worst of it, they would look at each other and smile as well. Appearances in such a case were everything.

Admittedly, to attain an appearance of calm during one of these attacks was not always easy; it had to be feigned sometimes. But a good commander had it down to an art. U-boat officers would do almost anything to keep up this appearance:

read, make small talk, gaze unconcernedly at the overheads, eat. The best of them would simply go to sleep, as Gramitzki did. If a captain managed to remain collected, if he was able to keep the crew calm and in good order during an attack like the one U-9 endured in May 1940, he won all around. He became more sure of himself as a captain. He won the instant respect of his crew, whether they liked him or not. And he may have been saving his life, for more than once boats were lost after their crews panicked.

Lüth, in the first attack of his career, and the worst, succeeded in all of these things. The siege of U-9 continued for several more hours, but the depth charges began to explode farther away. The noise of propellers grew more and more faint. The crew sensed it was over and they began to relax.

Finally in late afternoon one of the warships dropped a marker buoy over U-9's position; they had apparently decided that she had been destroyed, and in lieu of evidence to support their claim they were marking her grave for later. More charges were dropped, but they were sporadic and distant. At midnight Lüth made the decision to surface. At 0025, after 21 hours underwater, the bridge hatch was opened, letting in a stream of cool fresh air and leaving those below dizzy with relief.

Lüth emerged and immediately, about 300 meters away, confronted the dark presence of a British destroyer. As he looked, U-9's emergency lighting blinked on again, illuminating him from below in a column of bright yellow light. He kicked the hatch shut, cringing at the clank of steel on steel, all the while keeping his eyes on the silent, drifting warship.

No reaction. U-9 began to creep away, on electric power, for Lüth did not dare start his diesels yet. To compound the ordeal, the boat had to pass through a minefield to escape. Nerves were as taut as piano wire. Gramitzki remarked drily, "Well, if we wake up tomorrow, I suppose we'll have made it through."

Dönitz was waiting on the pier when U-9 limped into Wilhelmshaven at dusk on 28 May. He had just about given Lüth up, in light of which his remarks upon seeing him again were remarkably terse. "'Where have you come from? I thought you were all dead. The British claim to have sunk you.'"

"'Then the British spoke too soon,' answered Lüth. . . . 'They even dropped wreck buoys right on top of us—but they won't find us there now.'"[12]

Soon after Lüth had left the theater, Operation Dynamo, the evacuation of Allied troops from the beaches of Dunkirk, commenced. During this ten-day evacuation over 300,000 British, French, and Belgian troops were ferried back to Britain in ships, boats, barges, tugs, and small craft of every kind. Few German submarines were in position to interrupt them. U-9 missed the opportunity by hours.

Great Britain recovered most of its army in the evacuation, but it lost everything else. France was left to the invaders, and Paris fell two weeks later. The formal surrender was signed at Compiegne on 22 June.

4

A NIGHT OF LONG KNIVES

Between the Mull of Kintyre on Scotland's west coast and Fair Head at Ireland's northernmost tip stretches an invisible line marking the egress from the Irish Sea. Below this line for some thirty fathoms down is the water of the North Atlantic, cold, gray, and choppy. High above the line is the sky, also cold, and usually gray.

It is early afternoon, 20 September, the last day of summer 1940. Across the line, heading north, a ragged assembly of nineteen ships steam. They can scarcely be seen from afar. Moving frantically around them are three small warships like shepherds tending a flock. It is Allied merchant convoy OB 216 bound for North America. For most of the morning and all of the previous day, OB 216 assembled in the Irish Sea. There were ships in this convoy from the Bristol Channel, the Mer-

An Allied convoy catches the North Atlantic sun. Hundreds of these
convoys crossed the Atlantic during the war; most of them in the
early years lost ships to German U-boats. OB 216, the westbound

sey, the Clyde, and Belfast. The escort, based at the Albert
Docks in Liverpool, is pitifully small, but it is all that can be
spared.

Between that line marking the boundary of the Irish Sea
and the harbors of North America's eastern seaboard lie 3,000
miles of open sea, and hiding in that sea are enemy submarines, each waiting to attack convoys that dare to cross.

The commander of the escort has received his orders: "Take
OB 216 west. Protect her from attack as best you can. Ensure
her safety as long as you can. But leave her no later than 17°W
to her own resources." These are the orders given to all escorts.

At 2105 on 22 September, a cool, cloudless evening. OB 216
is steaming west over the Stanton Banks. She has crossed the

convoy attacked by U-138 in September 1940, would have looked like this as it left the Irish Sea. (Courtesy U.S. Naval Institute)

line, no enemy activity has been detected, and it looks as though she might, just might, have a clear path to open sea. This is on the mind of Second Officer Richard Chisholm of the *New Sevilla*—a freighter, first ship, third column—as he stands in the bridge. As if to reassure himself that his ship and the convoy are still intact, he glances at the *Boka,* first ship one column over.

And watches as she explodes before his eyes.

For Wolfgang Lüth it had been a long, boring, frustrating summer. In June he assumed command of U-138, the second of sixteen new boats similar to U-9 but with additional fuel tanks for increased range. U-138 was launched on 22 June, "hoisted off the ways and into the water by a huge crane," wrote her new Obersteuermann, Theodor Petersen, "just like a loaf of bread at the bakery."[1] The commissioning ceremony took place five days later at the Blücher pier in Kiel Harbor.

Obersteuermann Petersen was the senior enlisted man on board U-138. He had been a merchant seaman before the war, and he was the son of a merchant seaman. For almost three years he and Lüth would serve together in the U-Bootwaffe, a fact that makes him the best source of information on Lüth alive today. Theodor Petersen was probably Wolfgang Lüth's best friend in the service; he is certainly one of Lüth's strongest critics. The positions Petersen held—Obersteuermann in U-138, watch officer in U-43 and later first watch officer in U-181 as Lüth's second in command—lend weight to his opinion of Lüth, which is high but not uncritical. His doubts do not change the fact that, to Petersen, Lüth was a friend, a comrade, and a good man.

It is Petersen who describes the summer of 1940 as boring and frustrating. One of the unpleasant duties of assuming command of a new warship is taking her through an extended period of trial and testing. U-138 was no exception. Between her commissioning and 10 July, for example, she had acceptance trials at the U-boat Acceptance Command in Kiel; between 12 and 17 July, torpedo trials with the Torpedo Testing Command in Gotenhafen; the following week, tactical exercises with the Twenty-seventh U-Flotilla at sea; and so on and so on. According to Petersen the worst was in Danzig, where U-138 was put through her time trials: "We had to sail along this mile dead slow; One E machine at one half knot. Then back again with the other E machine, then with both. . . . It was *dreadful*. The whole affair was run by U-boat Command and they tested everything. We had a Captain Sachs on board, who supervised all of these exercises with an iron face. The tower could only fit two people, so Sachs and I sat in the tower and Lüth stayed down below to run the boat. I had to write down everything Sachs said: *Achtung! Achtung! Achtung! NULL!* Dreadful."[2]

On 1 August U-138 was sent to Memel, where she was to serve for thirty days with the Twenty-fourth and Twenty-fifth

A quiet moment in the bridge of U-138. Franz Gramitzki, her first watch officer, is seated at right. A very young Theodor Petersen is above him and in the center. The four men are listening to a radio that has been brought up. The news is probably good; this picture was taken in the summer of 1940, the "happy times" of the U-boats.

U-Flotillas as a training platform for new commanding officers. This annoyed Lüth immensely. Shakedown cruises and training were necessary, but they took time. Memel meant exile. Lüth wanted to be at the front. He had no desire to waste time in the Baltic, especially since everyone knew that England's surrender was imminent. The war would be over by Christmas, he believed, and he had reaped no glory, received no medals.

Lüth was not the only man who thought this way. The prospect of early victory seemed obvious in 1940. Great Britain was fighting a war it could not win, alone. The Luftwaffe was attacking British soil every day. Germany was preparing plans for an invasion.

The U-boats had the best of the battle. Those based in French Atlantic ports cruised in the shipping lanes constantly, enjoying what historians call the "happy times" of the U-Bootwaffe. They sank ships almost at will—at sea or within sight of land and safety, quietly or sending them up in huge fireballs. Sometimes nobody knew where a ship had sunk, sometimes everyone knew, for the wreckage would float for days and bodies would wash onto the beaches. Forty-two merchant ships, most of them carrying vital war cargo, were sunk in July alone, sixty-eight in August, sixty-six in September. In the first twelve months of the war, a total of 1.5 million tons of Allied shipping disappeared at sea. Ships sank because they were unprotected. Neither the men nor the warships nor the aircraft could be spared to escort convoys sailing everyday for Britain. The Royal Navy performed splendidly, fought fiercely and without quarter, but a fatal imbalance was clear to anyone who could add.

All of this was happening while hundreds of miles away Lüth and his bright new boat prowled the depths of the Baltic Sea. It is not difficult to imagine his elation and relief when, at the beginning of September, U-138 was finally sent to Kiel to prepare for operational patrol.

On her maiden patrol U-138 was destined for the Western Approaches, a patch of ocean extending from the Irish Sea like a funnel, north and west, and fading indeterminately into the Atlantic. This was the gauntlet all merchant traffic to and from the harbors of Great Britain had to run, the killing fields of Dönitz and his boats. U-138 left Kiel on 10 September. It took her a week to reach the Approaches—to cross the North Sea, leaving the Scottish islands to the south and sailing in a long, lazy zigzag toward Barra Head, a tiny point of land at the extreme southern end of the Hebrides.

Barra Head loomed before U-138 at dawn on 19 September. At noon on that day HMS *Scarborough* left the Albert docks. She was the ship of the escort commander of OB 216, a ten-year-old sloop of about 1,600 tons, only lightly armed with depth charges and two four-inch guns. The other escort ships were a contrast in black and white, symbolic of the Royal Navy's current makeup. HMS *Vanquisher* was an ancient Admiralty "V"-class destroyer, launched in the last war, leaky and creaking, while HMS *Arabis* was a brand-new *Flower*-class corvette, only four months old, the smallest of the three and carrying a single gun.

Immediately on departing the Albert docks, the three warships began to collect their errant charges. It was not easy. Every master had his own ways, each ship characteristics of her own. By noon the next day, 20 September, the convoy was officially formed, and at 1300 the leading ships of OB 216 left the Irish Sea and entered the Atlantic Ocean, jostling in rough columnar formation, blacked out, escorts arrayed against who knew how many unknown enemies. It was quiet for a while.[3]

Lüth spotted OB 216 in the early evening, as the ships sailed west toward the Stanton Banks. He was engaged in the pursuit of another convoy, maintaining periscope depth to avoid aircraft, when the leading units of OB 216 came out of the dusk and straight into his crosshairs.

"Steamer passing at 2,000 meters," he noted in the log at 2000, "bearing 70-90. Immediately afterward two more bearing zero in sight, then a convoy of eight columns, distance 400–500 meters, irregular station-keeping in columns, about thirty ships, course 270, speed seven." OB 216 was following a zigzagging course. The base course at that time was 275 degrees, the base speed eight knots. The weather was fair, cloudy with good visibility, wind from the west at force two.

At about 2015 Lüth moved between two of OB 216's six columns. It was the sort of unexpected maneuver that confounded many escort commanders of the day. The ships of the convoy, counting on the escorts for protection and not paying any attention to the waters between them, failed to sight the thin black periscope. The escorts, concerned with the threat from outside the convoy, also missed U-138. Nor did they pick her up on asdic, the primitive sonar system used for detection of submarines.

Thus hidden, Lüth planned his first attack at leisure, able to choose from ships only 400 to 500 meters away. Not that it mattered much; he could hardly miss from such a position. Just point the bow and fire.

At 2120 he ordered two torpedoes released.

At 2121 Richard Chisholm, on the *New Sevilla,* looked over his right shoulder.

At 2122 the *Boka* blew up.

Chisholm immediately ordered evasive action on his ship, but no sooner had he rung for lifeboat stations than the *New Sevilla* was struck on the port quarter. "A large sheet of flame blew up abaft the engine room skylights. The vessel heeled over about 20 degrees to port and then righted herself and was seen to be settling aft."[4]

The *Scarborough,* stationed in the starboard column of OB 216, heard a single explosion at 2126 and immediately turned away from the convoy. The *Arabis,* stationed to port, "went hard to port and full speed towards the spot where it was considered the submarine might be." The *Vanquisher,* stationed astern, headed out after the *Arabis;* she reported later that the *New Sevilla* had been hit first and then the *Boka.* Both ships were sure that the attack had come from outside OB 216. The convoy began a slow emergency turn to starboard, "somewhat hampered by SS *Defoe,* the last ship in the second column, which turned to port."[5]

There was confusion, too, in U-138, with "men running back and forth, one after the other, in order to keep the boat properly trimmed," while the torpedomen tried to reload tubes for another run. The U-boat was now between columns three and four of the convoy; all three escorts still searched for her outside. As Lüth's crewmen dashed noisily up and down the single narrow passageway, he and Gramitzki calculated the next director angle through the periscope. Petersen, hunched over a tiny chart table in near darkness, plotted as best he could from their shouted bearings the movements of U-138, the escorts, and the target ship.

At 2126 a single torpedo was fired at the *Empire Adventure,* the fourth ship in the fourth column and the third to come under attack in six minutes. "There was a violent explosion amidships on the port side," according to the official Admiralty report of the action, "and it is stated by the Chief Officer that, to the best of his knowledge, neither the submarine nor track of torpedo was seen. The explosion may have broken the back

of the vessel, and orders were given to abandon her at once."[6]
The orderly columns of OB 216 dissolved into chaos after
the *Empire Adventure* was hit. Lüth got one more glimpse of the
ships before he was forced to drop below periscope depth. The
Arabis began dropping depth charges, as her captain later
explained, to "scare the submarine."[7] Hardly the best move to
make under the circumstances, but there was no alternative.
The *Arabis* could not see U-138; she could not hear U-138; she
had no idea where to look nor, for that matter, what to look for.
The dropping of depth charges was at least something.

At 2200 U-138 re-surfaced beyond the convoy and Lüth saw
the *Empire Adventure* dead in the water, her back broken and her
hull twisted into a huge, dark, half-submerged chevron. He set
off immediately to regain OB 216. All three escorts continued
to search for him until about 2330, at which time the *Scarborough* directed the *Vanquisher* to remain at the scene and assist
in recovering survivors. The *Arabis,* after doing what she could,
was to rejoin the convoy.

Shortly after 2300 the *Boka* sank; twenty-eight of her crew
had been picked up by the *Arabis.* The *New Sevilla* was still
afloat, her entire crew removed. Only the "forecastle head and
poop" of the *Empire Adventure* could be seen by midnight; of her
crew of thirty-nine, twenty-one still had to be accounted for.[8]

That was not all for OB 216. Lüth caught up with the main
body again at 0200 and was able to sink one more ship, the *City
of Simla,* before running out of torpedoes. With that, after twelve
hours, he broke off his attack on OB 216, feeling "like a man with
no teeth at a richly laden table." He evaded a last asdic search,
turned west, and arrived three days later in Lorient.

OB 216 limped on and finally made it to Canada with thirteen ships of her original nineteen. On 24 September the flag
officer in charge, Belfast, wrote up the official report of the
encounter with U-138 and forwarded it to the commander in
chief, Western Approaches. His report virtually summarizes
the state of antisubmarine warfare in 1940.[9]

It is clear that the escorts had no idea of U-138's location at
any time during the attacks on OB 216. Their commanders all
assumed that the attacks had come from outside the convoy;

apparently none could conceive of a U-boat sneaking *inside* a convoy to attack. Also, the escorts began asdic searches immediately after the first torpedo hit in the belief that the attack had been made underwater. But Lüth attacked at periscope depth then submerged to remain safe from detection, masked by the hulls of the convoy and the noise of multiple turning screws. Finally, the lack of escorts was a critical shortcoming; at one time or another, all three escort vessels were forced to abandon OB 216 so as to look for Lüth.

As she steamed into port U-138 flew four white pennants from her periscope housing, one for each of the four ships sunk. A band played while the lines were tossed over. The boat would be in Lorient for ten days to refuel, provision, and be checked for damage.

The crew went on shore leave. "Lorient was not a pretty place," recalled Petersen, "but it had that French 'flair.' The people were all nice, we drank a lot of wine and champagne, and it was all free."[10] In addition there was the regular liberty train to Paris and the east, and resorts and hotels in the countryside for the exclusive use of U-Bootwaffe personnel. And Lüth arranged activities: soccer games against the crews of other boats, for example, and excursions into the countryside. "I remember," he wrote, "how my crew was once invited to ride [horses] by a local artillery detachment. We all mounted up, I next to the commanding officer trying to cut an irreproachable figure as I had been taught in school. But the men were unable to hold their horses and they began to gallop down the street . . . the commander and I were suddenly alone, because his troops had taken off to hunt my men down. After a while they all came back in triumph. . . . For two hours we rode like mad over hill and dale, never stopping to realize that we would be stiff as boards later on. . . . I am proud to say that nobody fell off."[11] But for some, playing soccer and riding horses were not enough. They visited the bordellos in Lorient, which were always open, or risked Lüth's displeasure by seeking out French girlfriends.

By this time Lorient had become a gathering point for U-boat officers of high visibility and unusual talent. Lüth was still a minor star in their constellation, for other captains were making their reputations in the Western Approaches as well as he. Günther Prien was in Lorient, the cocky commander of U-47 who sank the *Royal Oak* in 1939 and was building a solid tonnage base as well, Joachim Schepke, debonair and dangerous with the face and manner of a matinee idol, Henrich Liebe, still in command of U-38, Herbert Schultze, Viktor Schutze, Fritz Frauenheim, and Otto Kretschmer. All of them were aces, and most had been commanders since the war began. They were the "first generation" commanders, of whom Dönitz proudly wrote, "They threw themselves with daring, skill, and ripe judgment into this onslaught on the British lines of communication. . . . They felt that they were the 'Rulers of the Sea,' and more than capable of coping with any defensive measures the enemy might use against them."[12] They were the best and, from the British perspective, the most hated men in the U-Bootwaffe.

Günther Prien was the first of the great World War II U-boat aces, flashy and telegenic. After Scapa Flow he became the darling of the Reich's propaganda office and a service legend. He was the archetypal German submariner, the wartime movie German in dirty white sweater and beard, the man the Allies loved to hate.

We cannot know whether or not Wolfgang Lüth and Günther Prien knew each other. Given the smallness of the community, it seems likely that they ran into each other more than once before Prien eventually died at sea. Other than in skill and success, the two were similar in only one way worth noting; Wolfgang Lüth was a Nazi, and so was Prien. But Prien was also a professional seaman, having once held master's papers in the merchant marine, whereas Lüth entered the Reichsmarine straight out of school. Prien was North German; Lüth was a Balt. Prien was loud; Lüth was quiet. But the essential difference was one of character: While Prien was an effective leader, his men hated him; Lüth was just as effective, and his men loved him.[13]

If Günther Prien was the most famous ace in 1940, then Otto Kretschmer was rapidly becoming the best. Captain of U-

Otto Kretschmer. Kretschmer, captured at sea only eighteen months after the war began, still accounted for more tonnage than any other U-boat commander in the war. Wolfgang Lüth was second behind him. The other commanders called him "Silent Otto"; to his enemies, he was sinister, hated, and feared, but always respected. (Courtesy U.S. Naval Institute)

99, Kretschmer was the first among equals in the U-Bootwaffe, and it was to him that all the other men were—and are—compared.

In the relatively short time Kretschmer was at sea—a period of eighteen months that ended when he was captured in March 1941—he sank, or helped sink, Allied ships of almost 300,000 tons, a total never exceeded on either side. His name dots lists of commanders responsible for merchant shipping sunk in the North Atlantic like a chain of bullet holes from a machine gun. Graphic tales of his attacks on convoys, particularly in late 1940, are as common as the stories of the *Bismarck* or the *Graf Spee*. He was a fearsome figure.

"Otto Kretschmer was the most dangerous enemy of them all," wrote Donald McIntyre, the man who captured him. "Utterly fearless, supremely confident of his skill as a seaman and a fighter, and devoted single-heartedly to his career in the navy, he commanded his U-boat with the iron hand of a martinet, bringing his crew to the highest pitch of efficiency, and yet earning their complete devotion."[14] Referring to Kretschmer's quiet, brooding manner and utter disdain of publicity, traits that won him the nickname Silent Otto, as well as his gaunt bony face and grim countenance, McIntyre finished, "Compared with his fellow aces he was a sinister fellow."[15]

Otto Kretschmer and Wolfgang Lüth did know each other. They were passing acquaintances in Lorient, and in December 1940 they were formally introduced in the back seat of Karl Dönitz's staff car on their way from Paris to Cologne for Christmas. They spent most of this journey catching up on their sleep. While he was awake, Kretschmer had to fend off the repeated pleas of his commander that he be transferred to a training billet. Unfortunately for Kretschmer he won the argument.

Lüth's impression of him can only be imagined. He was Kretschmer's junior and painfully conscious of the man's aura. Kretschmer, however, regarded Lüth as essentially an equal: "We are alike in several ways. Neither of us was a gossip or a braggart, we both had strong nerves and we both kept our heads before the enemy . . . basically Lüth was a Prussian like me."[16]

U-138's second war patrol began on 8 October 1940. It was not as successful as Lüth's first. At a time when boats were returning to port with three, four, five kills, it was almost humdrum, but it is interesting for other reasons. It proves the ease with which German U-boats were able to find, attack, and sink Allied shipping in the Western Approaches. Lüth, though he stumbled through this patrol, encountered one convoy after the other without trying. It demonstrates also how little the various accounts of such attacks differed. The events of this patrol can be reconstructed, almost to the minute, by using U-138's log, charts, descriptions in Lüth's book, and records of the Admiralty.[17]

At 0800 on 14 October, U-137, miles away from U-138, sighted the armed merchant cruiser *Cheshire* north of the Irish coast and gave chase. She was still chasing at 1730. Her commander, Herbert Wohlfahrt, had lost contact with the ship several times, regained her, attacked, and missed twice. Wohlfahrt's pride was hurt; he would not give up on the *Cheshire*, not even after he saw a small convoy heading north over Vidal Bank. Instead of turning away from his prey, he radioed the position of the convoy to BdU and let it pass. This is where Lüth and U-138 entered in.

Lüth overheard the signal from Wohlfahrt to BdU. He also heard Claus Korth in U-93 report a second convoy headed south. He himself, in pursuit of an unknown westbound convoy since 1628, was now in good position to reach any one of the three. He decided to follow his original target. If contact was lost, he would go after Wohlfahrt's convoy headed north. If he could find neither of them, he was still close enough for Korth's southbound convoy. In any case, he wrote, "it will be a night of long knives. . . ."

At 2045, Lüth gave up on the convoy he had been pursuing and began trailing Wohlfahrt's northbound convoy. Almost at once, he heard something that made him conclude that Wohlfahrt had torpedoed two ships from the convoy, then lost it in the fog.

There is no record of any convoy losing two ships at this time. Wohlfahrt had not stopped chasing the *Cheshire*, and after twelve hours he succeeded in sinking her. Lüth confused his reports. The charts of U-138 indicate a very short track toward Wohlfahrt's convoy, then a 180-degree turn to the north, suggesting that Lüth moved tentatively after his prey and changed his mind after receiving the message. The log states only that Lüth headed for Korth's southbound convoy at 2045.

At 2150 U-138 intercepted another signal: Korth's convoy had changed course and was now traveling due west. Soon it was out of Lüth's range. "We were speechless," he wrote. "Three opportunities had been taken from us. We had turned a complete circle in the fog and had lost one target after another." Disgusted, he ordered a course change due east toward Barra and went to sleep, only to be wakened again at midnight by Gramitzki, who handed him a bottle of cognac. It was Lüth's twenty-seventh birthday.

At 0230 he was called again by the watch officer. "A wonderful report had just been made by the bridge watch: 'Bridge to Captain, birthday present in sight!' I hurried up . . . the 'birthday present' got bigger and bigger until it finally became an entire convoy stretched out before us."

It was westbound OB 228, the fourth convoy of the night to venture into the six-mile square that formed U-138's area of operations. In his log Lüth described a formation of eight columns, with three or four ships in each and what he thought was a light cruiser in escort. The moon was out; he did not want to wait until it set, so he put the moon behind him by steaming up the port side of OB 228, crossing ahead of it, and steaming back down its starboard side to attack.

This time U-138 did not dive. Surface attacks at night had by now become doctrine at BdU. They had the advantage of foiling both sonar equipment and Admiralty planners who did not expect surface attacks from U-boats. It was also much easier to direct a torpedo attack from the bridge than through a wet periscope lens.

The ships of OB 228 sailed on, oblivious to the danger threatening them. Lüth made these entries in his log:

0510. Fired with G7a at tanker in middle column. Bearing 90 [degrees], speed 8 knots, distance 3800 meters, torpedo depth 3 meters.

0512. Missed with G7a on a second tanker under identical circumstances. Distance 2500 meters. After 4 minutes, 40 seconds, the first G7a hits the tanker aft, a tall burst of flame can be seen and then clouds of black smoke. Estimated at 10,000–12,000 tons.

0515. Fired with G7a at a tanker bearing 100, speed 7 knots, distance 2000 meters, torpedo depth 3 meters. There were two tankers better situated in my field of fire, but I fired at the largest instead. Boat turns with hard rudder to starboard after the shot.

0517. After 1 minute 57 seconds the G7a hits the tanker aft, tall burst of flame . . . estimated at 10,000–14,000 tons. No radio traffic on 600 m wavelength.

The first ship hit was the British steamship *Bonheur;* she sank at 0522. The second was the tanker *British Glory,* which did not sink and actually made it back to port. It was Lüth's stated intention to remain in contact with OB 228 as long as possible, but a destroyer forced him below at 0900, and after he surfaced at 0920 he could only report OB 228's last position and then turn for Lorient. His second war patrol in U-138, eleven days long, was over.

It was British practice to interview survivors of torpedoed merchant ships in the hope that their observations might be useful. The form for recording such information, "Particulars of Attacks on Merchant Vessels by Enemy Submarines," was ridiculously out of date. It asked questions such as, "Was ship boarded by enemy and how?" and wanted the names and personal descriptions of the attacking U-boat's officers. This form was used to interview the master of the *Bonheur,* one Leon Otto Everett, after he returned to Belfast. His answers were terse and uniformly unhelpful. The last two reflect the frustrations of the moment with subtle grace: "General remarks by interviewing officer: Does he consider the Master complied with Admiralty and local instructions and did all in his power to avoid capture? 'Yes, but it does not appear than an after lookout was posted or gun manned.' Master's reasons for abandoning ship (where this was done) should be carefully gone into and fully explained. 'Vessel sank in 12 minutes.'"[18]

The phrase "night of long knives," used by Lüth to describe the night of 14 October 1940, had been coined in 1934 after the bloody Rohm Putsch. In naval history it applies more accurately to the nights of 18–20 October, four days after Lüth's operation. During that period two inbound convoys—the fast Halifax HX 79 and the slow Sydney SC 7—were attacked in the Western Approaches and torn to pieces by wolfpacks.*

The concept of wolfpack, or as it is called in German, *Rudeltaktik* ("pack tactic"), was developed by Karl Dönitz before the war. A wolfpack was a group of submarines, usually between five and ten, that operated together to achieve concentration of force. The first boat in a wolfpack to sight an enemy convoy would not attack; she only signaled her position and waited for the other boats to gather. The entire pack would then engage, with results far better than if they had attacked in scattered and uncoordinated bursts. During the first year of the war, there were not enough boats for wolfpack operations. It was only now that packs prowled the North Atlantic with such terrible success.

When U-138 arrived back in Lorient on 19 October to the usual music and flowers, Lüth was greeted on the pier by his flotilla commander and informed that he was to be relieved for command of another, larger boat. The U-boat captain was understandably taken aback. After months of training, months

---

*Convoy SC 7 left Sydney, Cape Breton, with thirty-five ships early in October. It was first spotted by Rösing in U-48 while passing to the northwest of Rockall on the evening of 16 October. Six additional boats were ordered to join him, among them Heinrich Liebe in U-38, Joachim Schepke in U-100, and Otto Kretschmer in U-99. Between that time and the morning of the nineteenth, SC 7 lost over half of its ships. Kretschmer waged particularly savage attacks throughout the night; U-99's log is often quoted as an example of his relentless drive and to demonstrate the hellish gauntlet through which SC 7 had to pass that night.

Convoy HX 79 was made up of forty-nine ships and was escorted by ten warships when Prien sighted it the next evening. Nevertheless, twelve ships were lost during an attack that lasted from 2100 until dawn the following day. Five U-boats, including those of Prien, Schepke, and Liebe, made successful runs on ships of HX 79.

During this forty-eight-hour period thirty-one ships were lost in two convoys and three more were damaged. No U-boats were lost. Rudeltaktik succeeded brilliantly. "These two catastrophic encounters," wrote McIntyre, "perhaps mark the very nadir of British fortunes in the Battle of the Atlantic" (*Naval War*, 65).

of drill, months of work with his crew, and then just twenty-six days on patrol, he was being told that he would have to leave his new boat.

At the change of command ceremony, already bittersweet because of this relatively early departure, Lüth had to tell his crew that two of them had been killed in an air raid on the Lorient railway station, one cornered in the lavatory of an outbound train by shrapnel and broken glass. Some of the surviving crew cried, Lüth related in *Boot Greift Wieder An*. He himself regretted only that the men had died on shore: "Death was for all of us a constant threat; better that it came in the fulfillment of our duty. This is what distinguishes the brotherhood of submariners: the feeling of unity that comes from knowing in the end we will all experience the same success or we will all die together."[19]

5

THE BALT
AND HIS MEN

By the time he left U-138 in October 1940, Wolfgang Lüth had sunk over 55,000 tons of enemy shipping. He had reported sinking almost 80,000 tons, and for this, on 24 October, he was given *Das Ritterkreuz des Eisernen Kreuzes*—the Knight's Cross of the Iron Cross. A photograph taken afterward shows him in blue uniform and garrison cap, the medal in place, grinning his peculiar gap-toothed grin and looking quite smug.[1]

He had several things to smile about. One was the Knight's Cross itself, an honor of real value in an era of superfluous decorations. It was the premier decoration of the Reich, replacing the imperial *Pour le Merite* of World War I (some of the very senior officers of the Wehrmacht, Erwin Rommel, for example, wore both). It was almost never given to enlisted personnel and only rarely to officers outside positions of command or high visibility. There were more prestigious Knight's Crosses: the Oak Leaves, Oak Leaves with Swords, Oak Leaves with Swords and Diamonds. But the simple black and silver cross dangling on a striped ribbon was sufficiently impressive. You either had it or you didn't. The Iron Cross, First Class, was not nearly as valued as the Knight's Cross, and the Iron Cross, Second Class — a *very* common award — was really of no consequence at all.

Traditionally, a submarine captain was given the Knight's Cross after he had sunk 100,000 tons of enemy shipping, the Oak Leaves after 200,000 tons. This standard was often relaxed, and there were exceptions. Günther Prien, for example, was given the Knight's Cross after he sank the *Royal Oak* in 1939. Lüth himself had not amassed the requisite tonnage, but he had sunk an enemy submarine in May, and he had been credited (prematurely) with a destroyer in April.

Knight's Crosses were awarded by the flotilla commander or by Dönitz himself; in a few cases the Führer would do the honors. If notification came while the officer was still at sea, his crew sometimes made a temporary cross for him to wear into port. A Knight's Cross was also a tribute to the recipient's crew. In fact, wrote Peter Cremer, who won his in 1942, "a captain with the Knight's Cross was particularly valued by U-boat crews; he offered a certain security, since a young and inexperienced captain who wanted at all costs [to win one] . . . would often act over-hastily and could put his crew at needless risk. . . . This at any rate was how the ordinary crewman saw it, which is understandable, for whatever his readiness to fight, or because of it, everyone wants to survive."[2]

Lüth had other things to smile about as well. He had been successful in two boats, and he had just been given a third, much larger and more powerful. He was beginning to make a reputation for himself; he was one of Dönitz's Lords of the Sea, an ace. He had seen the war; he had been to the front before the shooting was over.

Lüth's personal life was also bringing him happiness. On 25 September 1939, while on leave from U-38, he had married twenty-four-year-old Ilse Lerch, who lived in Sassnitz on the Baltic island of Rugen. Her father, Otto Lerch, was a ferry captain on the Sassnitz-Trelleborg line. Wolfgang and Ilse moved into the naval housing complex in Neustadt where several other U-boat officers and their families lived. Eleven months later in Kiel, on 30 August 1940, they had their first child, a daughter named Gesa.

It is safe to say that marriage and children, of which he had four, were the most significant, most satisfying, most sacred part of Lüth's life—more significant than his commissioning, more satisfying than his medals or any of his sinkings, more sacred than his command or even his oath. Lüth preached marriage and the family with missionary zeal to anyone, at any time, on land and at sea, in jest and in deadly earnest. Marriage, to him, was the only perfect state of man. "He used to come up on the bridge at night," said Theodor Petersen, "smoke a cigar, and talk about [its] benefits," this while his boat was in mad pursuit of a North Atlantic convoy, or while she was steaming lazily through the Mozambique Channel 6,000 miles from home.[3]

His zeal brought predictable results for his crews. Enlisted men who were husbands and fathers were marked. They were counseled to be faithful, to write often, to buy things for their wives, and to stay away from other women in port. As for married officers, Lüth would literally follow them around on liberty to make sure they behaved. "We all went out together," said one, "and some of the places we went had very pretty women inside. But Lüth always saw that we stuck to our drinking and kept our hands off."[4]

Single men were encouraged to get married as soon as possible, not just because marriage was the ideal state, but also because Lüth thought that married men made better sailors. Friendly persuasion from a commanding officer can be perceived as pressure by seamen, and no doubt some resented it. Once, at a party in Stettin for the crew of his last boat, Lüth visited every table to ask couples if they were married, and if not, why not. "Marriage wouldn't make any difference, sir," replied one man bravely, "except that we would have a marriage license." Petersen recalls that this sent Lüth into shock for some time.[5]

Wolfgang and Ilse Lüth. Of all that Wolfgang Lüth ever did, his marriage was to him the most important and the most satisfying. It made him supremely happy, and since he was so happy, it seemed logical that everyone else he knew should be married too. (Courtesy National Archives)

If marriage was good, parenthood was better. Those in his crew who were fathers were always recognized, and on special days like Father's Day, celebrated. To be a father was to be responsible, selfless, a leader, and an example. Lüth would do almost anything he could to help a man with a family, whether the favor was service related or not, whether the man was in his crew or had moved on. After Lüth had been reassigned permanently to shore in late 1943, for example, one of his former crewmen wrote to him saying that his wife was expecting their second child and they could not find a new place to stay. Lüth saw to it personally that the man's wife was moved to a larger apartment. The supplicant did not find this out until he was released from internment in June 1948 and saw his three-year-old son for the first time.[6]

It is no coincidence that National Socialist doctrine emphasized both marriage and children. Lüth "was always after us to have children," said one of his men, "in order to fulfill our duty to the Reich."[7] But it is a mistake to assume that Lüth was a devoted husband and father because he was a Nazi; more likely it worked the other way. The affection he showed was never forced. Though the Reich told a man he should have children, nobody told him he had to love them. An officer was expected to maintain a veneer of propriety in public, but he didn't have to in private, and he certainly didn't have to proclaim his affection from the rooftops, as Lüth did.

If the hatred of promiscuity had Lüth trailing his men in port, it drove him to perhaps further lengths at sea. It is hard to explain this puritan streak. Lüth was not a religious man. He was baptized Evangelical Lutheran, but he would never admit to being anything more than *Gottgläubig,* a believer in God, and he rarely saw the inside of a church. And yet he was obsessed with the spiritual condition of his men. He outlawed pinups in the crew's quarters; "if you are hungry," he would say, "you don't draw pictures of bread on the walls." He examined their reading matter closely for prurient passages and dirty pictures; anything he didn't approve of he threw overboard. He banned all leave three days before leaving port to keep his boats free of germs picked up in bordellos.

The officers fared no better than the men and probably worse. "You can't let them hang a picture of the Führer on the left side of the officers' mess and a picture of a girl from a box of French candy on the other side. That shows bad taste." He permitted no profanity in the mess, "not just for moral reasons, but because it is hard to stop such things once they have started . . . and above all because the men are quick to pick up the habit." Lüth recognized, however, that "officers have to be left alone often enough to give them time to grumble about the captain."

Morals or not, behavior like his was risky in the U-Bootwaffe; he was either irretrievably naive or a shrewd manipulator of men. If he had been the former, his crewmen would have loathed him, taken advantage of him, resented his meddling, and ignored his attentions. They did not. Lüth was naive in some ways, but never about men in U-boats: He knew perfectly well that crewmen did not pick up their bad language from officers and that many sailors frequented brothels. He might be shocked at his men's behavior, but he was rarely surprised.

And so when Lüth tried to correct their actions, he did so without malice, and hoped at least for respect, even appreciation. He created the same relationship with his crews that exists between father and children. He nagged and preached and worried, he praised and he punished. He encouraged them to stay in touch when they left his command, and if they needed help after leaving he felt obligated to lend a hand. Lüth's behavior was the very definition of fatherhood.

In the meantime, apparently, a network of support grew out from the Lüth home on Teufelsberg Street in Neustadt, with Ilse at the center extending lines of support to the wives of Lüth's officers and they, in turn, to the home of every man in his crew.[8] "One big family," remarked a former officer of Lüth's. It was a description that would have given his commander great pleasure.

On 21 October 1940 Lüth relieved Kapitänleutnant Wilhelm Ambrosius as captain of U-43. If not a spectacular officer, Ambrosius was a competent one. In contrast to Lüth's other boats, U-43 had enjoyed a measure of success under the command of someone else: Nine ships of 50,000 tons were sunk during Ambrosius's fourteen-month tenure.

U-43 was one of eight type IXA oceangoing submarines commissioned in August 1939 at the shipyards of AG Weser in Bremen. U-38, in which Lüth had served Heinrich Liebe as first watch officer, was of the same class. U-43 was 77 meters long, weighed 1,153 tons (three times as much as U-9), and had a range of over 8,000 miles (twice that of U-138). She carried twenty-two torpedoes and three mounted deck guns, one of them a 105-mm cannon.

The interior, her new captain later wrote in *Boot Greift Wieder An,* made him think of a hospital; the forty-eight man crew was berthed in four compartments instead of one, and he had a compartment to himself. "Not really a room, just a bunk in a little space separated from the passageway by a curtain. I do my paperwork on a tiny writing desk, and in order to wash, the desk is pushed up to reveal a washbasin."[9] It was much different from U-9 or U-138: "There was nothing like this on the smaller boats. We all slept in one room, the captain as close to the control room as possible in order to 'be there' faster. There was a reserve torpedo stored between our bunks and we all had to sit with our legs crossed like Arabs."[10]*

The boat was only one year old, but already she was showing her age. Shortly after Lüth left Lorient for his first patrol on 10 November 1940, a leak was discovered in one of the fuel tanks and the boat began to trail a heavy silver streak of oil. He returned immediately, and it took a week to isolate and repair the problem.

She left again on the seventeenth, steaming west to get as far from land as fast as possible, for enemy aircraft were beginning to surprise the boat on the surface. Since it was Lüth's

---

*Theodor Petersen reminisced: "Of all Lüth's boats, U-43 was for me the best and the most reliable; even though her hull bucked like an old horse, we always thought that everything was okay and nothing was going to happen to us" (letter to author, 30 October 1989).

first patrol in U-43, and many of the crew were new to the boat, he drilled them regularly in emergency diving, deep-water maneuvers, and torpedo handling. He had plenty of time for drills, because U-43 was assigned as a weather boat for part of the month and all he had to do was report conditions back to BdU. Weather-boat duty was universally hated. Again, the submarine was effective only when used in an offensive role to sink ships.

Not until December, two weeks out, was Lüth back in the battle. At 1843 on 1 December he intercepted a report from Ernst Mengerson in U-101 of a convoy in the area. This was possibly westbound convoy OB 251, which had been escorted by HMS *Viscount, Vanquisher,* and *Gentian* to longitude 17° 5′ W, or a fast eastbound convoy, HX 90, picked up by the same three warships and which Mengerson himself eventually attacked.

Lüth headed for Mengerson's position, steaming all night at top speed. The ships of OB 251 were first sighted at 0620 on 2 December. The sighting was made at about 18° 30′ W, just west of the drop-off point. The ships of OB 251 were no longer under the protection of an escort, but they had not yet scattered either, and several could be seen from U-43's bridge.

Lüth, if he had been cautious, patient, methodical, could have taken several of the unguarded ships. It might have been a massacre. Instead, because of his overconfidence, U-43 was lucky to escape after sinking only two.

At 0901 Lüth hit the motor ship *Pacific President* with two torpedoes. It was a fairly straightforward run, and the ship sank in three minutes.

Forty minutes later he fired two torpedoes at another British ship, the tanker *Victor Ross.* Both of them struck her, one forward, one aft. The tanker settled slightly, but she did not sink. In fact, she continued forward, dying slowly on her feet. Lüth came in to about 1,500 meters for the coup de grâce.

He fired. The shot went wide. Then Lüth came in closer, to within 300 meters of the *Victor Ross.* When he tried to line her up for a fourth torpedo, the tanker swung around to ram him. Lüth had stopped his boat to fire. As the *Victor Ross* began to steam toward him, his rudder was useless and he had no time to gather speed astern. The enemy knew it, and went for U-43 even as she fired her fourth torpedo. "A senseless situation . . . stupid." Lüth was forced to make an emergency dive directly in front of his attacker.

"Emergency dive" was a misnomer as far as the U-Bootwaffe was concerned; every dive was made in haste. But a boat with no way on could not dive as fast as a boat moving forward. All Lüth could do was "blow negative"—that is, force the air out of U-43's buoyancy tanks with pumps so that she would sink, more or less vertically, as the dying *Victor Ross* steamed directly overhead.

It was close, too close, but the *Victor Ross* missed in her last lunge. Lüth came astern of her to see the ship standing almost vertically in the water. His fourth torpedo had hit her squarely and she sank as he watched. Meanwhile, at distances of three to five miles from him, the other ships of OB 251 were running desperately due west.

Lüth did not give up; U-43 went after another knot of ships from OB 251 at noon. As she approached, one vessel emerged from a rainstorm and headed straight for her, forcing her down and dropping depth charges. When she resurfaced to attack, both periscopes were damaged.

Lüth did his best to follow the ships farther west, but early the next morning he was forced to turn back—not, he noted pointedly, because he was unable to attack, but because his tanks were leaking and his engines burning oil.

The ships of OB 251 had proven unusually aggressive; no more of them were lost to U-boats. Shortly afterward, the Anti-Submarine Warfare Division of the Admiralty wrote a detailed analysis of the attacks on OB 251 and HX 90, which concluded:

> U-Boat "S."
> 59. A U-Boat was estimated to be in [56–57° N, 16–18° W] at 1124/1 (Admiralty Message 1258/1/12).
> Convoy O.B. 251 passed through the southern part of this area during the evening of 1st December.
> It is therefore probable that it was this U-Boat which torpedoed *Victor Ross* and *Pacific President* on the morning of 2nd December and may later have been responsible for the loss of *Victoria City.*
> . . .

Shortly afterwards, this U-Boat, which is believed to have been that commanded by VIKTOR SCHÜTZE, returned to L'ORIENT.[11]

Reports like this were the product of extensive interviews, exhaustive research, and very good intelligence, but they were not perfect. This one is correct up to a point. U-43 was in the area on 1 December, and it was Lüth who sank the first two ships. But he did not sink the *Victoria City* (she disappeared and is assumed to have been sunk by U-140), and of course he was not Viktor Schütze.

The *Pacific President* was listed in U-43's log only as "a ship of 9,000 tons, three cargo hatches forward and four aft . . . very large, about 150 meters long. . . ." U-boat captains in the North Atlantic had neither the time nor the inclination to identify the ships they sank, not unless they could do it with the aid of shipping registers or intercepted distress signals. The troublesome *Victor Ross,* however, was identified correctly by name and tonnage. Lüth's helmsman, once a merchant seaman, had sailed in her in peacetime, and in a bittersweet flash of recognition just before the attack he blurted out her name. It was not a pleasant moment for the helmsman, Lüth wrote in *Boot Greift Wieder An:* "The loss of this ship hurt him as a seaman and we understood it well . . . it was a shame to have to sink a German ship, but it was sailing under an English flag; we all felt sorry for our helmsman, since a seaman depends on his ship like a farmer on his plow."[12]

It all sounds sympathetic on paper, but his words were only that, words, shameless platitudes on Lüth's part. "Lüth was a naval officer, not a merchant seaman," explained Petersen. "Of the special bond between the seaman, who earns his daily bread from sailing, and the ships that are so important to him, Lüth had no idea. No idea. He was certainly never troubled or depressed about sinking one of them."[13] It troubled Petersen, once a merchant sailor himself, to have to say that Lüth was so lacking in this regard, that never in Petersen's earshot did he utter a word of regret for what he had to do. "In this case we were of completely different natures. I went to sea when I was only fifteen and every ship was to me as my own. . . . Funny, wasn't it? I considered those ships (and I still do) a way of life, but this view of things was alien to Lüth, and I always had the impression that he wasn't particularly concerned about the men or the ships he sank."[14]

Perhaps the editors of *Boot Greift Wieder An*—who, after all, had every interest in making Lüth seem humane, a nice fellow in a bad situation—put these words of sympathy into Lüth's mouth. It should be noted, however, that later in the war the commander did grow somewhat more feeling, and that may have been because of the influence of men like Theodor Petersen.

It was only by chance that Lüth and Petersen remained together after U-138. Lüth was not permitted to bring anyone with him to his new boat, for she already had a wardroom and a crew in place when he arrived. Franz Gramitzki, left behind, soon assumed command of U-138 himself, and Herbert Wohlfahrt asked Petersen to come with him to Wohlfahrt's new boat, U-556. Lüth brought U-43 back to Lorient in early December and spent Christmas in Neustadt. Petersen was on his way to the Blohm and Voss shipyards in January when he ran into Lüth and Otto Kretschmer in the Hamburg-Altona railway station. "Why weren't you assigned to my boat?" Lüth demanded. Finding the answer unacceptable, and even though he already had an Obersteuermann for U-43, Lüth interrupted his leave, went to Kiel at once, and had Petersen's orders changed.[15]

It was an understandable move under the circumstances. Lüth did not know any of U-43's officers, and his first patrol with them had apparently done nothing to reassure him of their value. Many were novices. The boat's new first watch officer, Richard Becker, had only just entered the U-Bootwaffe from the coastal artillery. That was not a good sign. The new second watch officer, Hans-Joachim Schwantke—"'Nigger' Schwantke," said Petersen, "because he looked just like Clark Gable"[16] was also an unknown. (As it turned out, he did not have the fortune of battle on his side.) And many of the remaining crew were just out of U-boat school.

Petersen was the friendly face in a strange crowd. He was someone Lüth knew, someone who was competent and with whom he could talk. That, at sea in wartime, was of inestimable value. The two men traveled back to Lorient via Paris, spending two days there. They visited the Eiffel Tower and saw the Arc d'Triomphe; they went to Sacre Coeur and the Invalides; they walked along the Left Bank, where both had their portraits painted; and Petersen even managed to drag Lüth into the Lido to see a show. "It was a show called *Le Sport;* a man would call out 'tennis' and a naked girl would come out with only a tennis racket, or he would call 'boxing' and a girl would come out with boxing gloves on. . . ."[17] Petersen thought the show fairly tame; Lüth was "shocked."

On account of *Le Sport*, they missed the last train to Lorient.

THE END OF HAPPY TIMES

Early morning, 4 February 1941. The harbor in Lorient is dark. The boats drift quietly, their crews ashore; the sentries pace, their minds lost in silent thought. Tied to the shore with heavy chains is an old sailing ship, the *Ysere*. She has no masts, no crew, and no watch. The *Ysere* is dead, but they have dressed up her corpse to serve as a floating pier.

Tied to this pier is U-43. There are six men on board. The watch officer sits in the petty officers' mess, reading. Every hour he stands up, stretches, then makes a quick tour of the boat. He has no other function. The other men in the watch section are asleep in their bunks—that is, all but one. A single watchstander must remain topside at all times. It is a boring post. There is nothing to see and nowhere to go. The man crosses the gangplank from U-43 to the *Ysere*.

The rest of the crew and all of the officers are ashore. They
have just been told that U-43 will sail at dawn, and in the few
short hours they have left they intend to celebrate, sleep, say
goodbye. Where she is heading they do not know. Boats leave
and sometimes come back; anything can happen in between.

The man standing watch does not know where U-43 is going
either. He is cold, because it is February, and he is frightened,
because it is dark and he is the enemy in an occupied country;
not everyone in Lorient is as friendly as the waitresses. Both of
these things are on his mind.

He walks through silence broken only by the occasional rum-
bling sound of an engine, the distant laughter of a drunken
man, horns tooting over the water. Nothing else. Then he
hears something closer, almost at his side, a sudden, loud
sound, a *crack!* It is a pistol shot. The sentry stops in his tracks,
rifle ready. The sound echoes, and then silence again. He
turns and peers into the darkness, puzzled. He has heard this
sound before, but it hides from remembrance in quiet play.

A whisper from below, an almost silent bubbling sound, like
the foam in a beer, persuades him to look down. And then he
knows instinctively what has happened: One of U-43's mooring lines has snapped in two. At that very moment, or a split
second before, the sentry sees something else—a gurgle of
swirling white water where U-43's after torpedo room hatch
had been, a flash of red and white as her ensign goes under.
The entire after section of U-43 disappearing into the murky
waters of her berth.

To his amazement the boat he is supposed to watch is sinking, fast, and as he gapes another line parts with a creak and
a crack. The sentry runs stumbling over the gangplank between
the *Ysere* and U-43, jumps and falls onto the sloping deck of his
dying boat, clambers up the ladder and into her tower. Then
he begins to shout, hoping that they won't shoot him for what
has happened.

Theodor Petersen walked down to Lorient harbor later that
day. Instead of going directly to his own boat he went to U-65,
moored farther away. U-43 was scheduled to head south to an

operations area near Freetown on the west coast of Africa; U-65 had just returned from Africa, and he wanted to pick up some charts from her captain.

The crew of U-65 knew better. U-43 would not be going to Africa. They had just seen her sink. "When do you expect to get back?" one of the officers asked him solemnly. "About six weeks," he replied. They all screamed with laughter, pointing across the bay. There in the distance, the tip of U-43's tower poked forlornly from the center of an empty berth while hordes of men swarmed around her — divers, yardworkers, flotilla staff in official vehicles. The patrol was off.

They raised U-43 with cranes in mid-afternoon. Lüth and Petersen had been hanging around for hours, and when they were finally allowed to go below there was nothing but water, with charts, tin cans, coffee beans, and clothing all floating in a greasy oil slick. The sight, said Petersen, was "indescribable," and the prospects for him and Lüth were even more dismal. Having your boat sunk at sea was one thing; allowing it to sink in port, under guard, moored to a *tender*, was another. Everyone was asking how it had happened; everyone wanted to know where Lüth had been, what he had been doing, who exactly had been in charge.

It took several days to work out the answers. The problem concerned valves. There were literally hundreds of different ones in the type IXA submarine — valves to control the direction and flow of compressed air, breathing air, exhaust gases, and fumes; valves for salt water, fresh water, cooling water, bilge water, and sewage; valves for fuel oil, lubricating oil, cooking oil, and battery acid. The shiny steel forests of turnwheels and cranks and levers were ubiquitous, and utterly confusing to anyone but a trained submarine engineer. (The engineer himself could easily work his magic on them.) On the afternoon of 3 February someone had fooled around with the valves and vents in such a way that water began to seep into the bilges of U-43. The leak was so slow that it went unnoticed, but the boat had taken a lot of water even before crew members went ashore that night.

U-43 settled gradually during the evening and early morning. This went undetected by the sleeping watch section, by the sentry standing on the relatively solid deck of the *Ysere,* and by the watch officer, who had never served on a submarine and only just reported on board U-43. Sometime in the middle of the night, water reached the sill of the after torpedo-room hatch.

A directive issued by BdU said that in port all hatches were to remain closed. The watch officer did not know this, so the hatch was left open that night. When the stern of U-43 dipped below the waterline, water began pouring into the after torpedo room. She went faster and faster after that, parting her mooring lines, alerting the sentry, and prompting his mad rush to raise the alarm.

The watch officer was out of the boat within seconds, but he had no idea what to do, and it was probably too late anyway. He sent a messenger running back to the barracks to get help, but the rest of the crew, drunk or asleep or both, thought the man was joking and told him to go away. Meanwhile, one compartment after another filled with water; dirty bubbles and flotsam from inside the hull rose to the harbor's oily surface. The six watchstanders stood glumly on the pier, watching their boat sink.[1]

Next day the crew of U-43 paraded in the town square of Lorient. A few were repentant, some, nursing hangovers, secretly delighted at their luck, most still unaware of exactly what had happened. Wolfgang Lüth stood stiffly in front of the pack, his career hanging in the balance. He was doubly unlucky — Dönitz was in town.

Dönitz arrived in the square and they all braced themselves. But he didn't deal with the men of U-43 just yet. Instead, the admiral put on his "Uncle Karl" show to greet a crew in from a successful patrol and also parading in the square. As Lüth and his men watched, the other captain was congratulated, the other crew decorated with "lots of pretty medals," as Petersen described the humiliating scene later.[2] Finally Dönitz approached the crew of U-43. "You, through your own carelessness and neglect, have lost a valuable boat. You have betrayed my trust and you have damaged the prospects of our war at sea." Half the men would stay in Lorient to help clean up, the other half would be sent back to Germany for more training. "There will be no leave and no liberty,"[3] Dönitz concluded, and with that walked off, leaving the red-faced Lüth to contemplate his short-term future as a U-boat commander.

What the admiral said was true. In February 1941 he was critically short of boats. It enraged him that one could be sunk in harbor when he was continually trying to impress upon Berlin the need for more of them at sea.

Over the course of the following weeks an investigation was held and several men involved in the incident were punished. Surprisingly—perhaps more so to those in western navies accustomed to the idea that a warship's captain is always responsible for what happens under his command—Lüth escaped any formal retribution; in fact the incident seems not to have affected his career at all. As for the crew, those left in Lorient did have to clean up the boat, a dirty job, but those sent back to Germany for more training "had a good time in Plon sailing . . ."[4]

U-43 was not the same boat after she sank. She spent a total of three months in the yards. Her motors had to be taken out and replaced, as did most of the other electrical components. She was cleaned and rewired from stem to stern. But her batteries, for some reason, were not replaced, and because of the sinking they were never again able to hold a full charge. Lüth found himself at sea more than once with his electrical power down to a trickle because of that night in Lorient.

While U-43 convalesced in the yards, the Battle of the Atlantic raged on. U-boats sailed and ships were sunk, pennants flew, men died at sea, some won medals and others nursed wounded egos. The war at sea was not necessarily working to Germany's advantage.

Losses began to hurt the U-Bootwaffe. They were not great, not yet, but morale was badly shaken when three of Germany's best and most infamous U-boat aces—Günther Prien in U-47, Joachim Schepke in U-100, and Otto Kretschmer in U-99—

*In fact, there were fewer U-boats operating in February 1941 than in any other month of the war.

were captured or killed in the space of a month. Prien, the Bull of Scapa Flow, died first. On 7 March 1941 his boat exploded below the surface in a huge red glow after a depth charge attack by HMS *Wolverine*. He had been following convoy OB 293, waiting for support, when he made the mistake of coming too close. Schepke died ten days later. In an attack on convoy HX 112, he was crushed to death between the tower of his boat and the bow of HMS *Vanoc*. Then it was Kretschmer's turn. He participated in the same convoy battle as Schepke, in fact sank four ships from HX 112. But before he even had a chance to radio his kills back to BdU, HMS *Walker* attacked his boat and forced it to surface. He and most of his crew were taken prisoner. Captured after just eighteen months, he spent the next four years in England and Canada as a prisoner of war, but nobody on either side, in six long years of war, sank as many ships as Kretschmer had.

Next came a significant break in Allied attempts to read U-bootwaffe radio signals. Most signals were encrypted using the Enigma machine, for which the Kriegsmarine had several cyphers (the cypher for North Atlantic U-boat operations was called *Heimische Gewasser*). Many of these had been broken, but the primitive computers Britain used at that time to decrypt German messages often took days or weeks to produce results, and often the information (which was distributed under the Allied code word Ultra) was so outdated as to be useless. That changed in May 1941, when three British warships attacked U-110 just south of Iceland. She was forced to the surface, whereupon a boarding party shot her luckless captain, Fritz-Julius Lemp, and retrieved a working Enigma machine along with the documents and code keys for three months.[5]

Not surprisingly, U-Bootwaffe fortunes declined in the following months, and from that point on Dönitz remained in doubt about the Enigma cyphers his boats were using. But the experts reassured him over and over again that they were sound, and so he retained them until the end of the war.

Meanwhile, Allied shipping losses due to submarine attack dropped, though the number of U-boats at sea was on the rise. Antisubmarine technology improved; there were more war-

Kretschmer leaving HMS *Walker* after his capture in March 1941. His loss, and those of Günther Prien and Joachim Schepke the same month, marked the end of the U-boats' happy times. (Courtesy U.S. Naval Institute)

ships at sea and more air cover. And the tactics of the Royal Navy changed. Streetwise now, the British were learning German tricks. The loss of Dönitz's aces in March, proof of this, gave a tremendous boost to Allied morale. Despair was slowly turning into confidence.

Over the course of the previous year the United States had become more involved in the battle, although strictly speaking it was neutral. It came down squarely on the Allied side, Franklin Roosevelt never hiding his opinion that Germany was an outlaw state. At first help came in the form of equipment: Fifty aging American-built destroyers had already been commissioned into the navies of Great Britain and its allies, and with the passing of the Lend-Lease Bill in March 1941 Congress guaranteed billions of dollars more. Soon Roosevelt was offering more than money or materiel. Warships of the U.S. Navy began to patrol the western Atlantic in March. Officially their task was to guard a newly defined American security zone; in reality, it was to protect Allied convoys against German attack. By the summer of 1941 there were U.S. Marines in Iceland.

Roosevelt wanted war with Germany, grumbled Dönitz in his memoirs, and all Germany's efforts to prevent it would be doomed.[6] The calculated game of brinksmanship between the two countries was to continue for another six months, but the happy times of the U-Bootwaffe had ended.

Wolfgang Lüth was not a sentimental man. He knew that to win in war, one must be violent and one must kill. His men knew it too. But there was the realization among those who had to kill at sea that it was a tragic necessity best avoided.

Consider what happened in World War II when a merchant ship was hit by a torpedo. There would be the initial blow, followed by total confusion, then disbelief, then frenzied action. How much damage? Could the ship be saved? If so, damage control and firefighting teams would be called into action. If not, a race to lower the lifeboats would ensue.

The men in the area of impact were invariably pulverized, burned, or jellied by overpressure. Others were wounded, some severely, and required medical attention. If the hit was mortal, the ship would have to be abandoned—in good order if she was sinking slowly in the absence of fire; as fast as possible, every man for himself, if she was a burning tanker or an ammunition carrier. The sight could be horrifying, and was not easily forgotten by observers. "She was sinking fast," wrote Monsarrat in *The Cruel Sea,* "and already her screws were out of water and she was poised for the long plunge. The cries of men in fear came from her, and a thick smell of oil; at one moment, when they had her outlined against the moon, they could see a mass of men packed high in the towering stern, waving and shouting as they felt the ship under them begin to slide down to her grave."[7]*

Not all survivors made it into lifeboats by the time their ship went down. Many leaped from their ships into oil-covered water that was itself on fire, where they would be asphyxiated or burned to death. Or they were killed on impact after falling from the masts or bridge wings, or sucked underwater by the ship's descending bulk to drown.

A ship in shallow water would not disappear before coming to rest on the bottom; the wreck would later be indicated by little black dots on nautical charts. In deeper water a ship became an artificial reef, overgrown with barnacles and coral. A ship off the continental shelf might take twenty or thirty minutes to reach the ocean floor; the men trapped inside her would drown, or perhaps suffocate, and eventually even their bones would disappear.

Those who did not die at once and who did not have the luck to be rescued immediately were left alone in the water. Perhaps the shore was close or fate had landed them in a well-traveled shipping lane. If not, death could be slow. The men who died in the water became waterlogged and sank, only to rise again to the surface as their bodies decomposed. They were more fortunate, often, than those in boats. In a boat men waited days, maybe weeks, to die. They died of burns, broken bones, open wounds, and later hunger, thirst, exposure, the cold of the north or the heat of the tropics. Those who died were shoved overboard, if there was somebody strong enough to move them. Lifeboats have been found more than once with nothing but corpses, lying down, sitting up, looking lifelike from a distance.

Some went completely mad. They would see nonexistent ships, aircraft, and land. They would swim from safety to meet

---

*The scene in the movie *Das Boot*, after an oiler has been sunk and the men in the bridge of the U-boat are crying at the sight of it, is overdone. It does illustrate the point, however, that the distances involved in a torpedo attack tend to buffer the senses; when the buffer is removed, the shock that has long since deserted the infantryman is brand-new to the submarine sailor.

these apparitions. Drink gallons of seawater to quench their thirst. Stare at the sun in a desperate search for rain. Rave and scream, and then die too.

Lüth knew this suffering took place. He had seen it. But there is evidence to suggest that he did not really comprehend it and was unaware of his obligation as a commander (and a mariner) to avoid it as much as he could. Simply put, he had no sense of proportion when it came to war.

On 11 May 1941 U-43, fresh out of the yards, left Lorient and headed west into the open Atlantic. At 0245 on the fifteenth, Lüth sighted the French three-masted schooner *Notre Dame du Chatelet* on her way from France to the Grand Banks of Newfoundland. He sank the ship—not with a quick, clean torpedo run, but in a messy attack using all three of his mounted deck guns, as described in the opening chapter of this book. At first glance, the attack was nothing out of the ordinary for Lüth or any other captain. A ship was sighted in a war zone, engaged, and sunk—225 tons more on the books, another pennant for the periscope. Why then did Theodor Petersen, whose memory retains an image of Lüth screaming from the bridge, write that the sinking of *Notre Dame du Chatelet* "did Lüth no credit at all"?[8] It is an unusual remark for a U-boat officer to make.

Closer examination shows the sinking to have been a rather strange affair. Why did Lüth choose to sink *Notre Dame du Chatelet* at all? Why did he use his guns and not a torpedo? Why did he waste so much time and so much ammunition on what had become a blazing wreck? The answers, or lack of them, are interesting.

Notre Dame du Chatelet was a small sailing ship obviously useless for commerce. In *Boot Greift Wieder An,* Lüth suggested that she was a Q-ship, a trap disguised to lure U-boats and armed to destroy them as they approached. Petersen later wrote that Lüth suspected the ship of being an observation platform, of carrying agents whose job it was to monitor U-boat movements in and out of France's Atlantic ports.

Both of these explanations are dubious. First, a Q-ship lured attackers by presenting an attractive target, and *Notre Dame du Chatelet* was anything but an attractive target. Second, she was sailing hundreds of miles from land, much farther out than the normal dispersion points for U-boats. The real explanation was much simpler: The *Notre Dame du Chatelet* had the misfortune of straying into sight shortly after Lüth and his crew left France under the odium of utter failure and on unspoken probation for their sins in February. Lüth was out to sink something, *anything.*

As for the shellfire rather than a single torpedo, Lüth explained that in his book. Half his crew were new since the last patrol and most were rusty. They needed training badly, and *Notre Dame du Chatelet* provided the perfect opportunity for a gunnery exercise.

"I called Becker up," he wrote, "and gave him half an hour to get ready," that is, to ready the gun crews, to brief them, and to prepare the exercise. Half an hour was almost leisurely. U-43 was clearly in no danger: Lüth knew that the *Notre Dame du Chatelet* would not fire on him and that he could take his time.

But the training exercise Becker probably envisioned, a quick, orderly drill, rapidly degenerated into an undisciplined firestorm. Lüth did not want an exercise, or if he did at first he changed his mind somewhere along the way. He wasn't concerned about his men. As we have seen, when one of them washed overboard during the attack he was furious that a gun crew stopped firing to rescue him.

Lüth's sole object was to sink the *Notre Dame du Chatelet.* She had to be destroyed — never mind the cost in ammunition, or that in remaining on the surface, 500 meters from a ship on fire with all guns blazing, he may as well have been firing signal flares and tap-dancing on the fantail. Such unblinking concentration calls to mind a pyromaniac at a warehouse fire, not a captain in the bridge of a warship.

It is not condemnation that drives this discussion. Most historians shrink from the judgment of amoral acts in battle ("you cannot say unless you were there"). Rather, it is curiosity. Up to this point Lüth had been a professional and relatively restrained commander — callous, perhaps, but not unusually so, impetuous on his first patrol, but otherwise responsible. A second, much wilder Lüth appeared on the bridge that day. More curious, the new Lüth disappeared almost at once after the sinking, not to resurface for years.

It is an interesting puzzle altogether. Unfortunately, the patrol would not be remembered for this darker side of Lüth, or for the *Notre Dame du Chatelet*, or for the men who died in her. It would be remembered for the *Bismarck*.

The war at sea has produced many remarkable stories. The sinking of *Royal Oak*, the scuttling of *Graf Spee*, the raid on *Altmark*, the Channel Dash. The list goes on and on, and extends into fiction, film, television. But none of these stories approaches the hunting and sinking of the *Bismarck* for sheer excitement and human drama. It was a screenwriter's dream and an instant legend.

Wolfgang Lüth played a role in the story of *Bismarck*. As it happened, things did not work out to his advantage and he became, as many others, an observer. But for several days he had the potential to change the outcome.

The breakout of the giant German battleship *Bismarck* from the Baltic Sea into the Atlantic, code-named *Rheinübung* (Rhine Exercise), had been planned for some time. In March and April 1941, after the successes of other German warships and raiders in the shipping lanes, these plans were formalized, and on 19 May the *Bismarck* left Gotenhafen. The nine days of Rheinübung had begun.

Admiral Günther Lütjens, fleet commander for the operation, had agreed with Karl Dönitz that U-boats might be useful, even pivotal, given the right conditions. Dönitz would not take any of his boats away from their normal patrols during Rheinübung (a U-boat's job was to sink ships), but he did offer to keep Lütjens and his staff fully informed of U-boat dispositions just in case, and he assigned one of his own officers to the *Bismarck* for the breakout.[9]

As it happened, BdU was unable to provide direct support to Rheinübung until the afternoon of 24 May, after the *Bismarck* had engaged units of the Home Fleet in the Denmark Straits and sunk the battle cruiser *Hood*. After the *Hood* went down, Lütjens set off south with the battleship *Prince of Wales* and her two escorting cruisers *Suffolk* and *Norfolk* in pursuit. He then requested that a barrier line of U-boats be set up before his fleet. The object was simple: The *Bismarck* would cross the line safely; her pursuers would cross it and be sunk.

U-43 was patrolling as usual on 22 May. Lüth had just received a report from U-111 of a convoy and was steaming north to intercept it. At 2200 that evening, he received a preparatory signal from BdU directing him to join Lütjen's barrier line, which started just south of Cape Farewell and stretched southeast for 200 miles. Also ordered to the line were U-46 (Engelbert Endrass), U-66 (Richard Zapp), U-93 (Claus Korth), U-94 (Herbert Kuppisch), and U-557 (Ottokar Paulssen). These boats were a formidable combination. All their commanders would soon become aces; every one except Paulssen would eventually win the Knight's Cross; and one would probably have had another pennant if the *Bismarck* had lured her pursuers close enough.

At 1940 on 23 May a signal was overheard from the *Bismarck* stating for the first time that the *Hood* had been sunk and that she intended to pass over the line of U-boats at dawn. The boats were on the line, waiting, watching.

But things did not work out as intended.

During the evening of 24 May, the *Prinz Eugen* managed to detach and escape to the south. Shortly after midnight, the *Bismarck* dropped from the radar screens of the *Suffolk*. Lütjens was no longer heading west toward the barrier line; he had turned southeast instead. With his fuel dangerously low after engaging the *Hood* and the *Prince of Wales,* he meant to try for Brest on the far western tip of Brittany. Curiously, his movements were unknown to the enemy for several hours. Stranger yet, he did not know it, and he gave the *Bismarck*'s position away that morning with two long signals to Berlin. Within twenty-four hours, half the British fleet was pursuing her as she steamed hard for France.

It was a desperate race for survival, and the *Bismarck* lost it. In the course of an attack by Swordfish torpedo bombers from the carrier *Ark Royal* late on 26 May, a torpedo struck her astern, jamming her rudders and stopping her dead. She was cornered, and effectively doomed.

The *Bismarck*'s change of course on 25 May rendered the U-boat barrier line unnecessary. U-43's crew, clustered around the radio, could only listen to her signals fade with the miles. "I was in the radio room," recalled Radioman Herbert Krutschkowski. "I heard it. *Bismarck* reported that she had been hit and damaged in her rudders. Then she said she could no longer make way and that she was steaming in circles . . . we could not come close enough to save anyone."[10]

The only boat that could have assisted in these final hours was U-556, commanded by Herbert Wohlfahrt, but he had no torpedoes. Both the *Ark Royal* and the battle cruiser *Renown* passed before her that last evening, hurrying to the *Bismarck*'s scene. Wohlfahrt cursed himself, and in helpless fury watched the flashes from ships holding the *Bismarck* at bay.

At 0840 on 27 May the huge battleship, scuttled by her crew, capsized and sank after a sustained bombardment that included two torpedoes fired at close range. One hundred seven survivors were left in the water. Rheinübung was over, and U-43 set out to hunt for easier prey.

The boat returned to Lorient on 1 July. Lüth heard the news that U-138 had been lost, attacked and sunk off Gibraltar by five Royal Navy destroyers on 18 June. Gramitzki and his crew were prisoners. He also learned that U-556, the boat Petersen would have been aboard if he had not run across Lüth in Hamburg, had disappeared nine days later, and that most of Wohlfahrt's crew had been taken prisoner as well.

Meanwhile, events of immensely greater significance were unfolding. On 22 June German troops invaded the Soviet Union in Operation Barbarossa, and by 1 July German armored divisions had penetrated 200 miles east of the border. Petersen could not recall Lüth's reaction to this news; he kept any thoughts he might have had to himself (as he would six months later when Adolf Hitler declared war against the United States). He was probably elated. Like most Baltic Germans, he despised the Russians. Life for his family had been hard under their rule. They had persecuted his grandfather and locked up his father. Besides all that, the drive to the east was Reich policy, and Lüth was unswerving in his support of Reich policy. "He considered every move the Nazis made as having been willed by God," said Petersen. "He avoided any criticism of them."[11]

The Soviet Union's declaration of war had little immediate effect on the Battle of the Atlantic, since Russia had no merchant fleet to speak of. Within a year, pitched battles would be raging between U-boats and convoys on the long and cold Murmansk run.

Russian involvement eventually led to the loss of Lüth's first command, the little U-9, the Iron Cross Boat. After Lüth's departure in 1940, she had been taken out of service for almost three years. In 1942 she was disassembled, shipped from Hamburg to Dresden by barge, hauled overland to Linz, and barged again from Linz to the Black Sea port of Costanza. In 1943 U-9 was recommissioned as a unit of the newly formed Thirtieth U-Flotilla. The effectiveness of the Black Sea boats was questionable; they were able to harass and complicate Soviet maritime operations, but their success in numbers was limited. In August 1944, Soviet aircraft sank U-9 at her berth. It was an improbable end for such an illustrious relic, but it was an improbable war all around.

PROBLEMS OF
LEADERSHIP

Do not forget: it is the duty of the commander to have faith in his men and to be determined to go on trusting them despite being let down. For we have one great advantage over the Anglo-Americans: our young men are unreservedly eager to come to grips with the enemy and, so long as they are united in the National Socialist spirit and led with revolutionary ardor, they will return gladly, again and again, to the attack. But we must respect them and we must like them.[1]

These words were spoken by Wolfgang Lüth in 1943 to conclude a lecture, "Problems of Leadership on a Submarine," presented to a convention of Kriegsmarine officers in Weimar on the subject of military leadership. If a man like Lüth can be said to have left a legacy, this lecture is that legacy. It is the only part of him that has endured — enlivened by quote and requote, enhanced by synopsis, paraphrase, and comment long after Lüth himself faded into the mists of naval history.

Though "Problems of Leadership" was rambling and structurally unsound, it succeeded in capturing the essence of Lüth's approach to leadership. And in so doing, it showed the man at his best—a commander concerned for the welfare of his crew—and at his worst—a Nazi enamored of the ideology of Adolf Hitler's Reich.

In "Problems of Leadership" Lüth discussed, and illustrated with profuse detail, his unique leadership style. It was a style revolutionary in one way, in another based on simple common sense: Take care of your men, and they will take care of you. We in the postwar military cannot imagine any military commander thinking otherwise. But many officers in the German military establishment at the time, officers young and old, did not think it necessary to "like" their crews or to take care of them, any more than they accepted the idea of a crew as an extended family and the captain a surrogate father. It was not unusual for officers to be successful and disliked, even hated, at the same time.

It is hard to know exactly when Lüth's style began to take shape. As early as his first days in command of U-9, he gathered his crew on the bridge for the sinking of the *Flandria*, took them horseback riding in Lorient, and celebrated a crew member's birthday in the midst of a convoy battle. As time went on Lüth honed his style. It was based on the need to "keep the crew happy," a need that increased in direct proportion to the length of time a boat was at sea. Life in a German U-boat was dismal, no matter how you sliced it, but a short patrol affected the crew less. One or two ships sunk, the prospect of a good time in France—these kept morale afloat. A long patrol was different.

Lüth's early patrols in U-9 and U-138 were short, one or two weeks at the most. It wasn't until he took command of U-43 that they stretched into months. The critical point probably came shortly after 2 August 1941, for on that day U-43 left on a long and unsuccessful war patrol, one during which it finally became necessary to pay more attention to the crew than to tonnage figures. The patrol was a miserable experience for everyone. For six whole weeks the boat steamed back and forth across the North Atlantic. The fresh food went bad. The engines smoked. The batteries failed over and over again. A chronic fuel shortage developed, weather conditions were bad. And they did not sink a single ship.

Except for an inconsequential six-day patrol in March 1940, Lüth had never returned from an operational patrol without sinking a ship, usually several. Nor would he do so again. But in the summer of 1941, he failed. There were several reasons. The main one was Ultra. The breaking of the German military codes was beginning to have an enormous effect on the war at sea. The cracked Heimisch cypher, for example, was used for all tactical signals between BdU in France and U-boats at sea; with the Enigma machine and the code keys recovered from U-110 in May, these signals could be read in Great Britain almost as quickly as they were read by their intended recipients. Every time U-43 reported her position to BdU, the Admiralty knew exactly where she was. Every time BdU ordered U-43 to intercept a convoy, the convoy was rerouted. No wonder the number of ships sunk by German submarines in the summer of 1941 declined so precipitously. The pages of U-43's deck log remained as empty as the sea around her.

Another reason for Lüth's failed patrol was the increasing presence of American warships in North Atlantic convoy lanes. By late summer 1941, the U.S. Navy was escorting ships of every flag across the western half of the Atlantic. U-boats (by order of Adolf Hitler and not the exasperated Dönitz) were instructed to avoid confrontation under any circumstances, even though the Americans had no qualms about confronting U-boats.

On 14 August a convoy was sighted abut 450 miles south of Greenland, and Lüth recorded a *San Francisco*–class cruiser and a *Mississippi*-class battleship in escort. He could only steam alongside an hour or so, "for a last longing look at the battleship and the big steamers," before turning away. On 11 September it happened again. U-43 saw three destroyers and a cruiser steaming in formation to the south and made ready to

fire, but at the last moment the cruiser was identified as belong-
ing to the American *Pensacola* class.

President Roosevelt had calculated, correctly, that the presence of these ships in the convoy lanes was not in itself a sufficient excuse for Adolf Hitler to commit to war. But it was a
dangerous dance, and inevitably a German submarine fired
upon an American warship.

Early on 4 September the destroyer USS *Greer*, alerted by a
British aircraft, began to track the movements of U-652. The
Greer did not attack, but the aircraft dropped several depth
charges at the location. U-652's commander, Georg-Werner
Fraatz, believing the *Greer* was responsible, fired two torpedoes
at her. The *Greer* responded with a depth-charge attack of her
own, which also failed. Roosevelt called this attack by U-652
piracy, and declared that any German warship entering the
American Defense Zone would be subject to attack.

On 15 October a more serious incident occurred when U-
568 attacked and damaged the USS *Kearney*, which had been
escorting a British convoy. The United States expressed out-
rage all the same. Then, on 31 October, Erich Topp in U-552
attacked and sank the destroyer USS *Reuben James,* which
resulted in 115 deaths. The United States was still legally a neutral nation, but from the day *Reuben James* was lost a de facto
state of war existed between it and Germany.

A third reason for the failed patrol was plain bad luck. The
day after Lüth broke off his run on the *Pensacola*-class cruiser —
one of the escorts for eastbound convoy SC 42 — he fired six torpedoes at three different ships in that convoy, and all of them,
for one reason or another, missed.*

"Problems of Leadership" dealt primarily with Lüth's leadership style after it had been perfected in U-181 (four- and six-
month cruises gave him every chance to think of things to do
with his time). But he devoted an entire chapter of *Boot Greift
Wieder An* to "the lighter side" of U-boat life in U-43. Here
Lüth described the measures he took to keep the crew happy

---

*SC 42 lost thirteen ships in a wild convoy battle west of Iceland; it was
one of the few times that summer that Ultra failed the Admiralty.

during her long patrol. He started up games such as Diction-
ary, in which two teams would quiz each other on the mean-
ings of obscure words. He talked to the crew, read them the
news and discussed it, told them about the diversions of the
sea — the birds, the fish, the phosphorescence on the water, and
the northern lights. He encouraged individual reading, group
discussion, hobbies. One man built model submarines from
scraps of wood; Lüth had one at home.

He made a production of music. U-boat crewmen liked to
listen to records at sea; the sound of music calmed their frazzled
nerves. To us, the thought of playing records on a war patrol after
watching a helpless merchant explode and burn may be jarring.
As Nicholas Monsarrat wrote in his searing introduction to
Heinz Schaeffer's *U-Boat 977:* "She was sunk in the North Atlantic, breaking in two in wild weather. There was, of course, no
warning given; simply the sighting, the stalking, the hand on the
trigger, the sweet moment of murder. When it was all over, the
author tells us, when the survivors had been left to die, and the
wrecked ship extinguished by the sea, 'we put on some gramo-
phone records, and hear the old songs that remind us of home.'"[2]

Music was an integral part of life in U-43, both for enjoy-
ment and as a tool of command. Every time U-43 left on
patrol, the *"Englandlied"* ("We Sail against England") was played,
followed by *"Heute Stechen Wir ins Blaue Meer"* ("Today We Make
for Open Sea"). The boat steamed home to the strains of *"Blaues
Boot, Bring Mich Wieder in die Heimat"* ("Little Blue Boat, Take
Me Home Again"). A popular show on German radio during
the war was *Wunschkonzert* ("Request Concert"), and many
boats, including U-43, copied the format of this show with
their own record collections. Herbert Krutschkowski would collect requests from the crew and play them over the loudspeak-
ers in between marching tunes and classical selections. The
latter were Lüth's favorites; he introduced each one with a few
words about the composer, "and the men really did listen to the
piece with a little more appreciation." The last record was
always "Lili Marlene," a favorite of both sides during the war.

All of these — the records, the games, the hobbies, the discussions — served to lift spirits and break tedium. "The best, how-

ever, comes after all the torpedoes have been used up and the boat is on her way home. Then the crew can gather together in the control room or the bow compartment to sing; the *Siegeswimpel* [the victory pennants for sunken ships] are cut out, sewn and painted, and plans for the next liberty are discussed. . . ."[3]

But there were no pennants after this long and dreary patrol in the late summer of 1941. U-43 finally returned to Lorient on 23 September and went at once into the yards for repairs. One week later Wolfgang and Ilse Lüth's second child was born, a girl they named Ilske.

On 1 September 1941 Germany was two years into the war. During the previous six years approximately 230 U-boats had been commissioned into the U-Bootwaffe, of which forty-eight were sunk. The loss rate was still low, and simple arithmetic yields the fact that three times as many boats were in service as in 1939. And, there were still enough good officers to command them. Kretschmer, Prien, Schepke, and Wohlfahrt were statistics, true, but others were already replacing them.

Erich Topp had begun to make a name for himself with U-552, the Red Devil Boat, so called because of two dancing demons painted on his conning tower. Jochen Mohr had relieved Wilhelm Schulz in U-124, the "Edelweiss Boat"; he would go on to achieve fame greater than Schulz's and greater than that of many first-generation aces. Reinhard Suhren and Karl-Friedrich Merten both made their first patrols in 1941, and both would achieve the success of a Prien or Schepke. Bauer, Cremer, and Hardegen were just starting out, all of them good and all of them hungry.

But losses inevitably occurred when the number of boats increased faster than the number of officers ready to command them. The time it took to build a boat could be decreased; the time it took to train a good captain could not, and the consequences of drawing on undertrained men were just becoming apparent. For instance, the captain of U-570, lost in late August 1941, was a man named Hans Rahmlow, a promising officer but one who had been given command too early. He

Erich Topp. Topp, the third most successful U-boat ace of the war, was commander of U-552, the "Red Devil Boat." In October 1941, six weeks before Pearl Harbor, Topp sank the U.S. Navy destroyer USS *Reuben James* in the North Atlantic convoy lanes. His action heralded the beginning of an undeclared war at sea between the United States and Germany. (Courtesy U.S. Naval Institute)

was unable to control his crew, unable to get along with his officers, and in the end unable to handle crisis. On 27 August 1941 he surrendered his boat, intact, to aircraft of Royal Air Force Squadron 269 off the coast of Iceland. The exact circumstances of the surrender were more complex than this implies;

nevertheless, Rahmlow lived the rest of his life in ignominy.* Theodor Petersen himself benefited from the dilution of the U-Bootwaffe officer corps. By late 1941 Richard Becker had departed U-43, and Schwantke and Petersen both moved up a notch. Petersen found himself third watch officer.† Even if it was not entirely meritorious, the promotion says something about Petersen and his ability, for Lüth would not have recommended him without reason. The promotion did not involve a commission. Petersen was still a noncommissioned officer, and the Third Reich was still a class-oriented system. Rank mattered, not responsibility, because rank was visible and responsibility was not. This became glaringly apparent to Petersen when, as Lüth's career flourished, he began to receive visitors on board—important ones, not just minor functionaries. At the end of one patrol, the flotilla commander brought NSKK *Korpsfüher* Adolf Hühnlein down to meet Lüth and tour U-43. Hühnlein was introduced to her officers, one by one. Unfortunately for Petersen, when Hühnlein saw his insignia he would not shake the watch officer's hand. "I will never forget it," Petersen commented.[4]

Lüth's thirteenth war patrol began on a high note that quickly soured. U-43 left Lorient on 10 November. On the twenty-first, he and Georg Schewe in U-105 were ordered to proceed west to the Newfoundland coast and then south to penetrate the anchorage at Halifax, the principal assembly point for fast eastbound convoys. The operation was an ambitious one. But Lüth would never get there. Within five hours of

---

*Petersen was with Lüth when the news of Rahmlow arrived. "Well," said Lüth with lifted brow, "what can you expect from a member of the *Katholike Crew?*" and he told Petersen a story of how the Catholic Center Party, in exchange for their support of the 1927 Cruiser "A" bill in the Reichstag, had been promised an all-Catholic class at the Marineschule. The story is not true; it was probably not so much that Lüth disliked Catholics as that he appreciated a tidbit of service gossip. (Petersen, interview)

†The new second watch officer was a man named Helmut Munster. Although Munster has no direct bearing on this story, Petersen thought him worthy of a note because of his loud and tedious defense of the hollow-earth theory of the universe.

departing, Petersen told him that the charts he needed for the operation were missing. A signal from Schewe stating that U-105 was missing the same charts confirmed that it was BdU's fault, not Lüth's. "There will be hell to pay at BdU-Op for this," he told Petersen angrily.[5]

On 21 November Hitler directed BdU to send all available boats to the approaches of the Straits of Gibraltar and into the Mediterranean. Dönitz had no choice but to concur, however bitterly he protested that the real battle was still in the North Atlantic. The Admiralty welcomed this shift with elation and relief. The losses incurred by convoy SC 42 in September showed that there were still dangerous gaps in convoy defenses, and that they could not be plugged soon. After abandoning the Halifax operation, therefore, Lüth turned southeast toward the Azores. Because U-43 was so much farther south than usual (his track during this patrol was never north of latitude 40°N), Lüth encountered no traffic until the early morning of 29 November.

At that time convoy OS 12, southbound from England to the Cape of Good Hope, was sighted. More correctly, one of the escort destroyers was sighted at a range of 600 meters, steaming out of the fog on a collision course with U-43. U-43 may have been seen, but no asdic pings or depth charges were recorded during the fifty-five minutes after U-43 made an emergency dive. When she resurfaced at 0215, Lüth could see the convoy itself. At 0410 he fired two stern torpedoes at an innocuous steamer, the British *Thornliebank*, on his port side. The result was as spectacular as it was unexpected.

The *Thornliebank* was a munitions ship. There was a heavy shaking through her hull, then for hundreds of meters up the sky turned from black to orange to a hellish yellow. Debris skyrocketed into the smoke and seconds later came raining down on the water, illuminated itself like liquid fire. The blast from the explosion hit U-43's bridge watch like a freight train; the needle on the barometer dial in the control room spun completely around, then completely back. Petersen, standing in the bridge, cried out suddenly at a searing pain in his arm. He thought he had been hit by shrapnel, but days later an unex-

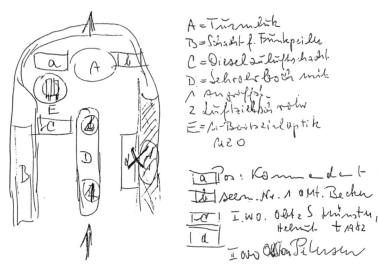

The bridge of U-43 when *Thornliebank* blew up. This drawing by Theodor Petersen shows the position of everyone in U-43's bridge, including himself (marked with an X). Closest to the exploding munitions ship, he was hit by a grenade. U-43 was seen in the light of the explosion and her attack was followed by a depth-charge siege of several hours.

ploded 105-mm flare grenade was found in the tower. Every ship in the convoy had started to launch them; they went up like fireworks.

U-43 fled to the north at flank speed, lit up like a cruise ship on New Year's Eve. One of the escorts turned toward her and approached at high speed, but Lüth was unwilling to dive until he could be sure his boat had suffered no serious damage. "I couldn't believe his cold-bloodedness," Petersen continued, "and I still can't. It was as bright as day because of the flares and a destroyer was coming up behind us, but he waited for Kaschner, the chief engineer, to report 'Clear for diving.' When the call . . . finally came back, we dived quickly and had to ride out a very bad depth-charging."[6]

Several days later the grenade was retrieved from where it had lodged next to a diesel exhaust vent, Lüth gave it a coat of lacquer and mounted it on a piece of polished wood for use as a desk ornament.[7]

Lüth sank two more ships on this patrol, but neither event was as spectacular. The first kill was the *Ashby*, a British steamer from convoy WS 12. The second, the Socony Mobil tanker *Astral*, was a big mistake, for Lüth sank her on 2 December, and she was flying the Stars and Stripes when she went down. He had sunk an American ship five days before Pearl Harbor and nine days before the United States and Germany declared war. It would have been embarrassing, to say the least, had the news come out, but oddly enough Lüth escaped censure, even notice, because nobody knew he was responsible for at least twenty years. The probable fate of the *Astral* only came to light in the early 1960s, and by then it no longer mattered.

In an article called "Overdue — Presumed Lost," published in the Naval Institute *Proceedings* in 1961, Edward Oliver addressed the issue of ships that disappeared without a trace during the war. Several, including the *Astral*, were listed by name and appeared in photographs.[8] Subsequently, a reader wrote to *Proceedings* to say, "quite calmly, as if he were merely correcting an oversight," that the *Astral* had been sunk in February 1941 by a U-boat. The date was way off, but his confidence prompted some research by Arthur Gordon, the author of a second article, "The Day the *Astral* Vanished." It is an account of how, if the reader was right, the *Astral* might have left traces after all.[9]

Gordon's argument can be summarized as follows: At 1701 on 1 December Günther Heydemann, in U-575, identified a U.S. merchant vessel sailing east at approximately 35° 25' N, 26° 30' W, about sixty miles south of the Azores. Under orders to let American ships sail, he "had to let her go with a heavy heart."[10] Information on the origin, destination, and sailing date of the *Astral* indicates that she was the ship Heydemann saw that day. At 2159 that very day U-43 fired a single torpedo at an unidentified merchant in the same area and then followed her through the night. At 0924 on 2 December, the U-boat sank her. Lüth described his victim as a 12,300-ton British tanker of the *San Melito* class, but descriptions in the two log-

The Socony Mobil tanker SS *Astral*. The *Astral* disappeared in December 1941 without a trace. In a magazine article twenty years later, Wolfgang Lüth was given credit, or blame, for her sinking: credit because *Astral* was a valuable ship; blame because Lüth sank the American tanker five days before Pearl Harbor. (Courtesy U.S. Naval Institute)

books and the positions of the two sightings indicate that Heydemann's ship and Lüth's ship were the same.

Gordon's article speculates on the question of possible cover-up; that is, did Lüth know afterward that he had sunk an American ship illegally, and if so, did he or BdU conspire to hide the fact? The author implies that Lüth did know she was an American ship after he sank her. Gordon cites two known facts: Heydemann knew, and Heydemann and Lüth met after the sinking and spoke. "Whether the truth was known to him and Heydemann as they compared notes at the time of their rendezvous and discussed the possible consequences, is not known. If an error had been made, and a US ship had been sunk due to a case of mistaken identity, it was too late then to correct it. From that moment on, the politics of war and the niceties of service loyalty may well have prompted the keeping of this guilty secret."[11]

This part of Gordon's theory is contradicted by two other facts: Lüth never acknowledged his "guilty secret" in U-43's log, and U-boat logs were known for their accuracy (there is only one known instance of a U-boat log being altered after the fact). As for the sinking, Lüth described it in the log in some detail. He also described the sinking in *Boot Greift Wieder An*. "The tanker offered a magnificent show as she burned . . . for hours afterwards thick clouds of smoke hovered so far above the location that we could see a couple of small bright 'fair weather' clouds underneath them. Over half the sky was covered with black smoke."[12] It is a safe bet that these lines would not have survived if BdU had had any idea of the *Astral*'s identity.

The fate of the *Astral* was forgotten after the United States declared war on Japan on 8 December and Germany declared war on the United States three days later. U-43 was loitering off Cape St. Vincent on the coast of Portugal when the news was broadcast. The crew was astonished; again, Lüth did not have much to say. He was, however, relieved that they would no longer have to play games with American warships.[13]

He returned to Lorient on 16 December. It had been ten months and three long patrols since U-43 went down in Lorient harbor. She was worn out, her batteries almost gone. Next time she left Lorient she was headed for a complete overhaul in the dry docks in Kiel. But not straight for Kiel. It was the mission of a U-boat to sink ships, and as long as U-43 was at sea, she was on patrol.

It rained hard as she left harbor that day in late December, and soon, wrote Lüth in *Boot Greift Wieder An*, "we were soaked to the skin. We had to sound fog signals on our way out of the harbor, because the rain was so strong that we couldn't see a hundred meters in front of us. Then a brisk wind came up to show us that things were just as nice at sea. The watch put their oilskins on and as we put to sea they all fastened themselves down to the bridge with tethers."

The sun did not come out until 1 January. When it did, Petersen told Lüth he was lost. The line of bearing taken that day showed U-43 off course and close to the southern Irish coast. Kaschner had a look at the compass and told Lüth flatly that the sun was in the wrong place. Lüth had him start up the reserve anyway, and U-43 was found to be sixty degrees off course.[14]

The weather worsened as the boat headed north. On 8 January the rain turned to hailstorms, and by the twelfth the boat was logging winds of over forty knots and a sea state of twelve

Wolfgang Lüth on the bridge of U-43. He looks cold because he is cold. During his last patrol as captain of U-43 in January 1942, his crew had to knock the ice off her rigging and superstructure with hammers. (Courtesy Horst Bredow)

to fourteen. During the afternoon of the eleventh Lüth surfaced in the midst of a convoy, about 500 miles southwest of Iceland, but with the weather so inclement he could do nothing about it.

> I watched as Strahlendorf pointed to something with his arm, but I could not see what it was. As the boat rose onto a crest I made out a ship, broadside on. At the same time Kliegel saw a destroyer behind us, also broadside. Both ships were fighting for their lives and we could do nothing; we could make no way against the sea. When after a few minutes the destroyer saw us, he tried to turn our way, but he came crossways to the sea and almost toppled over. He gave up and turned against the sea again. We dived, resolving not to let our quarry get away. Several hours later we came up again and saw another ship. But again the powers of nature worked to keep peace between us.[15]

At 0650 Lüth began to track the Swedish *Yngaren*, which he was only able to see at intervals as the two vessels rose and fell with the waves. He had to have his binoculars wiped dry continuously during the attack. He had no expectations when ordering two torpedoes fired at 0802. Both of them, however, hit.

The Swedish ship broke into two pieces. Her forward section sank first, followed by the stern, which turned turtle and stood vertically in the water before going down. And as she went, Lüth, standing in the bridge, hurled her agonies down the hatch to his crew: "Bow is gone," he screamed, "now the stern is up . . . she's gone."

It was quite a storm; one of the worst of the season. Later in his book, Lüth recalled the cries for help his radio room was receiving: "From one ship nearing her end we intercepted a distress call that sounded something like: 'Lifeboats carried away—cargo hatches full of water—I'm beginning to lose hope of ever seeing land again. . . .' The signal was very sad for us, because as seamen we appreciated the struggle between the seaman and the power of the sea . . ." It was the same gratuitous drivel Lüth's editors employed in recounting his experience with the *Victor Ross*; he himself really could not have cared less.

"GOOD LUCK AND GOOD SHOOTING!"

The boat was huge. When she left Kiel Harbor on the morning of 12 September 1942, her massive gray deck dwarfed the four boats behind her. The men clustered in her bridge were as small as bugs. She moved slowly, gracefully, in spite of her size, while escort vessels chugged around her like carefree pilot fish.

It was dawn, scattered clouds above and high visibility. The men in the bridge and on the weather deck, all of them sharp, shaven, and in clean uniforms, were formed in straight ranks. Inside, the cheerful notes of "Today We Make for Open Sea" played while men stumbled through spaces crowded with bags of potatoes and mounds of sausage and onions. The men down here were not paraded; they had jobs to do, and they could talk, argue, or curse as the spirit moved them.

U-181 was brand-new, untried, on her way out of Kiel for a maiden war patrol. In the bridge stood Kapitänleutnant Wolfgang Lüth, twenty-eight years old, bearer of the Knight's Cross, late of U-43, U-138, and U-9, at sea again for his fifteenth patrol.

Lüth had left U-43 in January. Three months later he reported to Deschimag Bremen Shipyards, and shortly after that he commissioned U-181. Over the next fourteen months the captain and his boat would become famous, the result of a spiritual symbiosis between man and machine that is uncommon but not unheard of in military history.

Without U-181, Lüth would probably have finished a decent career at the bottom of the North Atlantic, his name nothing more than a series of brass letters on the submarine memorial at Möltenort, or behind a green desk somewhere in Germany or France, duties restricted to the greeting of incoming boats and the signing of leave papers. Without Lüth, U-181 would have been nameless metal like a thousand other boats, lost, scuttled, or scrapped, paving the English Channel with steel or spinning compass needles in the Bay of Biscay.

Germany and the United States had gone to war in December 1941. Dönitz sent a few of his boats to the eastern seaboard at once, and their success surpassed his wildest dreams. It was a second "happy time"—almost 500 ships sunk in five months against a pathetic defense. Lüth, between commands, missed this campaign, no doubt to his bitter disappointment.

But the happy time didn't last. The Americans got smarter after six months or so. Their defenses stiffened, sinkings declined, U-boat losses rose, and Dönitz had no choice but to withdraw his forces into the mid-Atlantic. He considered other areas of opportunity; the sea was a giant chessboard for him, with pieces on both sides shifting continuously. Perhaps enemy defenses had softened in the Caribbean, perhaps in the Mediterranean or the Western Approaches. During this search he began to look seriously at the prospects of operations in the far south—the South Atlantic, the Cape of Good Hope, even the Indian Ocean. The cape route was a major supply line for the

Allies, especially in 1942, after Japan had entered the war and Britain had launched offensives in North Africa. In August Dönitz ordered four large type IX boats to the cape. *Gruppe Eisbär* (Polar Bear Group), he named them. In September he decided to send four more boats after them.

So U-181 headed south that September day in 1942. South past the Western Approaches, past Ireland and France, past Gibraltar, North Africa; south for over seven weeks and almost 8,000 miles to the Cape of Good Hope, where no German submarine had ever been before.[1]

It had been a long summer. Everyone was at the commissioning ceremony in Bremen, wives and families, the workers and supervisors who had built U-181, a band and color guard. The ceremony itself ended soon enough; Lüth was not a talker. "I do not know you," he said again, "and you do not know me. We will meet at the front." These were the same words he had used when taking command of U-9, U-138, and U-43. In defiance of naval tradition, he took the wives on a tour of the boat, pointing out each husband's duty station and the equipment he was responsible for (they were all appropriately shocked at the small size of the galley). He arranged for Ilse to have them over for tea. He even gave them a little lecture on the duties of a navy wife: love, support, understanding, children.[2]

Someone had invited a group of older men who turned out to be veterans of the imperial submarine fleet. They went about telling anyone who would listen what it had been like back in the early days of "real" submarines with kerosene engines and no toilets. "No wonder they lost the *bloody* war," Walter Schmidt, one of U-181's new crew, commented in later years. "We used to laugh at these men with the crowns on their badges just like the men in the new *Bundesmarine* laugh at us today from their newer and faster boats."[3]

The training that followed commissioning was drudgery, but Lüth was a seasoned commander by 1942 and he knew how to fill in the time. The men played soccer against the army in Bornholm, lolled on the beach in Hela, gambled in Zoppot, partied in Stettin. Lüth felt better this second summer in the Baltic. He

The commissioning ceremony of U-181, May 1942. Lüth is on the left, his crew (officers in front) opposite him. By most accounts it was an enjoyable occasion; in fact, Lüth went so far as to take the wives of his new crewmen on a tour of the boat, which was a major breach of naval tradition.

had his share of the glory, his medals, and nobody with half a brain thought the war was going to end by Christmas.

Technically stated, U-181 was a new type IXD2 oceangoing U-boat. Informally, she was known as a U-cruiser or a Monsoon boat, the first term in reference to her size, which was immense, the second in reference to her mission, unprecedented and only just defined. She carried twenty-six torpedoes, three deck guns, a crew of fifty, and fuel for a trip around the globe at ten knots. She displaced 1,800 tons, and the two giant diesels inside her hull could push her weight through the water at a maximum speed of nineteen knots, fast enough to raise a decent bow wave. Her magazines carried hundreds of rounds of high-explosive and incendiary shells, and the top of her tower, almost forty feet above the keel, bristled with the latest in electronic gadgetry, including the new Metox equipment.

The Metox, a primitive radar detector, was in theory able to pick up the searching radiations of enemy ships and aircraft. It was built in the form of a large wooden cross with a wire strung from point to point like the frame of a kite (hence its common nickname, the Biscay Cross). On the bridge the cross was wired to a simple processor in the control room, then to a speaker. It had to be removed for diving, and was often damaged after being tossed down the hatch in an emergency.

The custodian of the Metox was the boat's doctor, Lothar Engel. He had to make sure it was in good repair and that it was quickly and properly reinstalled in the bridge after a dive. Engel had been made Metox officer almost by default, having arrived on board in Stettin, one of the last in the crew. With nothing for him to do, Lüth shipped Engel off to Metox school.

Engel was a Prussian, born in Bromberg (Bydgosczc) and raised in Emden, a German port on the North Sea. "I had the sea in my blood," he acknowledged proudly.[4] He received his medical degree in 1939, completed the *Sanitätsoffizier* or medical officer's course in 1940, and was sent first to the Netherlands as an assistant medical officer treating downed German airmen and then to Brest as a medical officer with the First U-Flotilla.[5]*

Neither Engel nor anyone else could recall trouble with aircraft during the passage into the North Atlantic (perhaps because it became so much worse later on), but the Metox began to buzz and whistle almost daily, usually early morning, in anticipation of approaching bombers from RAF Coastal Command. It was nerve-racking in the extreme, because the standard response to a Metox warning was a fast dive before the aircraft sighted the boat.

Sometimes the Metox failed. On the afternoon of 18 September, as U-181 was sailing south past the Shetlands, her for-

---

*The other officers in U-181 included First Watch Officer Theodor Petersen, newly commissioned, Second Watch Officer Gottfried König, a young Leutnant zur See and earlier a midshipman in U-43, and an experienced but strict and high-strung engineering officer named Carl-August Landfehrmann. Everyone in the boat referred to him simply as LI, for *Leitende Ingenieur*.

ward lookout spotted a bomber coming in low from the clouds. He screamed the alarm. The entire watch section jumped for the hatch, and Lüth took the boat into a steep dive to 135 meters, too late to avoid being hit on the port quarter by a single bomb, which caused "minor" damage. Furthermore, the bomber brought with it an unknown number of surface vessels that dropped over thirty depth charges in an unsuccessful ten-hour search.

From then on the Metox was suspect. For at least two weeks, as the boat sailed past the British Isles and the Iberian Peninsula, the crew lived on the balls of their feet. Watch sections were especially jumpy. It had happened once, it could certainly happen again. Not until they passed Gibraltar did the routine become more relaxed. Log entries such as "Emergency dive because of aircraft" or "Destroyer in sight" gave way to "Phosphorescence on the waves" and the usual reports of distance traveled. The latter was calculated at noon and entered with an arrow pointing up to indicate miles on the surface and another pointing down to indicate miles submerged. The boat never came within sight of land. It was only mentioned in the position reports: "East of the Azores" on 2 October and "West of the Canary Islands" on the fifth. "We are now close to the island of St. Helena," noted the boat's newspaper one day, "where Napoleon was banished until he died."[6]

The weather grew warm and tropical. The crew took to clumping around on the weather deck in nothing but shorts and boots, their skin brown and their noses peeling. In the engineering spaces it was like a kiln, the temperature regularly exceeding 120 degrees. The machinist's mates took turns coming up to the bridge for a smoke and a look at the ocean and the sky. Africa's coast lay 300 miles over the blue horizon.

It wasn't just the heat that brought them to the bridge. U-181 was more comfortable than the little canoes like U-9, but comfort is relative. Not even seven large compartments and two berthing spaces provided enough room. At the beginning of a long patrol the boat was packed with provisions; with the space under the mess tables crammed, "you never knew where to put your legs when you were eating."[7] Traffic continually clogged the single passageway, and torpedoes were stored in every conceivable place, including the steel canisters on the weather deck.

The boat had a definite smell to it—a pungent mix of diesel fumes, battery acid, food, unwashed clothes, and sweat. Writers like to talk about the inevitable green mold that grew on bread and shoes in U-boats, but if a boat spent a fair amount of time on the surface, as U-181 was able to do, it kept mold to a minimum. Cleanliness was emphasized, if only out of consideration for one's fellow crewmen, and the crew always performed a minimal amount of "housework."

The heat was intense in U-181, and not just for the engineers. It caused rashes and blisters (the "red dog" they called it in the Kriegsmarine), and contributed to ringworm and lice. It made the food spoil faster. The best efforts of U-181's cook could not prevent food from tasting like diesel fuel or insects from proliferating. Little black bugs crawled through the rice, and cockroaches scurried all over the galley, oblivious to diesel oil, acid, sea water, overpressure, vacuum, and the unending persecution of disgusted crewmen.[8]

But neither the smell nor the heat nor the wet were real problems; submariners in every navy had been dealing with them for forty years. The real problem was boredom. It bred discontent and argument; it made men careless and slow to respond. It could be fatal, and it was the commander's job to prevent it. As always, Lüth was tireless in his own efforts to do so.

His campaign took him from one end of the boat to the other—up to the bridge, where he would quiz the watch section about possible emergency situations, into the bow compartment, where he bothered the midshipmen (he wanted them to realize that being a midshipman "is nothing like it is in the movies"), and even to the head, where he posted a clipboard and suggested that each visitor sign in and write something funny on it.

He arranged singing contests over the public-address system. He staged Olympic games with radio commentary and presentation of a medal. He put on a lying contest where everyone had to make up a tall tale. "Some of them," he declared, "were good enough to publish." He arranged a chess tournament and broadcast the results of each round afterward. He had a poetry contest with Lothar Engel's hygiene lectures as the springboard, and some of the winning entries are not really fit to print.

> It is important for everyone,
> to have a movement now and then.
> And the future isn't pleasant
> when nothing happens on the toilet.
> To wake your plumbing up again
> to bring your torture to an end,
> stay off the chocolate and the sweets,
> eat plums in giant quantities.
> The problem doubtless won't remain
> and you'll be free of rectal pain.
>
> * * *
>
> If the red dog hasn't bit,
> and if you regularly shit,
> if you brush your teeth each day
> to scrape the evening meal away,
> if you don't know the itch of lice,
> if you beware of social vice,
> then the police can certify
> you "clean enough for U-boat life!"
>
> * * *
>
> He who drinks in tropic heat
> will start to sweat excessively,
> and he who drinks iced *Kujampel**
> will soon get stomach cramp.
> Canned food, chocolate, cookies, too,
> will also make your stomach hurt.
> A daily movement is your goal;
> one gains from regularity.

The last poem was Lüth's. The humor disguises his deadly serious attitude toward the health and hygiene of his crew. He was particularly obsessed with stomachs and lower intestines, where, he believed, every other complaint originated. He en-

---

**Kujampel*, a mixture of water and concentrated strawberry syrup, was a staple in the boat.

couraged his men to visit the doctor for any perceived afflic-
tion. He made it a standing order that everyone wear woolen
bands around the stomach at night, he banned ice in the
drinks, and he watered down the coffee. The younger crewmen were forbidden to smoke on an empty stomach, and
nobody dared come back aboard with syphilis. Again, it was
the father looking after his children, the old man who made
sure they brushed their teeth and didn't go into the water after
eating.

Plans for the equator crossing took up at least a week. They
included writing a series of fake messages to and from King
Neptune, drawing up a formal plan of the day, with appropriate honors, ceremonies, and uniforms, and compiling a list of
initiates. One clever artist hand-lettered at least forty crossing
certificates (see illustration). These activities were interrupted
on the morning of 14 October when the bulkhead between the
port trim and buoyancy tanks gave way with a muffled roar.
Water gushed into both tanks when the flooding vent broke.
Divers had to go down and fix it.

U-181 crossed the equator at longitude 20° 5' W on 18 October. Initiates emerged unscathed from the subsequent "holy
baptism," during which they were "covered in oil, hit with
razor strops and pieces of wood, and being made to drink
strange liquids."[9] "The educational value of the ceremony, if it
is rough enough, should not be underestimated," commented
Lüth. "I am of the opinion that young men should experience
once in their lives how much a healthy body can endure."

Lüth read the war news out loud to his men and published
it in a boat's newspaper. He had them observe the sea and the
skies and the weather. Like U-43, U-181 had a phonograph,
and he added a new record to the repertoire; "Abendlied,"
sung by the Regensburg Cathedral Choir, was played every
night for tattoo. Lüth encouraged reading, rationing out six
magazines per week. After enough men had read a book or listened to a symphony, he set up a discussion group.

Discussion groups were part of a continuing series of lectures Lüth had arranged in which volunteer teachers talked
about any number of things. Classes were held in meteorology,

An Equator-crossing certificate. Dozens of these, lettered by hand with ordinary ink on ordinary paper, were awarded to crewmen after U-181 crossed the Equator in October 1942. She was one of the few boats to have had such a ceremony during the war.

for example, engineering, mathematics, medicine, and philosophy. Discussions centered around the war effort, the weather, whether horse meat tasted funny because the horse sweated through his ribs, how Swiss cheese got its holes, and whether or not cows made more milk if a radio was played nearby.

In "Problems of Leadership" Lüth claimed to have given his men regular lectures on history and politics. "The men must know what they are fighting for," he declared, "and they must be willing to risk their lives for it." By politics he meant the politics of National Socialism, to which he adhered.

National Socialism, or Nazism, is hard to avoid in studies of German officers of World War II. There is no use ignoring it. If the subject is left alone, suspicion will fester that a particular officer was a Nazi; it will taint our memories of the man. With Lüth particularly, it is better to state the truth at the outset and attempt to explain it than to say nothing and hope for charitable disinterest.

Naval historians, particularly German ones, like to point out that officers in the Kriegsmarine were apolitical and that most of them disdained the party faithful. Several members of Lüth's crew said the same about him. According to one man asked about these lectures, "We used to discuss this or that, what came in over the radio, for example, but we never got lectures about National Socialism. Lüth was no Nazi in this regard, but a good soldier through and through. Most Germans, particularly those in the Navy, had nothing to do with the Nazis."[10] Sadly he was wrong.

Lüth tried hard to be a good National Socialist. He did not apologize for it (which explains the embarrassing scene he made after sinking the *Sigurds Faulbaums* in 1940). He loudly proclaimed his fervor for National Socialism, for the party, for the Reich, and nowhere more so than in the pages of "Problems of Leadership," a document significant not just for its thoughtful and imaginative comments on leadership and personnel management but also for its surprisingly high content of lockstep Party ideology:

[Political lectures are] necessary to eliminate a certain passive philosophy in some of the men. On Sundays I sometimes dive and hold muster underwater to tell them something about the Reich and the centuries-old struggle for it, and about some of the greatest men in our history. On the Führer's birthday I tell them something about his life and about my visit to Führer Headquarters. Another time I tell them something about racial and population problems, all from the viewpoint of the struggle for the realization of the Reich. We speak about Germany, the Führer, and about the National Socialist movement.[11]

"Problems of Leadership" was delivered to an audience that included senior officers of the Wehrmacht and members of the Party elite. Lüth himself was wearing the highest military award the Reich could bestow. For these reasons one might expect the odd throwaway phrase about the advances of National Socialism, perhaps even a word or two about Jews. It would have been imprudent of him to leave such subjects out. But the language Lüth used is as strident and simple-minded as the words on any political poster in the Weimar railway station: "We had on board a volume of the 1933 issues of the illustrated magazine *Die Wochenschau*, a very good paper which still showed in its first numbers of January 1933 many pictures of Jews. The crew had never experienced anything like that. Then came the day of the assumption of power, the Reichstag fire, the day of Potsdam, the superhighways, the Reich Labor Service, and so forth. The men were surprised about many of these pictures, because they could not imagine that there had been times in Germany when all these things to which we are now accustomed were still being fought for."[12] These words go far beyond the bounds of political expediency and stray considerably from the subject of the lecture. They are words that make the naval historian flinch. They do not match the common perception of the Kriegsmarine as an aloof, apolitical entity, and in fact, are usually deleted when Lüth's lecture is quoted. The writer Harald Busch, for instance, included large sections of "Problems of Leadership" in his book *U-boats at War*, but he excised every last reference to Adolf Hitler, the Party, and National Socialism.[13]

Yes, Wolfgang Lüth was a Nazi. It should be noted, however, that his idea of National Socialism was dated. He spoke about the "struggle" as though he were still a youth in Riga and the year were 1933. He held the fairy tale view of early propagandists; the ideology he defended was not the ideology of Auschwitz or Dachau, but that of superhighways. When Jews were being killed by the millions in 1943, the idea of a Jew was merely an abstraction to Lüth. Four years after the war began and two months after Himmler's formal presentation of the Final Solution, Lüth's idea of National Socialism bore little relation to reality. "Lüth was enthusiastic about National Socialism," said Engel, "but only the good side."[14] Petersen said of him that he was "at least one-third Nazi," implying that Lüth could not have been completely corrupted because he never had the opportunity to see the bad side of National Socialism.

One may wonder why Lüth failed to apply his high personal standards to his political beliefs. One reason is that propagandists invoked the virtues of hard work, health, family, bravery, and patriotism to bolster the National Socialist program. Though they masked a Nazi lie, these virtues appealed to Wolfgang Lüth. Furthermore, Germany's peacetime concerns may have constituted what Lüth looked upon as the good side of National Socialism: the superhighways, for example, and more importantly, the move toward a united greater Germany. Finally, Lüth seemed to believe, as did many in his time, that moral responsibility could be at least partially abdicated in favor of a higher civil or temporal authority—that you could trust another to make decisions of conscience for you. "He considered every move the Nazis made as having been willed by God."[15] The will of God was the ultimate mandate. A person could always follow His will, incomprehensible though it was, with a clear conscience.

Two facts stand in his favor, however. By this time Lüth had accumulated more than enough rank, honor, and connections to apply for formal membership in the party. He never did. Second, whatever his personal views might have been, he did not try to enforce them in his boats. This may be why his crews remained ignorant of his beliefs. The lectures he claimed in "Problems of Leadership" to have given "about the Reich and the centuries-old struggle for it," about "Germany, the Führer, and . . . the National Socialist movement," did not in fact take place. "We never spoke about politics," said Engel, "and there weren't even any books about the subject on board."[16] Lüth was a good captain, and a good captain avoided lecturing his crew on the merits of National Socialism.

On 1 November, just before midnight, U-181 crossed an imaginary line at 34° S. She was due west of Cape Town; the cape itself, only miles away, was almost close enough to touch. U-181 had arrived. The passage took exactly seven weeks and one day. She had come over 7,500 miles. Most war patrols would have been over and done with long before. This one was only just beginning.

Lüth turned east toward the city, and at dawn on 3 November the American ore carrier *East Indian*, bound for New York via Trinidad with a cargo of manganese, was sighted from his bridge. Diving to beat the dawn, he decided at once to pursue her.

The *East Indian* was zigzagging. This was a problem. The director angle for a torpedo could only be calculated if a ship's track was known in advance; therefore, it was critical to calculate the course and length of each leg in the zigzag. The patient use of a stopwatch would yield both the base course of the zigzag and the zigzag pattern, but if the target happened to deviate at random from her pattern, the attack solution would be ruined.

After ninety minutes of patient maneuver, U-181 was brought into position for a run. She did not surface. At 0548 Lüth fired two torpedoes from 2,500 meters. "Ship zagged just before the shot," said the log plaintively, "but it wasn't a very good idea to shoot at this distance anyway." The torpedoes were wide, and Lüth had to start all over again.

The *East Indian*, unaware of her close escape, sailed blithely on toward the west, still zigzagging. U-181 surfaced at 0644 and followed her. It took nine hours for the U-boat to catch up to her prey again. There was not much else to do in the way of planning, since the zigzag had not changed and the *East Indian* had apparently not altered her base course southwest. Lunch was served.

At 1525 U-181 dived for her second run. At 1620 Lüth fired two more torpedoes. There was momentary alarm as the *East Indian* zagged again at the last moment, but within two minutes both torpedoes struck her amidships, each of them raising a huge column of white water.

She sank by the stern four minutes later. U-181 surfaced to find survivors floating in three rafts and a lifeboat. The master had drowned; the first officer was missing. The senior man in the lifeboat, the second officer, told Lothar Engel everything he was asked—name, tonnage, cargo, destination. Engel asked the man if he needed anything—food, water, medical supplies. He said no. Whereupon the boat was cast off with directions to the nearest beach. "The American had an extremely confident attitude," wrote Lüth in the log, "and he wished us a friendly 'Good luck' as we left."

This was a curious exchange. The second officer of the *East Indian* had no reason to be friendly. His ship had just been torpedoed, he was floating in a lifeboat, he was nowhere near land. . . . Yet Krutschkowski confirmed it: "There was a boat with six or eight sailors on it and in the back an officer with the tiller between his legs. I seem to recall he even gave the *Hitlergruss* and wished us good luck. He had a blue jacket on and khaki trousers with one leg torn off. He said 'Good luck and good shooting.'"[17] Perhaps the American was being ironic.

The sinking of the *East Indian* capped a satisfactory first month for the new campaign. U-181 was only the fifth U-boat in history to operate in the cape's waters; she was also the fifth to arrive in as many weeks. The four Eisbär boats had been in the area since the first week of October, and together they had sunk or damaged twenty-three ships, many within sight of the coast. One of their victims was the 23,000-ton liner *Orcades*. The *East Indian* had added a quick 8,000 tons to the total. The Eisbär boats had also been the first to confront cape defenses. By the time U-181 and the boats of the second wave arrived, these defenses were ready and willing to fight back.* Lüth found this out the hard way, but not before finding and sinking three more ships.

As U-181 rounded the cape the weather worsened, and a sea state of seven was recorded about 180 miles southwest of Port Elizabeth on the morning of 8 November. The Panamanian steamship *Plaudit* was sighted early that day sailing west from Calcutta to New York. Lüth gave chase, but rainy weather and heavy swells conspired to upset the boat's trim at a critical moment during the first torpedo run at 0815. U-181 followed the *Plaudit* for ten hours as the torpedo tubes were reloaded. By noon, the weather had worsened, the sea state hovering between seven and eight.

At 2055 Lüth lined the boat up and fired again. The *Plaudit* was hit this time, but instead of sinking she drifted and glowed in the dark for over an hour until Lüth decided to use his guns. He gave the order *"Artillerie klar!"* ("Clear for gun!"), then had the 105-mm cannon rigged. U-181 approached the *Plaudit's* stern, the sea state now registering ten.

The attack went slowly. Ammunition for the guns had to be passed by hand from the magazines to the gunners through the open bridge hatch. Every time the boat made a course or speed change, the gunners were called back into the bridge for fear they might be washed overboard. Finally, after eight hits, the *Plaudit* sank by the stern. Lüth approached the spot afterward to look for survivors, but there were none to be seen.

He did not have as much trouble with the Norwegian freighter *Meldahl*, which was hit on the morning of 10 November and went down in nine minutes amidst a floating field of aircraft parts.

For eight hours on 12 November, Lüth stalked a "huge steamer" of indeterminate registry. At 2000 he surfaced just

*On 8 October, for example, U-179 (Sobe) was sunk with no survivors by HMS *Active* off the coast of southwest Africa. Ernst Sobe was a twenty-year veteran of the Kriegsmarine. Despite the fact that he had been commanding officer of the Seventh U-Flotilla before the war, U-179 was his first submarine, and on 25 September he torpedoed and sank his first ship, the British *City of Athens*.

600 meters away from her for a ridiculously easy shot, but no sooner had he opened his mouth to give the order to fire than she turned her lights on. The log reported: "Ship identified as Portuguese *Mouzinho*, 8374 GRT, well marked as a neutral. The boat has wasted three cbm of fuel on this ridiculous chase." Tempers improved next morning when the American steamship *Excello* was sighted en route from Suez to Capetown and sunk about thirty-five miles from the South African coast.

Each sinking was capped with celebration on board U-181. The younger crewmen and those on their first patrol were the most enthusiastic. The veterans drank their share of the cognac, but sedately. It was a hell of a long way to come to sink a ship. Why, in 1940 you couldn't help sinking ships; they were asking to be sunk, and right on your doorstep . . .

"Success is easy to take," Lüth would observe in "Problems of Leadership." "It raises morale. But my efforts on board are directed towards keeping up the crew's morale when things are not going well; a good soldier can show his true mettle only when the odds are against him. . . ."

THE SECOND LÜTH

"ALARM!"

A lookout screams out, points, then jumps for the hatch in the center of the bridge. Nobody else can see what he sees, but his warning electrifies the rest of the watch. The other lookouts and the watch officer follow him instinctively, one after the other, like rats down a hole. They come crashing down into the control room, a wet pile of rubber-clad men. The watch officer slams and spins shut the hatch from below. One of the lookouts takes the plane controls, another the helm. Before they are fully in their seats, the boat is in a steep dive, bow down, stern disappearing in foam. Perhaps ten seconds have elapsed.

It is dawn on the cape. U-181 is seventy-five miles south of Durban. The seas are high, the weather is bad. "[A] good soldier can show his true mettle only when the odds are against him." The odds have caught up with Lüth here. His dictum is about to be tested by a warship of the Royal Navy.

The boat falls quickly to A plus 40,* rocking from side to side as she shakes the last few bubbles from her hull. The diesels are shut down and the electric motors switched on, pushing the boat through the water with just enough way on to keep her at depth. In almost slow motion, she levels off. The crew has executed the dive with the speed and efficiency that result from constant practice. They function like a single machine, without direction. Still, it is too little, too late.

Lüth is in the control room now. The watch officer explains to him that an enemy warship has been sighted approaching. Where was the lookout responsible for that sector, Lüth wants to know. Not paying attention, replies the watch officer. The miserable boy receives a sharp glance, nothing more, since there is no time. Twenty seconds have now elapsed.

The warship is the Royal Navy destroyer *Inconstant*, on routine antisubmarine patrol from Durban. She has seen U-181, is steaming at twenty-eight knots toward a swirl of white almost directly over the boat. The *Inconstant*'s depth charges, forty of them, have been primed in their racks. Her guns are manned in case U-181 should decide to resurface; her crew is in lifejackets and helmets, in case the boat should decide to fight back. She sends a signal to Durban: "U-boat sighted, send assistance."

The *Inconstant*'s asdic is on. Everyone in U-181 can hear it, a chilling sound like rain on a tin roof, like gravel in a can, like a skeleton being dragged across the hull. The crew can also hear the slow, dull grind of the *Inconstant*'s propellers overhead. Equipment is turned off, voices are lowered, nobody moves. A strange quiet falls as they wait and listen.

Thirty seconds. One minute. Five minutes. Ten. Still they wait.

And after an hour, the first explosion. A huge jarring crack like a hammer coming down on the hull. Then on its heels, four more, one right after the other. The boat rocks and shudders.

---

*The letter "A" represented 80 meters. It was a benchmark, a shorthand, used for entering depths in the log, but it differed from maximum depth, which in U-181's case was 200 meters.

All eyes are on Lüth's face, bored, emotionless, illuminated in strobelike pulses as the lights flicker and the seams creak.

The *Inconstant* and U-181 both sighted the other on the morning of 15 November. The resulting siege would last until midnight, sixteen hours of close combat between vessels invisible to each other.

The *Inconstant*'s asdic operators first detected U-181 at 0832. The warship dropped a single depth charge and then lost contact. In U-181 a spread of five charges, "very close," was logged; Lüth took her down to 460 feet and crept south, all unnecessary machinery turned off, bilges flooding, gas from batteries leaking into the passageway.

At 0906 the *Inconstant* dropped five more charges, logged in U-181 as "ten, very close," and the boat drifted down to 525 feet. A third spread of four at 0930 ("eight, close in") set the port shaft to rattling loudly, and five more at 1030 (also "eight, close in") made it worse.

The *Inconstant* tracked and dropped depth charges throughout the morning. By noon a serious leak had developed in an exit hatch, and the after main switchboard was in danger. No water remained in the trim tanks, and adjustments had to be made by hand. The log contained a running discussion of problems with the vent valves, through which water was escaping into the bilges. All nonessential crewmen stayed in their bunks, breathing through potash cartridges.

U-181 was now A plus 80, still 130 feet above her maximum safe depth, still trying to sneak away, still pinging on the *Inconstant*'s asdic. Lüth remained in the control room directing repairs. He gave no hint of his feelings, though he knew U-181 was in for a long and perilous day. "There are two destroyers overhead," he wrote in the log at 1130. "It looks as though they intend to starve us out."

Depth-charge attacks could easily confuse the senses. Lüth counted two ships; Krutschkowski said later he thought there were three coming in and out of Durban in shifts —"one in Durban Harbor refueling, one on the way and one overhead all the time."[1]

But only the *Inconstant* and a lone Lockheed Ventura were present for the first eight hours of the attack. Not until mid-afternoon did reinforcements—two corvettes, HMS *Jasmine* and *Nigella*—finally arrive from Durban. The three ships hovered over U-181 with sporadic depth charges and asdic pings until at least 1700, when the *Inconstant* had to depart.

By then U-181 was rattling and creaking heavily, the bilges were flooded, seams were leaking, lights were out. The *Jasmine*, the *Nigella*, and two smaller craft sent out later kept her down for three more hours. The search was not called off until nightfall. And when the warships were gone, Lüth waited. Not until midnight did U-181 surface for a blast of cool fresh air.

Lüth was almost casual about it. "Boat and crew behaved well," he jotted down afterward. The hours under attack had not made a great impression on him. Despite some significant damage, "the crew was able to go about normal repair duties with no fear of oxygen depletion"; the boat could have endured twice as long with her reserves of air and battery power. The experience did not compare with that of U-9 in May 1940, when every major piece of equipment had been damaged or broken and she had been left for dead on the bottom of the English Channel.

Lüth might have been interested to know that the *Inconstant*, after all that, had reported only a "doubtful contact" to Durban, and that according to the authors of *War in the Southern Oceans*, the "*Inconstant*'s attacks were remarkable for their persistence and accuracy in a single ship hunt. . . . Had U-181 been kept down until the arrival of aircraft next morning, the 'starvation' process might have borne fruit. However, from a strictly academic standpoint, the cool and experienced Lüth certainly seems to have earned his escape."[2]

Forty years later Krutschkowski echoed his captain's nonchalance: "When one is young one doesn't worry about such things,"[3] he said. Another crewman, Josef Grobelny, thought it was the worst experience he had ever had in the U-Bootwaffe.[4] Engel was philosophical: "We were all soldiers; it was understood that we could die. If we were lucky enough to see the sun rise over the bridge next morning, we knew that we had lived to see another day."[5]

As for the lookout, who suffered through the bombardment with the knowledge of having failed in his duty, Lüth did not punish him: "The looks he got from his shipmates when the depth charges began to explode were punishment enough. . . . Obviously some of the punishments laid down in the disciplinary code cannot be applied to a U-boat in wartime. . . . Suppose I gave a man two weeks in the brig. He couldn't serve it until the end of the patrol anyway, so we would have to continue on, sharing the same successes and failures until we got home, all of us in high spirits and with a sense of accomplishment. Am I now supposed to send this man off to the brig? I'd be very stupid to do so."6

Of course Lüth did occasionally have to punish a man on the spot, usually for crimes of intent like insubordination, theft, or fighting. But his punishments were simple, imaginative, effective, and rarely by the book, because as he had observed, the book was not written for the U-boat:

> Once I had a chronic grumbler on board who also liked to be disobedient to his superiors. . . . He crabbed about everything, [like] some types in civilian life. Once, when we had had no success for weeks and his grumblings threatened the morale of the crew, I called a muster. I dived to forty meters, got everything well settled, left three good men in the control and electric motor compartments, assembled the crew and addressed the man in a loud voice: "Either you return with me as my friend, or when you return I shall send you to a penal colony at the Eastern Front. For the time being you will draw two weeks extra duty according to an exact schedule." I gave him this in writing and had him sign it. Then I had it printed in the ship's paper which hangs on the bulletin boards, one across from the radio room and one at the head in the aft compartment where it could be read with the necessary leisure.7

Insubordination was a serious offense in the Kriegsmarine, almost as serious as mutiny, and the punishment for insubordination could be severe. But Lüth treated the chronic grumbler as though he were nothing more than a teenager with a bad attitude. Dressing him down before the crew worked; Lüth had no more trouble with him. "He [the man was never identified] became an excellent man, and I have recommended him to my successor as a combat helmsman," Lüth reassured his audience in "Problems of Leadership." That was a good recommendation indeed.

Lüth's style of leadership would not have worked in any boat. It was uniquely suited to his circumstance. The combination of his personality, the length of U-181's war patrols, and the character of the German seaman in general made it succeed. Picture Lüth trying to present "Problems of Leadership" to a roomful of American submarine commanders during the war. They would have laughed out loud at the idea of speeches on meteorology, the banning of pinups, poetry in the head, and enforced chastity.

The same can be said of Lüth's philosophy of discipline—that its effectiveness depended on circumstance. In Lothar-Günther Buchheim's book *Das Boot*, the boat's unctuous first watch officer, an avid Nazi whom the rest of the crew hates, is always reading from a notebook. Not many readers realize it is a bound copy of "Problems of Leadership," for Buchheim does not credit Lüth. What he does do is show how ludicrous the words, especially those on punishment, sound. Lüth's penalty for insubordination was three days of sleeping on the deck, for breaking the boat's crockery, three days eating out of tin cans. For the crew of Buchheim's U-boat, on a short patrol in the North Atlantic, broken crockery is the last thing on their minds. How can you worry about the china when depth charges are exploding around you and every moment might be your last? Buchheim quotes paragraph after unvarnished paragraph, and they do sound ridiculous because the words no longer match the circumstances. He cheats the reader at Lüth's expense, and that is unfortunate, since Lüth was closer to Buchheim's ideal commander than most of his peers.[8]

To die under the *Inconstant* would have been bad enough, but worse considering Lüth had learned only hours before that he had been awarded the *Eichenlaub*, the Oak Leaves for his Knight's Cross. He was the 142nd man in the Wehrmacht to have them, the sixteenth in the U-Bootwaffe. The Oak Leaves were much more difficult to get than the Cross alone. To win them a commander had to sink 200,000 tons of enemy shipping, a requirement often relaxed (perhaps almost always— only one man, Kretschmer, had reached the requisite number). Lüth had reported a total of 201,000 tons, but the real figure was closer to 170,000, and the award had been initiated before that was reached.

The physical difference between the two awards was slight: A small silver oak leaf was attached to the medal ribbon and the cross hung from the leaf instead of the ribbon itself. The real difference lay in the person who presented the award, often Adolf Hitler himself, and in the promise that any holder of the Oak Leaves would be entitled to an estate in conquered lands after the war.

Earlier, BdU had given U-181 and other boats in the area "free maneuver" east of Cape Town. On 16 November U-178, already farther east, had reported sinking two ships in the approaches to Lourenco Marques. On the basis of this report, and because cape defenses had recently seemed to pose a great deal more danger, Lüth decided to head toward Lourenco Marques as well. U-181 left at once upon intercepting the signal, and arrived there on 19 November.

Lourenco Marques was the capital of Portuguese East Africa and a major neutral port. The city itself (now called Maputo) was located at the mouth of the Espiritu Santo River, which runs into Delagoa Bay at the extreme southern tip of the country, less than fifty miles from the South African border. The port of Lourenco Marques was significant for two reasons: First, it was the port closest to the Rand, the industrial and mining center of South Africa. Second, it had one of the best deepwater harbors in the world. Before the war Lourenco Marques was a popular liberty port, although Lüth had never been there. Karl Dönitz, as captain of the cruiser *Emden*, had contracted malaria in Lourenco Marques during a visit in 1935.[9]

By 1942 Lourenco Marques had become a supply point of major importance for Allied shipping. Its neutrality was guarded zealously by ships and aircraft of the Portuguese fleet (immune from attack by direction of Erich Raeder), and until

November 1942 ships entering and leaving Lourenco Marques were relatively unconcerned about submarine attack. This innocence did not last.

Right after U-181 arrived, she sank the Norwegian tramp *Gunda*. As the Portuguese were picking up her crew, U-181 sighted another ship in the beam of the Point Inhaca lighthouse and hit her with a single torpedo. Two lifeboats full of survivors were left in the wreckage, but neither would allow Lüth to approach within hailing distance. He had to pull someone out of the water to determine that the victim was the Greek ship *Corinthiakos*. (He was gracious enough not to throw the man back, finally persuading one of the lifeboats to paddle over and pick him up.)

At midnight on 22 November, U-181 sank the American freighter *Alcoa Pathfinder*. "The survivors described the officer who questioned them (apparently Lüth himself) as speaking 'Oxford English' in an accent which was German in character," stated the authors of *War in the Southern Oceans*.[10] It was not Lüth who spoke to them, however. It is safe to say that Lüth could not speak Oxford English; his own officers disagree over whether he could speak English at all. But there is no disagreement about one thing: Lüth never spoke to survivors. He stayed in the bridge, one eye on the horizon, the other on his enemies, who might at any moment pull out a pistol or a machine gun and put a hole in his boat. It was Engel who usually did the talking.[11]

In spite of his good fortune, Lüth was not satisfied. Merchant traffic in the approaches to Lourenco Marques turned out to be lighter than expected. Several times in the previous days aircraft had driven the boat down, and strong tides made underwater attacks almost impossible. Toward evening on 22 November Lüth decided to head south along the coast in search of targets. The move proved to be the right one, for soon he sighted the Greek steamship *Mount Helmos* en route from Suez to Capetown.

It was the start of an unusual week for Lüth. During the next eight days he saw and sank four enemy merchant vessels along the east African coast. This in itself was not unusual, it was how he sank them. As during the *Notre Dame du Chatelet* incident back in May 1941, when the shooting got out of control, a new Lüth surfaced, stalked U-181's bridge for one short week, then disappeared like a whisper in the wind. This man was no hero. He acted in a callous, malicious manner. But the curious thing is that he also acted unprofessionally, even incompetently. Lüth was normally a cautious and responsible captain, and the sudden change is inexplicable.

The *Mount Helmos* went first. U-181 tracked her for four hours before attacking at dawn on 23 November. Then, though she swerved sharply at the moment of firing, a single G7e electric torpedo hit her amidships after a thirty-seven-second run. The crew of the *Mount Helmos* abandoned ship at once, but despite the large hole in her side the stubborn old steamer was still afloat an hour later. Annoyed, Lüth called away his gun crews, then set upon her, point-blank, as he had done with the *Notre Dame du Chatelet*. He brought U-181, on the surface, to within 800 meters of the *Mount Helmos* and opened fire with all three of his deck guns at once. The barrel of the 37-mm gun exploded almost at once; the other two guns—the 105-mm cannon and the 20-mm antiaircraft gun—kept firing for the next forty minutes. After sixty-five hits, the *Mount Helmos* finally went down.

Excessive, perhaps, but nothing really to criticize. Most captains, including Lüth most of the time, would have used a second torpedo to administer the coup de grâce.

Later that day, U-181 fired a torpedo at the British steamer *Dorington Court*, en route from Australia to Lourenco Marques. She was hit, but remained afloat. Lüth fired ninety 105-mm shells at her from 800 meters, damaging his boat's antiaircraft gun, and the *Dorington Court* sank after sixty hits on her stern. Ninety is a large number of shells. Lüth's log entry in this case is striking: "In spite of so many hits by explosive shells, the ship never really caught fire. This made it harder for us to leave the area." Which raises the question whether Lüth was trying to sink the *Dorington Court* or set her on fire.

At 2030 on 28 November U-181 sighted an old Greek steamer, the *Evanthia*. Once again a fired torpedo hit the vessel but she did not go down. Lüth proceeded to sink her with an unbelievable 107 rounds of mixed incendiary and high-explosive cannon shells from 600 meters away. And again he was disappointed: "Unfortunately, this ship didn't burn either, and retreat was difficult." Here lies the answer to the question of the *Dorington Court*: Both she and the *Evanthia* were set afire to illuminate U-181's retreat.

To sink a ship with guns was acceptable in certain cases. To blow one to bits with eighty, ninety, one hundred rounds of high explosive was usually not. The *Plaudit*, a ship of comparable tonnage, was sunk in high seas after only eight hits. When it was necessary to use artillery, a commander would shoot to sink as quickly and efficiently as possible. He would not waste time or ammunition trying to start a fire for any reason.

The fourth ship was the ancient Greek freighter *Cleanthis*, sighted northeast of Cape Corrientes at 0115 on 30 November zigzagging south toward Lourenco Marques. Lüth tracked her for four hours. At 0511 he fired two electric torpedoes, the first from 500 meters, the second from 600 meters. He was close enough to the *Cleanthis* to read the name from her stern, but both torpedoes missed. Then guns were spotted on her deck. "Next to the bridge are two raised machine gun platforms," Lüth noted in the log, "and two more next to a 40-mm cannon on the stern." U-181 retreated to about 3,000 meters while Lüth decided what to do next.

The *Cleanthis* was a good opportunity. There were two ways to go about sinking her; the more prudent was to fire a third torpedo. Three torpedoes for one ship may seem prodigal, but Lüth had fired four to sink the *Meldahl*, and during his second patrol in U-181 he would use that number several times to sink a single ship. The less favorable alternative was guns.

Less favorable because the *Cleanthis* was armed. Any attack on her threatened a duel, and an artillery duel between a U-boat and a surface ship was contrary to both BdU doctrine and common sense. The U-boat, according to BdU's *Handbook for U-Boat Commanders*,

> is not constructed for gunnery action on account of its limited stability, its low and unsteady gun and observation platforms

which are directly exposed to the sea's motion. Strictly speaking, the U-boat is inferior to every surface warship in an artillery battle. . . . The U-boat, as opposed to its surface opponent, is rendered completely vulnerable in every artillery duel since one hole in the pressure hull can prevent the U-boat from being able to dive and thus easily leads to the loss of the boat.[12]

One lucky shot from the *Cleanthis* and U-181 was dead.

BdU's advice notwithstanding, Lüth chose the less favorable alternative, preparing for the attack as though the crew were all headed across town for a rumble. He broke out the boat's machine guns and passed them around. They were useless at U-181's range, 3,000 meters, even dangerous. But using them made sense in view of his philosophy about "getting the crew involved." Lüth, in letting his men spread over the main deck with machine guns, gave them a sense of armed combat that sailors rarely experienced. They could think of themselves as real soldiers in a real fight instead of technicians who operated weapons only to observe the mayhem from a distance.

At 0531, from 3,000 meters, U-181 opened fire on the *Cleanthis* with incendiary and high-explosive shells. The crew continued shelling uninterruptedly for thirty minutes. The purpose of this, according to Petersen, was to ensure U-181's safety: "I think [Lüth] said 'First the bridge and the radio room,' so we shot at those. The crew abandoned ship as fast as lightning and headed for the coast. I seem to remember that this ship had a gun on her stern, and a single hit [from it] would have been fatal for a U-boat. It was Lüth's view, therefore, that the crew not even be allowed to think about using the gun."[13] Lüth's men destroyed the radio room (too late to stop a single distress call from going out) and shot the masts away, whereupon the *Cleanthis* lost her steering and began to burn.

> 0600. 80 rounds of 105-mm ammunition have now been fired at a range of 2,000–3,000 meters. About 70 hits aft and starboard side. The inside of the ship is smoking. The boat has only one round of 105-mm left, closes to 400 meters, and puts the round after careful aiming into the stern under the waterline. At the same time the 20-mm gun fires explosive rounds into the stern and the port side. Now the ship finally begins to sink.

0655. Steamer has sunk by the stern. Several bodies are floating around the after deck gun.

These seamen may have lived if Lüth had not resorted to artillery fire. U-181 had used all of her remaining ammunition in the attack. The log specifies that it was her very last shell, fired by Franz Hawran, the boat's 105-mm gun captain, that finally spelled the *Cleanthis's* end. She rose on a swell, bared her hull, and it hit.

In emptying his magazines, Lüth rendered his guns useless for the rest of the patrol. With the *Notre Dame du Chatelet*, he had justified such waste by citing a need for training. But the crew of U-181 needed no such training. Nor could he claim to have been in danger from the *Cleanthis's* guns; his first shots went unanswered, and halfway through the attack the ship was abandoned.

By the time of the last shot, U-181 had been on the surface for half an hour. There is no record of her submerging before another hour was up, when the *Cleanthis* finally sank. A captain who spent that much time on the surface during and after an artillery battle, especially when the enemy had made a distress call and then burned, endangered both his boat and his crew.

Perhaps that was why Lüth did not remain to interrogate survivors, as he usually did in U-181. (When the *Gunda* was sunk earlier that week, he had hunted around for hours in search of a survivor to talk to.) Perhaps he did not want to face them after such an attack. For their part, the survivors believed that U-181 was a Japanese boat and that Lüth had been trying to kill them all.[14] Their perception of how a German U-boat commander was supposed to act toward "seamen like us" certainly did not match his. Thirteen men had been killed in the attack, twelve injured, and he left them in the water without a thought.

The incidents with the *Cleanthis* and the three victims that preceded her do not show Lüth at his best. As if to make up for that, the month of November 1942 brought his career to an all-time high.

November 1942 initiated what historian John M. Waters called the "bloody winter" of 1942–43.[15] The Battle of the

Atlantic was never more fiercely fought than during the four or five months that followed. It was a period in which both sides seemed to know that the balance would be tipped, one way or the other, for good.

One hundred eighty U-boats went to sea in November, three times as many as BdU had had, working or not, in 1939. Together they sank 120 enemy ships, three-quarters of a million tons. Wolfgang Lüth sank 10 of those 120 ships on his own. In November 1942, he was the most successful submarine commander in the world.

After sinking the *Cleanthis*, Lüth headed south and then west along the South African coast toward the cape, at first avoiding land so as to intercept traffic reported by U-177 and U-178, then after East London approaching the coast to meet oncoming Australian traffic.

Late on 2 December the U-181 sighted and sank the Panamanian steamship *Amaryllis*, leaving six men behind on a raft and a herd of drowned livestock in the water. Crew members hauled a wet sheep aboard and slaughtered it for meat, an almost unimaginable luxury. Lüth, worried about a lack of fuel, then decided to head home with two torpedoes intact.

U-181 spotted nothing of promise during the passage around the cape except for the well-lighted and -marked hospital ship *Dorsetshire* heading for Durban. On 19 December the haunting sight of a fully equipped but empty lifeboat from the liner *Orcades* was recorded in the log. U-172 had sunk the *Orcades* on 10 October, resulting in the loss of forty men. The ship's last recorded position was some 1,000 miles southeast.

The crew of U-181 celebrated Christmas, with a tree of wire and toilet paper dyed green, somewhere between Ascension and St. Helena. "Merry Christmas to everyone at home from the South Atlantic," radioed Lüth to BdU on Christmas Eve. "58,000 GRT sunk at this time. We are celebrating in tropical heat with accordion and tree at a depth of thirty meters."

On Christmas Eve an imitation Santa Claus, who wears only a bed sheet in the tropics, stands in the festively decorated bow compartment and presents every man with some candy and a

Lüth in the bridge of U-181 as she returned from her first war patrol in January 1943. Twelve pennants are flying behind him, one for each of the twelve ships he sank during the patrol. Ten of them were sunk in one month.

book with a dedication. All of this of course is accompanied with appropriate phrases and verse. We sang Christmas carols and the captain gave a Christmas speech. After the celebration we ate supper on the gaily decorated mess tables; the officers' mess was dissolved and the officers ate with the men.[16]

It had taken forty-nine days for the boat to sail from Kiel to Cape Town. It took thirty-five days to sail back from Cape Town to Bordeaux, base of operations for the Twelfth U-Flotilla and U-181's new home.

Before U-181 reached Point Hand, the first of the tactical points in the approaches to the Gironde, Lüth took her down one last time. He assembled the crew, thanked them for their efforts over the past four months, and warned them about security, posting a sample letter home on the bulletin board: "Dear Erika, I have returned safely. We were very successful and sank several steamers." The men were lectured about venereal disease, encouraged to buy things for their families, and told to stick to Bordeaux and those places of leave that BdU approved. Finally, Lüth restricted them to the barracks their first night in port to settle everyone down.

U-181 tied up inside one of Bordeaux's huge concrete submarine pens at 1700 on 18 January 1943. The last entry in the log reads simply, "Boat was at sea for a total of 129 days and sailed 21,369 miles. Twelve ships were sunk in the Cape Town-Lourenco Marques area for a total of 57,500 GRT." The actual total was slightly higher than that; for once, Lüth had underestimated.

10

DEATH AND FLYING FISHES

The essence of Wolfgang Lüth's leadership style could be found in the relationship between him and his men; and to know Lüth, you had to know them.

"My men come from all over Germany," Lüth said in the prologue to "Problems of Leadership." And so they did: from every corner of the Third Reich, from every background, from every stratum of society. But under Wolfgang Lüth they became something more than the sum of their individual selves.

It was not unusual, for example, for someone from Königsberg (now Kaliningrad in the Soviet Union) to rub shoulders in the torpedo room with someone from Mulhausen (now Mulhouse in France), for a captain from Latvia to have to make himself understood by men from Bavaria or the Tyrol or Friesland, for men to scatter like leaves in the wind to Berlin, Frankfurt, Hamburg, Dresden, Düsseldorf, and Lübeck when their boat came home.

These were some of the men in U-181 with Lüth: Herbert Krutschkowski, chief radioman; Joseph Grobelny, electrician's mate; Walter Pfeiffer, machinist's mate; Franz Persch, electrician's mate; Walter Schmidt, torpedoman's mate; Franz Hawran, boatswain's mate; Heinz Schulz, seaman; Karl Kaiser, Siegfried Nagorny, Johannes Fröhlich, Wilhelm Williger. Over fifty crewmen were enlisted in U-181 at any one time, perhaps a hundred men altogether. The opinions they had of their commanding officer are not as useful as those of the officers because, paradoxically, the were so uniformly favorable. None of Lüth's enlisted crewmen could say a bad word about him. They loved him. At the end of a long interview in which he provided a mound of useful information about U-181, Walter Schmidt cried. *"Es gibt jetzt keinen solchen Mann,"* he said in utter despair.[1] There are no men like that anymore. The officers knew better. Their opinions, while still favorable, tended to be more objective and candid. The officers knew, for example, that Lüth was crazy about National Socialism; the enlisted men swore as one that he had had nothing to do with it. The officers recognized that he was a prude, a meddler, and sometimes cruel; the enlisted men saw only his courage, his competence, and his kindness.

There are reasons for the difference. The crew lived farther apart from Lüth than his officers; rarely did the crew socialize with him except as a group, and rarely were they involved in decision-making. They did their jobs, Lüth took care of them, and they benefited from his success. He "respected them and he liked them," and they knew it.

Men like these were standing on U-181's weather deck when she pulled out of Bordeaux on 23 March 1943 for her second war patrol. Nobody knew it then, but U-181 would spend the next seven months as sea. She would not return to Bordeaux for 203 days, nor at any time before that touch line to pier or anchor to bottom. Nobody knew it then, but when she did return to Bordeaux, her crew would be heroes of the Reich and

Lüth the most decorated man in the U-Bootwaffe. Nobody knew it then, but this was to be the last patrol of Wolfgang Lüth's life.

The men on deck stood stiffly, proudly, their eyes fixed on the city, their thoughts on recent memories. The men below-decks worked, talked, and laughed in a mad jungle of levers, pipes, sausages, and potatoes. Most of the talk was about Bordeaux and the good times they had had there: the pretty girls, the bordellos and taverns—King Kong, Place Gambetta, Fassle—and the trouble they got into. They talked about visits home, their parents and families, their sweethearts and old friends. Or they talked about the trip to Posen.[2]

In February, Lüth had taken some of the crew east to Posen for a visit. Posen was the capital of Wartheland, the new German province created after the invasion of Poland in 1939. Why would an entire U-boat crew travel a thousand miles by train to visit the dreary capital of an occupied Polish province when they could go to Paris instead? Because they had been personally invited by the *Gauleiter*, the provincial governor.

U-181's patron and godfather was Arthur Greiser, an unsavory senior functionary of the Third Reich and the Nazi Party. Earlier he had been head of the German government in Danzig. Later he would briefly be considered a candidate to replace Hans Frank as governor of Poland itself. Greiser met Lüth in the summer of 1942 on a visit to U-181 in Stettin. Greiser was part of the entourage of Wilhelm Frick, the Reich's interior minister. After Frick departed, Greiser remained for a time and began a friendship with Lüth. It may have been because he knew Lüth's parents were living in Posen (they had been resettled there after the war began), or because he genuinely liked Lüth. Whatever the reason, he "adopted" U-181, kept in touch with her always, sent gifts to the crew (the books and records were Greiser's), invited them to Posen, and more or less became an ex officio member of the crew himself.

Greiser's friendship was good for Lüth in one way: The man was important and he had influence. In another way it was a tragedy, for Greiser was as evil a man as the party produced. "All gentleness toward Poles must be avoided," he stated pub-

licly, "and loathing for the Poles sown in every German heart.
. . . God has helped us conquer the Polish nation, which must
now be destroyed. . . . In a decade the fields of Poland will be
heavy with stacked wheat and rye, raised and harvested by Germans, but not a Pole will remain."[3] His words had teeth; he
presided over a diabolical killing frenzy. "He was personally a
very nice man," said Lothar Engel, "but the Poles hated him.
. . ."[4] Passionately. After the war they hanged him.

It was an awkward situation for Lüth. You couldn't really
say no to a man like Greiser; if he wanted to be your friend,
you were stuck with him. On the other hand, to say yes was to
associate yourself with him, and Lüth knew very well what
Greiser was. The dilemma of the German military was how to
stay close enough to the beast without being consumed. Some
managed to remain aloof or detached without seeming subver-
sive or disloyal. Some did not, and to this group belonged
Lüth. By accepting Greiser's gifts and then his invitation, he
came too close to the beast.

When the crew of U-181 arrived in Posen, they were hosted in
an ostentatious and well-choreographed fashion by the entire
local Nazi apparatus, Gauleiter himself in the lead. They stayed
at the Hotel Ostland, which, according to Petersen, was one of
the three best hotels in the Reich. A full bottle of schnapps had
been placed next to each bed. Prominent citizens of Posen
invited the crew in groups to their homes. Parties were thrown.
The men were given a tour of the city, and they all signed the
guest book at City Hall. A picture of the crew shows them lined
up inside City Hall to greet the mayor of Posen.

"For several weeks," read the wrap-up in U-181's newspaper,
"the local edition . . . has not been published because the publisher was away on leave. Some of [the crew] was away too, on
a visit to Posen. They could tell some real tales. . . . But you
all know who you are! It was a journey which began in high
spirit at the train station and ended at the station in equally
high spirit."

The passage out the Gironde and through the Bay of Biscay
was nerve-racking. Three times on 24 March U-181 had to dive

after sighting aircraft. Each time the Metox was conspicuously silent. In the distant rumblings of depth charges, the men heard play out the unpleasant fates of other boats. This was the sort of experience, Theodor Petersen wrote, that produced "saucer-eyes from the younger men, quiet smiles from the older ones."[5]

Meanwhile Petersen, after serving with Lüth for almost three years, had been sent back to train for command of his own boat. U-181's new first watch officer was Gottfried König, who only two years earlier had been a midshipman in U-43. The times, it seemed, had made promotion in the U-Bootwaffe almost as quick as death.

The boat sailed steadily southward. "We have now crossed the Tropic of Cancer," wrote the anonymous editor of U-181's newspaper.

> Some of our shipmates have already started taking off all their clothes and are now running around half-naked. But it's really not that warm; the captain, for example, is still wearing his long underwear! After much hard work the mess left behind by the *Werft* [shipyard] is being cleaned up and it's slowly getting more comfortable around here. Now there is carpeting in the officers' and petty officers' spaces. All personal effects have been stored back behind the piping, the leather jackets under the mattresses, books under pillows, and the boat smells pleasantly of bad hair oil and other French odors. The Obersteuermann has taken out his card table again.[6]

Boredom threatened, and Lüth began his eternal search for ways to keep the crew happy. Chess and card tournaments resumed. "Today at 1630 a *blitz* tourney will begin in all spaces," the paper announced. "Entries accepted by Bootsmaat Hawran until 1600. Everyone will be paired off; ten seconds for each move! Judges will sit at each board with stopwatches. Pieces touched must be moved, pieces let go must be left where they stand. Whoever goes over the limit three times will be the loser. Now is the chance for those weak but enthusiastic players!"

The men made plans for the equator crossing, and invented less wholesome ways of passing time. Several formed a secret club in the after torpedo room. Lüth put a stop to it, comparing such practices to the Ku Klux Klan or the Masons. Forbidden jazz concerts took place in the forward torpedo room. Lothar Engel says this was Krutschkowski's doing; whenever Lüth was safely out of earshot in the bridge he pulled out his records—"Tiger Rag," "Alexander's Ragtime Band," and "We Will Hang Out Our Washing on the Siegfried Line"—all of them picked up in France and Belgium. The men thought they were very clever that way.[7]

Lüth was not stupid; he knew about the records but pretended not to notice. His taste did not run to jazz. He preferred classical music, kitschy folk tunes, marches—the "acceptable" music. "A German must not like jazz," he went so far as to say in "Problems of Leadership." "It has nothing to do with whether or not he *really* likes it. He simply must not like it, just as a German man must not like a Jewess." Good Germans did not like jazz, and that was that. The party decreed it.

Fortunately for Lüth, his adherence to the party line was not always so blind. If jazz kept the crew happy, then he was prepared to ignore it. Besides, he had a vice of his own: smoking. His men liked American music; Lüth liked British cigars. He had boxes of Upmanns, part of the huge stores left behind by the British Army in their haste to escape fallen France. He smoked one every night on the bridge, and even passed them out to his officers on Sunday morning.[8]

So much for purity—a German officer in his U-boat smoking a British cigar within sight of Madagascar, instructing his watch officer on the joys of matrimony while being serenaded from below by the muffled strains of "Tiger Rag."

And then there were the flying fish. According to Franz Persch, engineering mate, the fish "flew out of the water for distances of 200 meters, at a height of 50 cm, and when we surfaced in the morning haze they would hit the conning tower and fall to the deck. Members of the watch used to grab them right away and throw them down to me through the bridge hatch. Once someone missed the hatch and threw a fish down the voicepipe, where it stuck. Naturally all hell broke loose after the heat started to rot it. . . ."[9]

Persch was somewhat of a free spirit. He left home without permission at the age of fifteen to visit the 1937 Paris Exposition, and by the time he was seventeen he was traveling throughout Europe and North Africa with little cards that read, "Studies and recreation have taken me, a young German, out into the world to visit other lands and to meet other people. Help with my travel costs by purchasing this card." In U-181, while others read books or took part in discussion groups, Persh would occupy himself in a corner with his strange, malodorous hobby. For this he was known as the Poisoned Dwarf, a term that seems not to have offended him in the least. He explained what he did with his fish: "[T]he insides were taken out . . . we had tobacco and cigarettes on board, but the damp made them go off . . . quickly. I treated the entire skin with tobacco juice and stuffed it with tobacco. The fins were stretched out and nailed to a piece of wood to dry (the fin span of these fish was between 40 and 60 cm). At the end of the patrol everyone in the crew had one of my 'flying fish' to take home with him on leave."[10]

Just before midnight on 10 April, about 400 miles southwest of Freetown and close to the equator, U-181 sighted a ship in the moonlight. She was the British refrigerator ship *Empire Whimbrel,* bound for home. Lüth decided to make the *Empire Whimbrel* his first kill of the patrol; had he known what lay ahead, he would have let her sail in peace.

"We are in front of her and she bears 225," he recorded. "As she zags to zero we attack, but this time she does not zig back after twelve minutes as before, but turns 90 degrees after three." In this first attack, at 0330, Lüth fired two torpedoes; both missed as the *Empire Whimbrel,* being prudent, zagged suddenly to 160. Three more attacks proved equally fruitless. Apparently unaware that she was under attack, the British ship steamed serenely away in the phosphorescence.

By zigzagging at random, the *Empire Whimbrel* had prolonged her life for several hours. Shortening his range would not help Lüth because the target was blacked out. So he waited for dawn, then approached to about 450 meters.

At 0550 he fired two more torpedoes. Both hit the *Empire Whimbrel,* the first aft, the second forward, sending the crew running for her boats and prompting a distress call from her radio room. At dawn the *Empire Whimbrel* was abandoned and adrift, but she had not sunk.

The guns on U-181 had not been fired since the sinking of the *Cleanthis* almost six months before. They were dirty and clogged with grease. The last gunnery exercise had also been months before, and it is a safe bet that some of the men on the boat had never fired them. Nevertheless, Lüth—the young FLAK-Leiter of the *Königsberg,* the man who shot the *Notre Dame du Chatelet* to matchsticks, the captain who emptied his magazines to set the ancient *Cleanthis* afire—called his gun crews away once more.

The first shell, fired from the 37-mm gun, jammed in the barrel and exploded with a giant crack, steel splinters flying in every direction. It was over in a split second. The barrel of the gun splayed out like an open umbrella from which the cloth has been torn away. Men staggered, deafened or in shock, covered with blood, screaming and cursing and crying.

As the smoke cleared and senses returned, the awful extent of the blast became clear. Wilhelm Williger, the boat's cook, was writhing in pain, his knee shattered by shrapnel. A second man, Boatswain's Mate Kuhne, had a broken elbow, and a third, Seaman Erich Will, had a fist-sized piece of steel imbedded in his back, though he had been standing several meters away in the *Wintergarten,* the aft section of U-181's huge tower structure. There were multiple cuts and bruises as well.

Kuhne, then Williger, were handed down into the control room. In spite of his own wounds, Will helped with the delirious cook. The table in the wardroom was cleared and Williger laid across it. After a rushed examination, Lothar Engel amputated Williger's left leg at the knee. Schmidt administered chloroform and Krutschkowski acted as the nurse, handing Engel his instruments and mopping up blood.

The amputation was performed under almost medieval conditions: The heat in the boat was 50° Celsius, the light poor, hygiene dreadful. The barrage of the *Empire Whimbrel* continued topside. Engel's operation was a failure, and the cook died at 1130 from loss of blood.[11] The other two were luckier. A piece of gun barrel measuring 10 cm by 4 cm was removed from Kuhne's elbow, and Will, Engel determined, probably had lung damage.

Williger was buried at sea on the equator. The order of the day for Monday, 12 April, gave details in preparation:

> 0900: Uniform for the crew: short brown trousers, tropical shirts.
>
> 1000: Dive for burial service of Wilhelm Williger. Two men will stand as honor guard at Williger's bier. After the dive the guard will be increased to four. The crew will be assembled by the Chief Engineer. At the entrance of the Captain, the crew will not be called to attention, but will rise or sit quietly.
>
> Address by the Captain.
>
> *Ich Hatt' einen Kameraden* ["I Had a Comrade"], sung together.
>
> Boat will then be made ready to surface. The crew will proceed slowly to diving stations.
>
> At a command from the captain, Williger will be brought up to the bridge. Ten men in attendance (besides the watch). Number One will pipe the side.[12]

Lüth sent a message to BdU requesting that a boat en route to France be made available to pick up Will; U-516 appeared on the horizon shortly before the burial service ended. Kuhne remained on board. The entire affair had a noticeably sobering effect on the men of U-181. Lüth had never before lost a man at sea. Many of his men had never seen death close up (the effects of a torpedo attack did not count, since they could not be seen). The phonograph languished in silence. The celebration of the equator crossing was canceled. After twenty hits from her 105-mm cannon, U-181 sank the *Empire Whimbrel,* but nobody took much notice. Nobody wanted cognac.

The burial at sea of Wilhelm Williger, elaborate under the circumstances, tells us something more about Lüth—his inordinate love of ritual. "Military ceremony is necessary from time to time to stimulate the enthusiasm of the men," he stated in "Problems of Leadership." Parading the crew to bury a shipmate at sea was a proper demonstration of respect and sorrow; it also reminded them that they were a military unit and not rabble.

On a practical level, a ceremony every now and then kept the crew acceptably groomed and at least minimally clean. If anyone had a clean shirt, for example, he was to wear it on Sunday, a day Lüth made special with later reveille, better food, a holiday routine, and so forth. Sunday was a ceremony in itself. Moreover, a good ceremony was just as effective as a chess tournament or a song contest in fighting boredom.

"This morning we received the following message from Führer headquarters," said an item in the boat's newspaper on 16 April. "'To Kapitänleutnant Lüth: In recognition of your heroism I award to you as the 29th soldier of the Wehrmacht the *Eichenlaub mit Schwertern zum Ritterkreuz* (Oak Leaves with Swords to the Knight's Cross).'" Wolfgang Lüth was the fourth man in the U-Bootwaffe to win the Reich's second highest military award.*

Almost immediately messages of congratulation began to pour in, first from Dönitz, then from the Twelfth U-Flotilla, another from FdU West (the overall commander of U-boat flotillas in France), then a brief note from Erich Raeder, now in semi-retirement. The Italians sent their best wishes, as did the city of Posen and its mayor. Arthur Greiser was effusive: "We of the *Reichsgau* Wartheland look proudly upon you, you who have led our U-boats to new glory with tenacity and daring. I wish you and your entire crew the very best on the occasion of the Führer's award. With comradely greetings, yours, Greiser. There will be a celebration indeed next time you are in Posen."[13]

The message from Führer headquarters also included notification of Wolfgang Lüth's latest promotion, to *Korvettenkapitän*. Anyone who continued to address him by his former rank, announced the newspaper, would be subject to a fine of one mark.

U-181 did not waste time at the cape on her second patrol. Defenses there had stiffened considerably since November,

---

*The three before him were Otto Kretschmer (given his Swords in Bowmanville POW Camp, Ontario, by the camp commandant), Erich Topp, and Reinhard Suhren.

and Lüth routed the boat eastward around the cape. At 0800 on 10 May Inhaca Point Lighthouse was sighted. For the second time in six months, U-181 was outside the port of Lourenco Marques looking in.

The next few days resulted in frustration. Lüth wasted substantial amounts of fuel in pursuit of merchant ships that turned out to be Portuguese, and there were frequent patrols by Portuguese aircraft and the gunboat *Bartolomeu Dias,* a small but dangerous warship built for colonial use in 1934. At one point Lüth found himself chasing the Portuguese ship *Mouzinho* once again. On 19 May a notification from BdU brought a small respite to the frustration. Lüth's third child and first son, Wolf Dieter, had been born. The crew delivered the news to Lüth in verse: "From far away to the Cape we hear: / A little boy Lüth has now appeared. / It proves what we are often told: / Persistence has its own rewards."

On the afternoon of 26 May a well-marked neutral merchant ship was sighted leaving Lourenco Marques. Quickly identified as the Swedish motor ship *Sicilia* from Göteborg, she was not in the register of shipping. For Lüth, already exasperated at having to let so many Portuguese ships pass, this was cause for suspicion. "I intend to stop [the *Sicilia*] with a warning shot," he wrote in the log, and "after the papers are brought over and the crew are off, to sink her. We are close to land, in fairly shallow water, so a prolonged artillery operation is not acceptable; the coup de grâce should be with a torpedo."

U-181 trailed the *Sicilia* through the night. Despite such confident plans, Lüth could not make up his mind about her. According to Schmidt he spent the hours pacing back and forth in the control room wondering out loud what he should do.[14]

Sinking an obviously neutral ship with no good cause was risky, particularly in view of an earlier warning to him (which he had entered into the log) that such an action "would have severe political consequences." To stop a merchant ship for inspection, as Prize Regulations still required, was even riskier, since merchant ships did not always follow the same regulations and would often open fire. On the other hand, the *Sicilia*

The sinking of the Swedish freighter *Sicilia*. This sinking was unusual in that Lüth attacked and sank *Sicilia* in accordance with the obsolete Prize Regulations: he stopped her with a shot across her bow; he

was worth a closer look. To stop her with a warning shot would be vaguely chivalrous. At least it would entertain the crew.

At dawn Lüth maneuvered U-181 6,000 meters from the *Sicilia* and fired a single cannon shell across her bow. No response. He followed it with nine more in quick succession, each closer to the *Sicilia*'s bridge than the last, until finally the ship stopped and the crew took to their lifeboats. The master and first officer were brought on board U-181 for examination of the *Sicilia*'s papers. They were incomplete, and the ship's manifest looked suspicious. The deck log had been "left behind in the excitement," the master said. He acted peculiar during the interroga-

brought her master on board U-181 for interrogation; he gave her crew half an hour to abandon ship. A member of U-181's crew took these pictures as a single torpedo was fired at *Sicilia*.

tion. Lüth was sure he was lying. The man was a Swede named Jansen. He willing admitted that he had played this game before, once having spent four months in an Argentine hospital ship after a ship of his had been sunk in similar circumstances. "He was very understanding about it," said the boat's newspaper, "and stated that he sailed for money, not for politics."

Lüth and Jansen conferred with one another, then sent the first officer back to the ship for her deck logs. After examining them and questioning Jansen again, Lüth made his final decision to sink the *Sicilia*. He entered seven cautious paragraphs in the log explaining why: She was not registered; her papers were incomplete; she had made previous trips to such Allied ports as Rio de Janeiro, New York, and Philadelphia; her master had been involved in another sinking; the cargo had been purchased by English agents in Lourenco Marques; the Swedish consul in Lourenco was an Englishman; and finally, BdU's standing orders required that any ship in such circumstances be sunk.

The crew were given thirty minutes to pack their bags. At 1000 Lüth took U-181 in to 400 meters, pointed her bow at the *Sicilia*'s midsection, and fired a single torpedo, which struck her amidships. A crewman on U-181 took pictures of the *Sicilia* as she was rent in two and sank. Jansen remained calm, even cheerful, until his lifeboat cast off. At that point he began to wail loudly about cannibals. That part of the African coastline to which he had been directed was not far from civilization. Though there is no record of his fate, he was probably not eaten.

Mother's Day and Father's Day being of special significance to Lüth, they were observed every year in his boats. He celebrated Mother's Day by having the best remaining stores of food served and menus printed up. Father's Day was a slightly wilder affair that took place in the officers' mess; every father in the crew got a glass of Malaga for doing his duty for the Reich. "It was determined that eight fathers had a total of twelve children," Lüth wrote. "Nine of them were girls; that's always a sign that the man dominates his marriage." Those who were not fathers got only beer.

U-181 sank the British steamship *Harrier* the next day, 4 June 1943. "Hit astern after twenty seconds [from only 400 meters]," the captain recorded. "Giant column of fire. Pieces of shrapnel fly in all directions. There is a strong smell of gasoline and nothing more to see of the ship except for small fragments no larger than a man's arm. . . . then there was only a large oil slick . . . and some small pieces of wood you couldn't heat a room with. The crew probably still doesn't know that their ship was blown up. . . ."

They didn't. A small ship of perhaps 200 tons, the *Harrier* was carrying explosives. She had been vaporized. Never mind: U-181 had now sunk four steamers for a total of 13,852 GRT, each steamer averaging 3,463 GRT. Lüth hoped to rack up an average of 5,000 GRT per ship for this patrol. The last two ships had cost only two torpedoes, so sufficient ammunition remained for at least five more kills.

In June the boat's newspaper ran a news item from the daily fleet broadcast: "The first U-boat with the new anti-aircraft assembly has just left harbor. It was attacked yesterday by eight aircraft from a carrier. One was shot down, four damaged, and the other three turned away, leaving the U-boat with only minor damage." It was an upbeat item, and true besides. New boats with extra armaments were indeed setting out to sea. But that was only half the story. Things had to be bad for Dönitz to arm his boats and direct them to engage aircraft on the surface, violating his own principles of submarine warfare. Operating as a surface warship, the U-boat could only lose. The extra guns and larger towers that began to appear on Atlantic boats after 1943 said in veiled terms that Germany was losing the war.

Early in 1943 defeat had come in the sands of North Africa and under endless Russian skies. In March of that year, however, U-boats were still fighting and winning. They sank so many ships and with so little punitive effect that the war actually seemed lost on the Allied side. "[T]he Naval Staff were later to record that 'the Germans never came so near to disrupting communications between the New World and the Old as in the first 20 days of March 1943,' and 'it appeared possible that we should not be able to continue [to regard] convoy as an effective form of defence.' This was tantamount to an admission of defeat."[15]

That was what the crew of U-181 thought when their boat left Bordeaux near the end of March. It was what they thought in May upon receiving the signal about newer, bigger boats. But circumstances would change by May.

In April the war at sea finally began to turn against Germany. The numbers were just too great, the odds too long. Every advantage the Allies had came together in April. They had ever more warships and ever more merchants, built as fast as toys in the factory and tossed into the water. They were reading German signals and radio waves, their radar screens made U-boats look like steel mountains, and their sonar searched out prey as easily as if the water were glass.

An Allied convoy later in the war, as seen from an escorting aircraft. The photograph itself demonstrates something that most U-boat commanders were learning the hard way: the airplane made all the

May was the decisive month, over forty U-boats lost. The long and bitterly fought Battle of the Atlantic ended — even if the fighting did not — when Dönitz withdrew his boats that month from the North Atlantic. With that, "the Battle of the Atlantic was won, a complete and decisive victory."[16] Dönitz himself would not admit this was anything more than a tactical pause, a regrouping of effort. "In the future as in the past the

difference in the war at sea, and by 1943, Allied air superiority at sea was unchallenged. (Official U.S. Navy Photograph)

main operations area of the U-boats is in the North Atlantic . . . the battle there must be resumed with all hardness and determination as soon as the boats are given the necessary weapons."[17]

Miracle weapons, they were called. He had been promised boats that sailed faster and stayed underwater longer, for days, even weeks. They were equipped with "smart" torpedoes that homed in on sound or looked for targets, noiseless engines,

A U-boat under attack by a U.S. Navy PBM in the South Atlantic, May 1943. U-43, under the command of Lüth's old first watch officer, Hans-Joachim Schwantke, met an almost identical fate in July, lost with no survivors off the west African coast. (Official U.S. Navy Photograph)

and asdic-proof hulls. All of these things were on the way; he *knew* it. And as he waited, his boats disappeared.

U-43 was lost in late July. She was headed for a minelaying operation in Lagos Harbor, the kind of operation Lüth and everyone else hated, the kind with every risk and no reward. Two aircraft sighted her on the surface as she fueled a larger boat. The planes were flying from the deck of another Allied innovation, the aircraft carrier, in this case the USS *Santee*. One plane came in low and strafed both boats, one after the other. The second followed with depth charges and torpedoes, one of which followed U-43 underwater and hit her dead amidships. "Oil gushed up, bringing with it splintered wood, paper, and what looked like pieces of cork. Down below, U-43 had disintegrated, destroyed finally by her own mines."[18]

Hans-Joachim Schwantke and all of his crew were dead.

11

THE LONG PATROL

Josef Dick is from Cologne. At various times he has been a draftee in the Tank Corps, a minesweep sailor, and a Diesel-maat in U-boats. He speaks with a pronounced Cologne dialect, Kölsch, incomprehensible even to other Germans; it is responsible in a roundabout way for his nickname *Mömmes* ("joker")[1] on board U-181. Although his usual work station is the main engine room aft, Dick is over the side of U-181 in a canvas diving suit and lead boots. It is 9 May 1943. The boat lies dead in the water because of a steel fishnet tangled in one of her screws. Dick is a qualified diver, so he has been given the job of freeing it up.

The boat is drifting in the Mozambique Channel, midway between the east coast of Africa and the island of Madagascar. Miles from either shore, she still faces the constant danger of air attack. A double watch is posted in the bridge and the guns are manned. The rest of the crew clusters on the stern, watching Dick at work.

Dick is cutting the fishnet away with an electric torch whose elements have to be changed periodically. Every few minutes Franz Persch leans over the side, reaches below the surface, and takes the spent torch from Dick. He changes the element and hands the torch back down to Dick. It arcs violently, breaking the water's surface with a huge blister of frothy bubbles and a bright blue flash of Motorenwerk Mannheim diesel generator electricity. This bothers Dick, but not Persch, an electrician before the war, who claims, "I used to test sockets with my fingers."[2]

The crew, including Lüth, watches this bizarre little circus intently. The weather is warm and pleasant, and until the fishnet is freed there is nothing else to do. A far cry from convoy war in the north. Then someone cries out, "Shark!"

The effect is instantaneous. Dick hears the cry somehow, and still holding the torch, squeezes his body between the two screws as far as it will go. The 20-mm gun spins around and fires blindly into the water. Everyone cranes his neck for a look. Sure enough, there is the big fish, languidly touring the boat's circumference. It doesn't look threatening.

"Don't worry about the shark, Dick," Lüth tells him. "We'll watch it." Someone scuttles away to get the boat's fishing tackle and some bait. Dick isn't so easy. Sharks eat people. Hurriedly he hacks away at the net.

The fishing line's huge hook is baited with chicken bones leftover from lunch, then dropped in the water. The crowd on the stern watches as the shark snaps at the bait. There is a fight, blood and foam on the water, another burst from the machine gun. Soon the shark is hanging from the bridge railing, "at least two meters long."[3]

Lüth considers it a gift from the gods, as good as that sheep from the first patrol. Shark meat is delicious, he declares; it will be served for dinner. But to his displeasure, and everyone else's delight, the cook does not know how to prepare it. He boils it, bakes it, then fries it in oil. The result is a greasy rub-

Josef Dick's shark hangs from the bridge railing. The hunt and capture of this shark was a welcome diversion in an otherwise boring patrol. It meant that Lüth himself would have to invent one less thing for his crew to do with their time. As far as he was concerned it meant dinner too, but the cook mangled it to the point where it had to be thrown overboard.

ber, awful to look at. Several hours later the remains are tossed overboard.

Lüth saves the jaws as a souvenir. Before the end of this patrol, all the teeth will be missing.[4]

The meeting between Dick and the shark was a godsend for Lüth, in spite of what Dick or the shark may have thought. It distracted the crew from thoughts of war and gave them something to write home about. When Dick went over the side with his torch in May 1943, Lüth needed a diversion badly.

U-181's second war patrol was supposed to have lasted eighteen weeks. She had been fueled and provisioned for that amount of time. The Enigma keys she carried were good for only five months. Her crew looked forward to liberty in Bordeaux no later than 1 August.

But on 17 May, two days before the shark appeared and nine weeks into the patrol, Lüth received a signal from BdU instructing all type IXD2 boats in the area to refuel at sea in June. The additional 200 cbm of fuel to be pumped into each boat would increase the maximum length of their patrols to twenty-six weeks. U-181 would remain at sea until the end of September—a patrol lasting over six months.

Today, a six-month submarine patrol is unremarkable, if not commonplace. In 1943 no submarine in the world had made a patrol of such length. A war patrol of two months was considered long, and most were shorter than that because of restricted fuel, provisions, and torpedoes, equipment failures, or the loss of the boat herself. The effects of extended patrols on crews had thus never been measured. Large surface warships could and did remain at sea for months at a time, but there was no comparison between living conditions in an aircraft carrier or battleship and those in a submarine. It was like the difference, as Lüth put it, "between life in the city and life in the countryside."

Neither official records nor subsequent personal accounts indicate that the reaction of Lüth's crew to the extension was negative. Nor did the performance of the crew appear to suffer during the remainder of the patrol. But the danger always existed that it would, sooner or later, since each day brought a new experiment, each hour a new record. Lüth evidently thought it would be prudent to insert the following exhortation in the boat's newspaper on 11 June:

We are now in a fairly remote area, where there is a chance for ships but little danger of being surprised by aircraft. Use the time to come up on the bridge. Bathe on the weather deck; do a few arm stretches or knee bends. Keep in mind that no U-boat as yet has been out for half a year, and that everyone will have to exercise some self-discipline in order to keep fit. We are living like cavemen, with no distinction between night and day, so make sure you don't fall into the dull routine of watch, meals, toilet, and sleep! Make sure you don't get fat, and that you don't become neurotic. Listen to the reports of current events (whether they make you want to smile or be sick). They will give you an idea of

Wolfgang Lüth in an unguarded moment on the bridge of U-181. He is wearing what had become the standard uniform for crews in the Indian Ocean, shorts and boots, and his beard has already taken on its distinctive "fringed" look.

what's going on around you. Don't play the same old games; try something new. Read a decent book for a change, or listen to music and sing along, especially in the evenings.

U-181 left Lourenco Marques that morning for the last time. "In your beam we found no fortune," wrote a poet in the boat, "we could no longer stay. / But we will always think of you /

Beloved Inhaca." As the Inhaca Point light receded, so did the prospect of easy killing and quick glory in southern waters.

As the Battle of the Atlantic went, so did the battles on the periphery. The year 1943 would not repeat the successes of 1942; fewer ships would be sunk at the cape during the entire course of 1943 than had been sunk during that flurry in October and November 1942. While U-181 was in Bordeaux a third wave of large boats, *Gruppe Seehund,* had been sent to the cape, but their successes were unspectacular, even disappointing.

For Lüth it was a challenge. To compensate for the drop in sinkings BdU had been increasing the size of his operations area almost daily, and by the end of June it included almost all of the western Indian Ocean. Lüth took advantage of the increase, left the coast, roamed the sea to his limits, and through sheer doggedness—one ship here, one ship there—was able to add continually to his tonnage total, now fast approaching the bona fide 200,000 mark.

Lüth's replenishment area was a remote point in the Indian Ocean some 700 miles south of Mauritius, the nearest landfall, and 1,700 miles east of Durban. The replenishment ship was a merchant tanker, the *Charlotte Schliemann,* now a supply and part-time prison ship for the Kriegsmarine. She was homebound from Japan when ordered to fuel U-181 and four other boats in the cape area.

U-181 sighted the *Charlotte Schliemann* early on 22 June. Two boats, U-178 and U-196, were already tied up and fueling, another two, U-197 and U-198, approaching. These five boats represented the entire German submarine presence in the Indian Ocean for the month of June. They would have meant a certain medal for any bomber pilot who strayed over.

Lüth was not summoned alongside the *Charlotte Schliemann* for fueling until early on 23 June. U-181 had to spend the night circling her as a picket boat. As if this didn't irritate him enough, the Japanese provisions finally sent over to him were insufficient. "[T]he meat and vegetables are particularly meager, and taking into account the possible length of this patrol, they won't even last as long as the fuel," he complained. The crew was less dissatisfied; they took turns in the *Charlotte Schliemann's* showers while 280 cbm of diesel oil was being pumped into U-181's tanks, extending the boat's maximum possible patrol to over seven months. Her bilges were packed with Japanese lard in ammunition boxes, and one of *Charlotte Schliemann's* crew was sent over to replace the departed Williger.

His name was Müller, a merchant sailor, willing enough, but unaccustomed to military life. His first mistake was to wear a straw hat when reporting on board. The second, to Engel's amusement, was to greet his new captain with a breezy "Hello!" rather than the customary salute.[5] Müller was promptly assigned to an experienced petty officer for an abbreviated two-week course in military training.

The new man's swearing-in ceremony is another example of Lüth's fondness for ritual:

> We submerged for the occasion, decorated the bow compartment with flags, and turned the administration of the oath [the *Fahneneid*—the personal oath to Adolf Hitler] into a real ceremony. The man had previously learned the oath by heart. In my address I told him about the duties of a German soldier. The crew attended, dressed uniformly in brown tropical shirts. All hands got decent haircuts for the day. Appropriate songs for the ceremony had been prearranged and everything went off perfectly. We also made the young man a present of "Duties of a Warship's Man" which had been handlettered by a member of the crew. . . . He became an excellent man who later won the Iron Cross.[6]

For Lüth, nobody was beyond redemption.

With replenishment complete at 1500 on 26 June, Lüth headed north, still complaining about the lack of food and essentials. "Boat is ready for service until 10 October, fuel on board 415 cbm," he said in the log. "I have decided with regret to have a practice dive only once every three days in order to reduce stress on the air compressor. There weren't any spare parts on board [the *Charlotte Schliemann*] and the parts provided for in port will not last if the compressor is run every day."

He sailed toward Mauritius and arrived off Port Louis, the capital of that tiny island, early on 1 July. Just before midnight the next day he sank the small British steamship *Hoihow* with two torpedoes and left four men on a raft. The engagement seemed to set off a hornet's nest of activity. Soon he was picking up signals on the Metox.

On 6 July, a large ship that U-181 pursued heading toward Cap Est on the Madagascan coast had to be given up after she evaded two torpedoes. With the first miss, "a lot of men [came] out of opened hatchways, one after another, as though something had disturbed their sleep—the noise, for example, of a torpedo having just passed under the keel." (This was Lüth in a rare mood; he seldom joked in the log.) The second torpedo missed entirely and exploded twenty-six minutes later at the end of its run.

During the pursuit of this vessel, BdU informed Lüth that his operations area had been increased in size again. He now had "free maneuver" in an area that included most of Madagascar and all of the Mascarenes, extended up the east African coast almost to the border of Tanganyika, and was "almost as big as the Reich" itself. The boat traveled farther north and farther west, coming within sight of Tromelin on 8 July and Tamatave on the twelfth.

Tromelin marked the boat's greatest distance in navigable miles from Bordeaux. On 15 July a lookout sighted the British collier *Empire Lake,* and Lüth sank it at dusk with two torpedoes. "Five men have been left floating on a piece of wreckage," noted the log cold-bloodedly. "Due to the high sea and the 180-mile distance from land they will probably not be saved."

They were eventually saved, but not by Lüth. At first glance his remark would seem to reinforce Petersen's portrait of him as unfeeling and callous. Actually he was doing more for survivors in U-181 than ever before.

The charitable explanation for this change would be that over the years Lüth appreciated more the consequences of a torpedo and the incredible risks the merchant seaman ran in wartime. Perhaps with heightened awareness of his own crews' needs came the realization that others were also worth considering. The cynical explanation would be that he was looking for information. Lothar Von Arnauld de la Perière, the leading ace of

World War I, always acted in accordance with Prize Regulations because, as he put it, it was necessary to document one's claims. Indeed, the logs of U-181 are full of specific data on ships, tonnages, cargoes, points of origin, and destinations, all taken from interviews with crewmen in lifeboats. Moreover, it was less dangerous to linger on the surface of the Indian Ocean, for whatever reason, than it was on the Atlantic.

Next day at 0935 U-181 sank the British *Fort Franklin* only fifty miles south of *Empire Lake,* and over the next three days Lüth scored two more — the British steamers *Dalfram* and *Umvuma.* In spite of his success, Lüth chose to leave the Mauritius area shortly thereafter. An asdic search conducted by a British destroyer made him think that Port Louis was on to him. It was, but for reasons he did not suspect: High-frequency direction-finding equipment (HF/DF) as far away as South Africa had picked up his last signal to BdU.[7]

Lüth's last ship — the last of the patrol and the last of his career — was sunk four days after that, alone and in midocean. As fortune would have it, this is the ship we know most about, thanks to a survivor of Lüth's last successful torpedo run.[8]

Donald Crawford, a seventeen-year-old midshipman, was serving on the British refrigerator ship *Clan Macarthur.* On 7 August, after a long and tortuous passage from Glasgow in convoy, the *Clan Macarthur* arrived in Durban, where Crawford recorded "a dose of jitters due to a rumor that U-boats were operating in the area . . . a lot of tonnage had been sunk en route for Mozambique and Mauritius and the story going round was to the effect that a German officer had been picked up with restaurant and cinema tickets in his pockets, indicating that he had been around for a while."[9]* She left Durban twice in two days, once on 8 August, to be turned back because of a U-boat scare, and again for good on the ninth, bound for Mauritius with a cargo of livestock and medical supplies.

---

*Crawford's consternation was no doubt real enough, but this rumor had long since become sea lore. A similar story had already made rounds up and down the eastern seaboard of the United States. The tickets were for shows in Boston or New York, depending upon which version you heard.

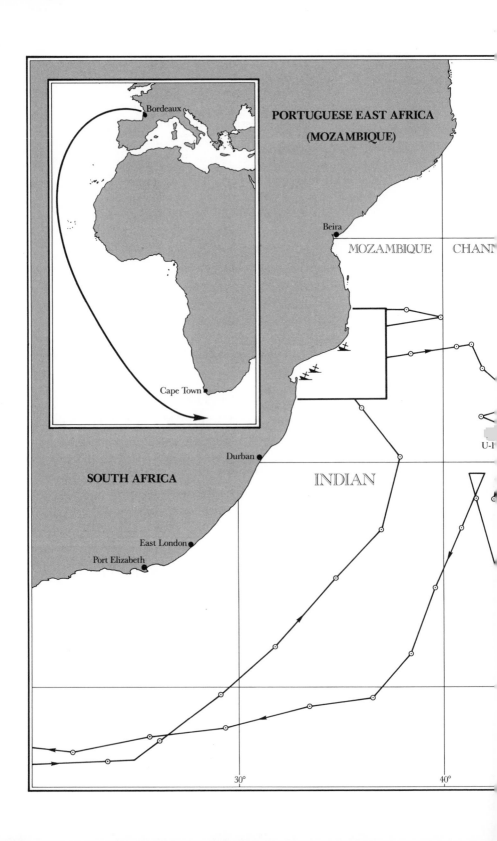

PORTUGUESE EAST AFRICA
(MOZAMBIQUE)

Bordeaux

Beira

MOZAMBIQUE   CHANN

Cape Town

U-1

Durban

SOUTH AFRICA

INDIAN

East London

Port Elizabeth

30°   40°

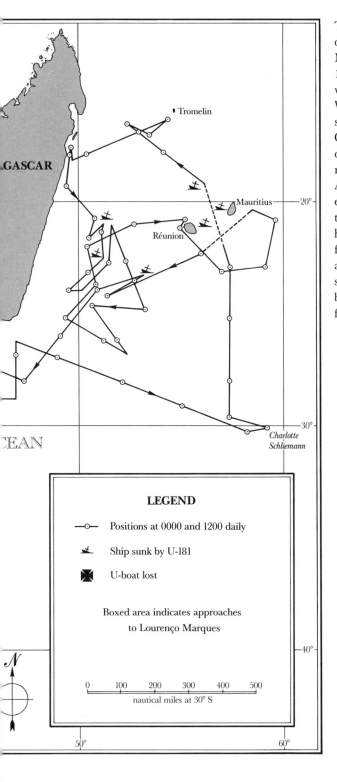

The track of U-181's second war patrol, from March 1943 to October 1943. During this patrol, which lasted 203 days, Wolfgang Lüth sank ten ships and won the Knight's Cross with Diamonds; his crew became media heroes; and the Battle of the Atlantic was lost. For several days after U-181 returned to Bordeaux, she held the endurance record for a single patrol, but another boat was still at sea: U-196 (Kentrat), who broke, then held the record for the rest of the war.

LEGEND

—○— Positions at 0000 and 1200 daily

✖ Ship sunk by U-181

✖ U-boat lost

Boxed area indicates approaches
to Lourenço Marques

N

0   100   200   300   400   500
nautical miles at 30° S

Shortly before noon on the eleventh, lookouts in U-181 sighted her halfway between Durban and Madagascar, sailing northeast.

Lüth decided to follow the *Clan Macarthur* until moonset early the next morning. He did not want to face her guns and he was unable to attack submerged because of her pronounced zigzag, though by 0100 her base course had been calculated and the pattern worked out. It was an almost leisurely pursuit; during the night, members of the crew were allowed on the bridge for a look, and they took turns thumbing through the register in an attempt to identify the large ship in the distance.

At 0332 Lüth attacked, firing two torpedoes from a distance of 900 meters. One of them struck the *Clan Macarthur* amidships, the other aft. Crawford, in his stateroom, was awakened by a "huge bang" and thrown to the deck.

[T]he door [swung open with] a harsh smell of cordite. The Fourth Officer poked his head in and shouted to us to dress as we had been pipped. My duty was to report to the bridge and so I pulled a battle dress over my pajamas, pulled on my sea boots, grabbed a three-pound bag of peppermints out of a drawer (leaving a brand new watch there) and stuffing the peppermints into the blouse of the battle dress, made my way to the bridge.

The Captain was already there and I joined him and the Officer of the Watch in destroying ship's papers. It seemed that we had been hit through the stern funnels at about no. 4 hatch and our propeller shafts were broken. We had no power at all and we were stopped. Nevertheless, pumps were brought into action and we manned the guns. The hope was that the bastard would surface, in which case we would give him some stick.[10]

Lüth had no such intention. He watched patiently from fourteen feet below as the *Clan Macarthur* lowered her boats. She was settling at this time but did not look as if she would go down soon. Eventually, at 0347, U-181's radio room detected a distress call. At that time Lüth fired a third torpedo, his coup de grâce. With a thunderous noise it struck the huge ship forward, and quickly she began to sink. Crawford, taken off in one of the last lifeboats, recalled "an urgent need to get clear of her before she sank. The end of a ship is unpredictable and it is obviously wise to give as wide a berth as possible before she goes."[11]

"Loud sinking noises to be heard," noted Lüth in the log, "and shortly thereafter a tremendous depth-charge explosion. The boat [U-181] is about 700 meters from the location, but nevertheless leaps in the water and several things fall from the shelves. Several [of the *Clan Macarthur*'s] lifeboats are destroyed." As the *Clan Macarthur* went under she was rent by a fourth explosion, a huge eruption from deep within her hull. It shattered a lifeboat still hanging in her falls and killed every man inside.

Those in the remaining lifeboats mistook the last explosion for a fourth torpedo. Crawford believed this until 1984, when he saw the log of U-181. Then he decided that the explosion had something to do with the cargo on board—not the livestock, nor the medical supplies, but another cargo. Though he would not say much more than that, he admitted that the *Clan Macarthur* had been carrying another consignment, classified and unknown even to him.*

It took eight minutes for the *Clan Macarthur* to sink. Crawford watched her. "The call went up shortly that she was going and I still see her there, solid and proud. She was on an even keel. . . . The last sight of her was tragic. Water pouring over her welldeck bulkheads and through her rails. Steam hissing, spars floating. Before she disappeared finally there was a dreadful cry from her, then a roar of water going down her funnel. Then just a swirl of water."[12]

Only after the *Clan Macarthur* was gone did Lüth bring U-181 to the surface. He stood in the bridge while Engel descended to the weather deck to speak with survivors. Crawford said he was quite pleasant: "'Good morning, gentlemen. I am sorry that we have had to sink your ship, but it is the fortunes of war. What is the name of your ship? Where were you bound? What were you doing? When did you leave the UK, etc., etc.' We

---

*In fact, every inquiry he made about the *Clan Macarthur* since the war went unanswered, and the mystery of that last explosion remains, thanks to red tape and Great Britain's Official Secrets Act.

told him all sorts of rubbish which he took in good part. One of our gunners called him a cheeky bastard and we worried a little about that, but again he laughed and brushed it off."[13]

The wounded in Crawford's lifeboat were taken aboard U-181 for treatment, then given sugar and water, nothing more, from U-181's dwindling stores. Lüth got the information he wanted — the name of the ship, her tonnage, crew size, and destination — from the men in another boat. He was anxious to be off; dawn was breaking and any time the enemy might respond to the *Clan Macarthur's* call for help. Crawford recalled the moment of departure: "I remember this figure on the U-boat, high above us on the conning tower, looking down at us only occasionally. He seemed to be looking all around the horizon most of the time and after a while showed an anxiousness to move away. Quick orders and we were cast off. The questioning officer wished us good morning and safe rescue. A very German voice shouted 'Keep clear of my propellers, I am submerging.'"[14]

The lifeboats, surrounded by dozens of men in the water, drifted off alone, one hundred miles from land. Lüth had promised to signal Mauritius for them. After U-181 had steamed a safe distance, he did so. But the survivors did not see help for weeks, not until each man had experienced his own calvary on the open sea.

[M]any of our men were lost to sharks. One could see the little red light that was attached to life jackets as men floated in the water. On all too many occasions, as we tried to close on that little red light and pick up the survivor, we listened to a scream, saw a great frothing in the water and in many instances the light disappeared. In other instances, when we arrived at the light and tried to pull its owner aboard, there was only part of a human frame. . . .

The days were painfully hot and the nights almost unbearably cold. The sea was at times . . . quite lumpy and at others, flat calm. We encountered quite a substantial storm which threw us about . . . a lot but it was one of those storms that arrive without rain, a damned nuisance [because it did not provide] us with drinking water.

Some days after the drifting, we held a council to determine
. . . whether we should try to use one of the boats to make
shore, but the islands previously referred to [Mauritius and
Reunion] were quite small and the chances of missing them
were far greater without any form of instrumentation. . . . It
was agreed, before we grew too weak, to tie the rafts and the
boats together in a roughly loose chain in order that we should
at least all remain together and all . . . be saved, or all . . . lost.

As days passed and we . . . became weary, our wounded
grew more restless as they needed medical attention, or they
died one by one and slipped quietly away from us. . . .[15]

After two weeks adrift, the survivors of the *Clan Macarthur*
were finally located by a Catalina bomber, which for five days
attended to their needs from the air. The Free French sloop
Savorgnan de Brazza then arrived and took them to Tamatave.
According to Crawford, 42 of an original crew of some 150
lived. The *Clan Macarthur* lost more men than any other ship
sunk by Lüth.

U-181's celebration of the sinking of the *Clan Macarthur* was
capped by a message from Führer headquarters. Lüth had won
the *Eichenlaub mit Schwerter und Brillanten zum Ritterkreuz* (Knight's
Cross with Oak Leaves, Swords, and Diamonds), effective 9
August 1943. It was the highest military award the Third Reich
could bestow; Lüth became the seventh man in the Wehrmacht
and the first in the Kriegsmarine to receive it. The crew, swell-
ing with pride, celebrated in the officers' mess with beer and
cognac.

On 15 August BdU notified Lüth that a meeting at sea had
been set up between U-181 and U-197, commanded by Robert
Bartels, so that Bartels could give Lüth the Enigma keys he
needed to finish his extended patrol (the code in use at that
time was a variation of Enigma called Bellatrix). One hour
later, Lüth received a signal forbidding further use of the
Metox radar-detection equipment.

The effectiveness of the equipment had been diminishing
steadily over the past year; again and again, boats using Metox
found themselves under attack by enemy aircraft with little or
no prior warning. Scientists in Germany trying frantically to

determine the reason for this eventually discovered that the equipment itself emitted low levels of radiation that could conceivably be detected. Actually, this was not the reason. By this time aircraft carried newer sets operating at a UHF frequency undetectable by Metox. In the mistaken belief that his boats were being betrayed by their own equipment, Dönitz made the desperate decision to pull the plug. At midnight another signal came: "All crystals out of the Metox and locked up by the captain. Execution of this order to be recorded in the boat's log."

On 16 August, en route to meet Bartels, U-181 sighted an unidentified steamer. Lüth followed her for six hours and at 1937 he fired a G7a air-driven torpedo, the last one on board, the last shot of his career, from a range of 600 meters. It missed.

At 1500 on 17 August U-181 reached the rendezvous point, approximately 500 miles southeast of Durban. U-197 was not there. At midnight Bartels signaled, "KQ6676 *Empire Stanley* sunk," and asked for a new rendezvous. The two boats finally met at 0900 on the morning of 19 August. Bartels turned over the code keys, and Lüth told him of four ships that had been sighted while U-181 was waiting. This being of interest to Bartels, he decided to remain in the rendezvous area.

Lüth himself could not afford to wait: U-181 had a measly 200 cbm of fuel in her tanks and almost no food. The two boats parted cheerfully, U-181 turning southwest for the cape. It was the last anyone would ever see of U-197 or Robert Bartels.

The next day U-181 and U-196 met at sea so that Lüth could pass the keys he had received along to the latter's captain. At 1535, shortly after they parted, a distress call shattered the otherwise peaceful afternoon. It came from U-197, under attack several hundred miles away. "Aircraft has attacked us with bombs. Marginally able to dive. KQ87," radioed Bartels. A second signal followed almost immediately: "Aircraft has attacked with bombs. Unable to dive. KQ52." Bartels was clearly desperate, but his position reports were contradictory.

"The two locations are 250 miles apart," recorded Lüth in the log. "KQ52 seems more probable. Distance from us 250 miles." The besieged boat sent out three more signals, each giving the same information. Then, at 1830, the radio went dead. Those who listened were left to imagine the worst.

BdU did not hear the signals directly; U-198 picked them up in the South Atlantic and relayed them back to Germany. At 2240 BdU responded. Despite a critical fuel shortage in U-181, she and U-196 were directed to turn back and search for U-197.

Lüth could not have known then that, indirectly, he was responsible for U-197's demise. A Catalina bomber from St. Lucia Airfield in South Africa (RAF Squadron 259) had been dispatched after a South African HF/DF station intercepted a signal Lüth sent the night before while waiting for Bartels. The station took a line of bearing on U-181.

Bartels made a fatal error by staying in the area of the rendezvous. The Catalina, looking for U-181, sighted U-197 at 1510 and immediately attacked with depth charges, prompting the first two signals from U-197. Another Catalina was summoned from St. Lucia after the initial sighting. The first bomber circled U-197 for the rest of the afternoon and waited while Bartels sent off one distress call after another, trying desperately to defend himself with his 37-mm gun. At 1900 the second Catalina arrived on the scene. The two aircraft made alternate bomb runs on U-197. "In a third run at about [1930], Bartels evidently misjudged the aircraft's course, turned parallel to it, and was straddled by six depth charges dropped from 75 feet. Debris flew into the air, and the U-boat disappeared, leaving a large patch of oil on the surface. [Aircraft] C/259 watched the attack and reported that 'a large upheaval of oil was seen gushing to the surface and spread over a large area.' The two aircraft remained for half an hour but saw nothing more."[16] The fate of Bartels was nothing out of the ordinary in BdU's experience. Report after report had been received, each one the same: "Attacked, aircraft," or "Attacked, sinking." No warning, no indication from Metox, no defense. BdU's inability or refusal to relate cause and effect only aggravated the situation. If the Germans had even suspected the Allied use of

U-181 returning to Bordeaux after a record-breaking second war patrol, October 1943. The number on her tower is the tonnage for both her patrols, and she is flying forty-eight pennants, Lüth's total for fifteen patrols (both numbers are incorrect).

direction-finding equipment, BdU would have terminated the lengthy signals from boats at once.*

Lüth searched two days for Bartels and found nothing. On 24 August he finally turned for the cape. With him in stages, some earlier, some later, went the other boats of the fourth wave. BdU was calling them home.

The return passage proved uneventful. Despite Lüth's concern, U-181 did have fuel enough to reach Bordeaux, although he was forced to let pass any enemy traffic encountered en

---

*This connection had already been made by U-181's radioman; in *Haie in Paradies,* Jochen Brennecke cites a conversation between radioman Paul Wurmbach and Lüth's successor Freiwald in which Wurmbach relates his suspicions about the use of direction-finding equipment.[17]

Another shot of U-181's bridge taken from the main deck. The crew has broken ranks early, but it was an excusable breach of decorum under the circumstances.

route. U-181 rounded the Cape of Good Hope on 2 September, and the postponed equator crossing ceremony was held three weeks later.

On 1 October the Bellatrix keys that Bartels gave to Lüth expired, and from that point on U-181 was unable to decode incoming transmissions or to transmit coded signals of her own. Lüth could not even send his expected position reports, a sign usually interpreted by BdU to mean that a boat had been lost. "I assume that any important signals for me will be sent RHV [clear text]," he wrote in the log, but none was received. Only after he had come within thirty-six hours of Bordeaux would Lüth risk a clear-text signal to request escort into the Gironde. The reception of this signal caused a minor stir at BdU. For the second time in the war, it had given up Lüth for dead.

Lüth and Lothar Engel, U-181's doctor. Engel and most of the crew have just received the Iron Cross; Lüth is wearing his new Knight's Cross with its diamond-encrusted oak leaf for the first time, but it is partially hidden by his beard.

U-181 sailed into Bordeaux on 14 October 1943, the day before Lüth's thirtieth birthday. The usual practice for a successful boat returning to port was to fly white pennants from the periscope housing representing the ships sunk during a patrol. U-181 hoisted forty-eight pennants that day, one for each ship Lüth sank during the course of his career—from January 1940 (the *Flandria*) to August 1943 (the *Clan Macarthur*). It was as though the crew knew, even then, that this would be Lüth's last patrol.

Lüth stood in the bridge, conning the boat and smiling broadly while the pennants flapped behind him and the crew caroused on the weather deck. The shattered barrel of the 37-mm gun, opening up aft of the Wintergarten like an ugly black flower, was the only indication that not everything had gone well. But it had been so long since Williger's death that the grief had dissipated, and in the flush of recent success the useless gun had become just another fixture.

Nobody knew of U-181's arrival until almost the last moment. Lothar Engel was unforgivingly disappointed at the reception on the pier. After all, U-181 had just finished what was then the longest patrol of the war; her captain had just been awarded the highest decoration in the Wehrmacht.[18] A band, however, did play, as one by one the crew of U-181 crossed over, unshaven, smelly, exhausted, and not altogether firm on their feet. "When you've been at sea for that long, you can't walk more than a couple of hundred meters before you have to stop and massage your legs," explained Walter Schmidt. "Everyone had a beard as well . . . mine was eighteen centimeters long."[19] Lüth stood before his crew as he was officially greeted by Hans Rösing, FdU-West, and Klaus Scholz, Twelfth U-Flotilla commander. Both men congratulated him warmly for his award and for the patrol. The crew was inspected and given less spectacular awards like the Iron Cross and the submarine badge. Karl-August Landfermann became the second chief engineer to be awarded the Knight's Cross.

That evening the crew attended a raucous dinner party at the base. Lüth took the seat of honor between Rösing and Scholz; each man had a cigar and a drink while the obligatory speeches were made and the letters from home distributed in huge stacks. Afterward at the base barbershop a camera crew arrived to film the barber cutting and shaving each man. Thousands at home in Germany watched newsreels of Herbert Krutschkowski fingering his beard one last loving time, then running his fingers down a bare chin afterward.

Along with Krutschkowski's whiskers, the long patrol of U-181 was history.

12

EVENING SONG

"The Führer Receives Korvettenkapitän Lüth." The front page of the *Bremer Nachrichten* was one of dozens during the week of 25 October 1943 that had Wolfgang Lüth's name splayed across it. Underneath was a short column about him, his men, his family, the service, and the German soldier/sailor in general, accompanied by a photograph of him and his boat. For on 25 October, at Führer headquarters, Adolf Hitler awarded Wolfgang Lüth the Knight's Cross with Oak Leaves, Swords, and Diamonds.[1]

The presentation was recorded on film, too, by the Reich Propaganda Office: a smiling Lüth walking toward the headquarters building in gloves and greatcoat; Hitler holding the medal in its case and then presenting the award; the quick choppy handshake, the stiff bow by Lüth. You can almost glimpse the gaggle of prompters in the background: "You must line up here. At this point extend your left hand to take the case while at the same time taking the Führer's hand in your right. Bow after the Führer gives you the award, and do not, under any circumstances, speak to the Führer unless the Führer speaks to you."

According to Walter Schmidt, Hitler did speak to Lüth and at length, bemoaning the situation in the east and the state of the war effort in general. And Lüth spoke to Hitler. The cameras, however, did not record him with an empty beer bottle on the top of his head demonstrating how a U-boat was brought to periscope depth—improbable, ridiculous, and yet several people have verified it.[2]

Lüth's first official portrait with his new decoration was reportedly made on this occasion by Heinrich Hoffmann, Hitler's personal photographer. The portrait now hangs in the Marineschule. Hoffmann's image of Lüth resembles the images of the other great aces: blue uniform, Knight's Cross, cap on, slightly cocked, icy glare. But it is different in one significant way. Lüth's glare, so necessary for infamy, is unconvincing, not at all like Otto Kretschmer's black glower or Erich Topp's cold, unsettling gaze. Instead of looking sinister, as he should to fit the stereotype, he seems quizzical, lost in the photographer's lens.

And what of this award, the Knight's Cross with Diamonds, the highest decoration in the German armed forces?* Did Wolfgang Lüth deserve to wear it? Or was he given it for convenience because the Wehrmacht had noticed an imbalance? Of the first six winners of the Diamonds, most were Luftwaffe officers or high-ranking army commanders.

The answer is a qualified yes, Lüth did deserve his Diamonds. But if he did, then so did several other men. Kretschmer springs immediately to mind. So does Topp, who together with Karl-Friedrich Merten was nipping at Lüth's

---

*Hermann Göring received a special Knight's Cross in gold, but it was hardly for valor and nobody else was eligible.

heels in the race for tonnage.* Both men spent most of their time at sea in the North Atlantic. Lüth sank half his ships in the South Atlantic and Indian oceans, where shipping was less protected, the enemy less in evidence, the weather better. And yet Lüth would have been on anyone's short list for the award; the incredible fact that he had spent four years at sea and was still alive, after all the other candidates had been transferred to shore, or were in captivity or dead, may have tipped the balance in his favor.

Lüth probably did receive the award as a representative of the U-Bootwaffe in general, but that does not detract from his achievement. The submarine service was in sore need of recognition. Times were bad, and although morale in the service had not slackened, Lüth's Diamonds gave it an added boost. War correspondent Edgar Schröder said as much in an article that appeared on 2 November 1943. "In the person of Korvettenkapitän Wolfgang Lüth, the Führer has decorated the entire U-Bootwaffe, and with it the entire Kriegsmarine."[3]

The question of merit arises because of another event as well. In 1944 Kapitänleutnant Albrecht Brandi was given a Knight's Cross with Diamonds. Brandi was no Lüth. If he did not deliberately falsify his claims, he inflated them with flagrant ease. At various times Brandi claimed to have sunk one battleship, two cruisers, several destroyers, and a huge amount of merchant shipping; in fact, he ended up with a rather mediocre record at best. Brandi's award casts a shadow on Lüth's. It was obviously given for expedience rather than merit, and his example is always available for those who argue that German military honors weren't worth much more than the metal from which they were minted.†

*Maybe Lüth thought Merten a little too close. "Karl-Friedrich Merten," he said cattily to Theodor Petersen one day, "got his Knight's Cross without ever being in a convoy battle" (Petersen, letter to author, 7 October 1986). It wasn't true, but it demonstrates the size of the average U-boat commander's ego at least.

†"Only one U-boat captain seems to have hoodwinked the High Command," wrote Richard Compton-Hall of Brandi, "and he was awarded the

Brillantenträger Lüth
von Feindfahrt zurück

Als erster Offizier der Kriegsmarine erhielt Korvettenkapitän Wolfgang Lüth die höchste deutsche Tapferkeitsauszeichnung

Rechts: Nach der bisher längsten U-Boot-Feindfahrt: Die Wimpel des Sieges wehen über der Brücke. 45 Schiffe, darunter ein feindliches U-Boot, hat Lüth auf 15 Feindfahrten versenkt

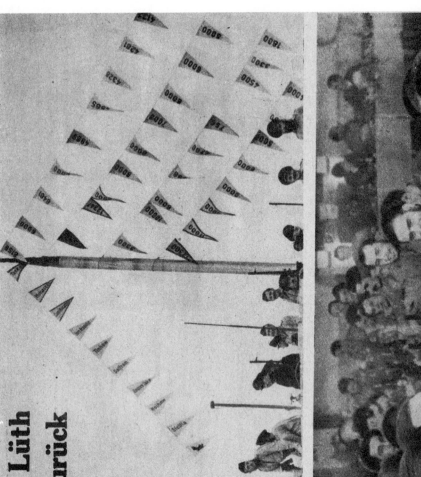

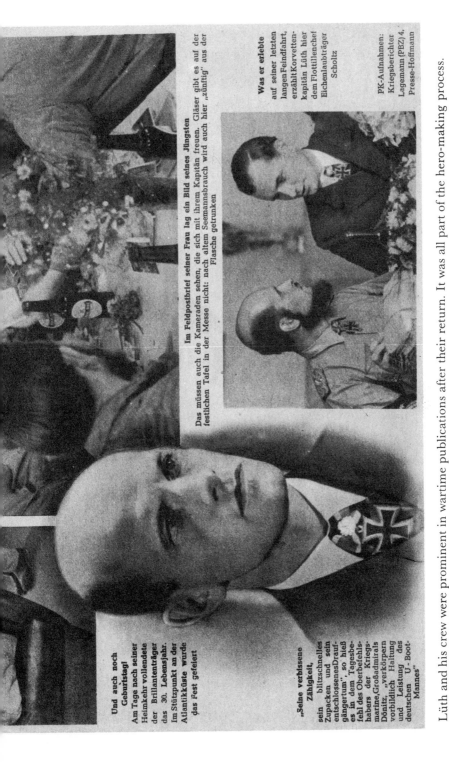

Und auch noch Geburtstag!

Am Tage nach seiner Heimkehr vollendete der Brillantenträger das 30. Lebensjahr. Im Stützpunkt an der Atlantikküste wurde das Fest gefeiert

„Seine verbissene Zähigkeit,

sein blitzschnelles Zupacken und sein entschlossenesDraufgängertum", so hieß es in dem Tagesbefehl des Oberbefehlshabers der Kriegsmarine,Großadmirals Dönitz, „verkörpern vorbildlich Haltung und Leistung des deutschen U- Boot-Mannes"

Im Feldpostbrief seiner Frau lag ein Bild seines Jüngsten

Das müssen auch die Kameraden sehen, die sich mit ihrem Kapitän freuen. Gläser gibt es auf der festlichen Tafel in der Messe nicht: nach altem Seemannsbrauch wird auch hier „zünftig" aus der Flasche getrunken

Was er erlebte

auf seiner letzten langen Feindfahrt, erzählt Korvettenkapitän Lüth hier dem Flottillenchef Eichenlaubträger Scholtz

PK-Aufnahmen:
Kriegsberichter Lagemann (PBZ) 4, Presse-Hoffmann

Lüth and his crew were prominent in wartime publications after their return. It was all part of the hero-making process.

In any case, the media had been extolling Lüth and his crew at length, for if the service needed heroes, the nation did as well. In the young men of U-181, these needs were met for a short while. According to one account, "In the six, eight, ten weeks that a U-boat remains at sea the crew does not lose spiritual contact with dry land. Lüth and his men, however, hunting in the expanses of the Atlantic and Indian Oceans, were during the latter part of their operation like men on an island, almost like men on a strange star in the isolation of limitless space. They did approach land at one time or another where, as Lüth describes, they could sense strange smells from the *kraals* where black men danced, but each time the sea drew them back, and another week, another month began at sea."[4] It is unlikely that Lüth or anyone in his crew ever smelled a kraal, but that was not important. Lüth was to be a hero, and heroes were made. The article went on to describe the new hero: "'My height is between 1.77 and 1.79 meters (according to the tape measure),' answered [Lüth] with his endearing dry humor. The thin lines, the gray-blue eyes, which are sharp despite obvious overwork, do not make Lüth look any different than the average young officer, but his head is a different matter. Here one is struck not so much by the long U-boat beard, but by the unusually high forehead. A dark wreath of hair covers only his temples, giving him the appearance of being tonsured; he has taken, so he says, 'quite a bit of joking for it in the Navy.'"[5]

Several of the crew were singled out for attention by the press as well. An equally fawning article by naval correspon-

---

highest decoration of all" (p. 62). But Jürgen Rohwer observed, "I think it is a difficult problem with submarine success reports. Brandi was a young commander, coming into the ranks of the U-boat aces only in 1943. At that time it was very difficult to observe successes. Most of the hits were reported only according to acoustic observations, which were often very difficult to get, and there were many sources of false reports, especially when the U-boat used the acoustic homing torpedoes. Maybe Brandi interpreted his acoustic observations in some too optimistic way, but he was not a special case in this connection and he made a great number of patrols and daring attacks on Allied warships" (letter to the author, 14 March 1985).

The petty officers of U-181. They were strangers when the boat was commissioned in 1942; after eighteen months and two long patrols they were more like brothers, members of "one big family."

dent Herbert Sprang described in great detail each man in the crew (for some reason, security perhaps, identifying them by initials only). He devoted a paragraph to Franz Persch and his strange collections, a paragraph to Josef Dick and the shark that almost ate him — in fact, a paragraph for everyone. And why not? Paper was cheap, and these men were heroes too. The article went on for three effusive pages and concluded, "A colorful collection of the best in German manhood, with incredible feats of heroism hidden by sheer number; a small selection of Lüth's petty officers which symbolize the entire boat, the entire service. These are accomplished soldiers with skill and experience, tested by the worst of war and still men of kind and tender German heart; the elite of our officer corps."[6]

The reporters followed Lüth to Neustadt. "Korvettenkapitän Lüth is now at home," announced one newspaper. "The *Rathaus* [town hall] of the small Holstein town is festively decorated, with bright flags in the streets and villagers gathered in the square. The U-boat commander who was given the 'diamonds' on 9 August by the Führer . . . is greeted by the *Burgermeister,* then surrounded by children; he listens attentively to

Wolfgang Lüth during his last night with the crew of U-181, November 1943. He is demonstrating for them what he had shown the Führer two weeks earlier, although this time he has no beer bottle on his head. (Courtesy Otto Giese)

what a small girl wishes to say, his face serious. [He] inspects the front of an honor company to the accompaniment of the 'Presentation March.' Suddenly he sees his wife in the doorway, a small daughter in each hand. . . ."[7]

Lüth returned to Bordeaux the first week in November. His larger family was breaking up: Promotions were posted and positions shuffled; some of the men departed for other commands, some for school. New men arrived, including Otto Giese, U-181's new second watch officer. On 11 November Lüth and his old crew gathered for the last time. Giese recorded the scene in detail in his diary.

> 11/11/43 Lüth arrives on the scene [in Bordeaux], returning from leave. The crew hailed him jubilantly! . . . The decision, if I will stay on board as 2WO, rests with Lüth. He will render the new commandant (Kpt.z.See Kurt Freiwald) a hundred percent boat and he does not know me.

11/12/43 *Kameradschaftabend* [fellowship evening] U-181—the crew bids farewell to Lüth. Lüth described his meeting with the Führer in the quarters of the Naval High Command.

11/13/43 Very exquisite farewell celebration (officers' circles) for Lüth and Gysae in the Officer's Club. . . . Dinner: Mimosa-eggs, bouillon, omelettes, veal with mayonnaise and asparagus, mushrooms and assorted fresh vegetables, pommes frites and creme pudding. Drinks: Vermouth, red wine, champagne. Afterwards, until 0300, celebrating in the bar.[8]

Other recollections of that evening came out in correspondence with Giese. "I vividly remember . . . the admiration and love . . . which they [the men] held for him. There was much laughter and jubilation over the way he explained to the Führer how he attacked his ships, especially his 'alarms' and crash dives with the boat which only took a few seconds to get to periscope depth. . . . Apparently the Führer had a good laugh and was highly impressed by Lüth. Of course during the evening this maneuver was practiced repeatedly by the whole crew under his command."[9]

Lüth remained with the Twelfth U-Flotilla in Bordeaux as a staff officer. In December, he presented "Problems of Leadership" in Weimar. That lecture, as we have seen, was seminal. It was received with wild enthusiasm by the Kriegsmarine establishment, was adapted for immediate use in the officer-training curriculum, and has since become something of a minor classic in the study of naval leadership.

Shortly after that, Lüth's *Boot Greift Wieder An* appeared. "Not something I would like to do again," complained the author to Theodor Petersen.[10] To write it, he had to fill out a mound of forms, petition to join the Reichsschrifttumskammer (the Reich Authors Guild), a pseudo-official organization to which all writers in Germany had to belong, submit a full family history, and even produce a certificate of Aryan ancestry. His coauthor Claus Korth, an officer of somewhat lesser accomplishment, irritated Lüth by demanding of Propaganda Minister Joseph Goebbels that the first printing of *Boot Greift Wieder An* be doubled.[11] (In spite of that, the book has never been popular; copies are rare today and no translation exists.)

What now for Wolfgang Lüth, Dönitz's fair-haired boy, *Brillantenträger* (Holder of the Diamonds), acclaimed lecturer, published author, and hero of the Reich? He could not go back to sea. His loss would be even more traumatic for the service than the deaths of Prien and Kretschmer so long before. Other officers in his position—Topp, Rösing, Merten—had been given operational flotilla commands. In January 1944 Lüth was sent east to Memel to take command of the Twenty-second U-Flotilla, a training flotilla. Ordinarily, such a position was a career grave. It had been for Lüth's predecessor, Wilhelm Ambrosius. It was not a job one would have expected for Lüth, and he must have been let down.

But Dönitz knew what he was doing, and he had made an excellent selection. The Twenty-second U-Flotilla trained officers for service and ultimate command in the U-Bootwaffe. The life expectancy for a new commander was something like four months, and every man in Memel knew it. These young men needed someone who could inspire them, who could reassure them that their sacrifice and devotion would not be taken for granted. Wolfgang Lüth, the best and brightest officer in the service, was their man.

One of the officers who trained in Memel during Lüth's tenure was Leutnant zur See Herbert Werner. In his autobiography, *Iron Coffins,* Werner tells of a dinner party on the liner that served as Lüth's headquarters in Memel. His class had finished their training, and Lüth, after his speech of congratulations and farewell, began to hand out their assignments from BdU. Werner had been made commanding officer of U-415. He took the telegram with a forced smile. "It was as good as a death sentence, for . . . the obsolete U-415 had already outlived too many patrols. This honor, this bright new command, was merely a matter of changing vehicles for an early ride to the bottom."[12] Lüth, under the cheerful veneer of congratulations and good wishes, knew the odds for men like Werner. Fortunately for Werner, he survived the war against those odds.

Lüth's awareness of the danger, although he would never have admitted it, was a factor in his recommending his former first watch officer, Gottfried König, for a teaching command.

"Because of Lüth I was eventually assigned to a training boat in Danzig," recalls König. "It was not much to my liking at the time, but Lüth actually saved my life by doing so, since almost all the operational boats after 1944 were lost at sea."[13]

Lüth served in Memel from January to July 1944. On 15 July he was reassigned as a division officer to the Marinekriegs-schule-Mürwik, the same institution he had attended only ten years earlier.* He was promoted twice during his two months in this position, first on 1 August to *Fregattenkapitän*, and then on 1 September to Kapitän zur See. The second promotion made Lüth, at age thirty, the youngest full captain in the Kriegsmar-ine. He had to be a full captain in order for Karl Dönitz to per-sonally appoint him commandant of the Marinekriegsschule, a position of some prestige normally held by a flag officer.

Lüth had not been forgotten after all. Sensitivities being what they were in the U-Bootwaffe, however, someone was bound to complain about being passed over for the position, and eventually someone did—Hans Ibbeken, captain of U-179 and once, in 1938, Wolfgang Lüth's flotilla commander. It wasn't so much that Ibbeken was senior to Lüth, said Petersen, or that he wanted the position. Ibbeken harbored a grudge: Both men had been on patrol in the South Atlantic at the same time in 1942, and the day after Ibbeken reported sinking the British merchant steamer *Adviser* off the coast of South Africa, Lüth saw that ship under tow.

"Never mind," Dönitz had said to Lüth. "If anyone doesn't like it, I'll make you an admiral." He named Lüth comman-dant anyway. "It was all so easy then," said Petersen wistfully as he recounted the story.[14]

Lüth's was not an easy job. The Marinekriegsschule was as distinguished and as venerable as she had ever been; war had not altered that. But war, and wartime exigencies, had made some changes inevitable. The curriculum had been modified to eliminate courses considered superfluous to the need at hand; riding and fencing were out of place in 1944. "Branch" schools had been opened in the nearby communities of Meier-

*The name of the school had been changed in 1943.

wik, Husum, Schleswig, and Heiligenhafen to accommodate the increased need for officers. As commandant, Lüth became responsible for the training of hundreds of officer candidates in each of these locations. Most of them would not have passed the rigorous prewar admissions process; none of them had any expectations upon commissioning except capture or death. It was difficult to believe that Lüth himself had been one of these young men only ten years earlier, and that things had changed so much since.

Lüth relieved Konteradmiral Waldemar Winter as commandant on 17 September. One of the first officers to see Lüth afterward was a young Leutnant zur See, Karl Peter, who needed help in finding an apartment. "I was a division officer at the Marineschule, just married, and my wife and I lived in Flensburg. One day our landlady gave us notice because my wife was expecting a baby. It was a very bad situation for us. I came to Lüth and asked him to help us find a new place. That was when we first became acquainted. He did help us and soon after that he was the first guest in our little apartment."[15] Lüth could appreciate Peter's position; on 7 November he and Ilse had another child of their own, a boy named Jan.

The war dragged on to its inevitable end. Germany died slowly in its boots. The Allied invasion came from the west. Someone tried to assassinate Hitler. France was freed. The Russians invaded from the east. Still they fought. The war at sea had ended for all practical purposes that day in 1943 when Dönitz withdrew his boats from the North Atlantic. But U-boats still patrolled, sank ships, and were sunk themselves in large numbers until the very last day. The miracle weapons for which the U-Bootwaffe prayed—the submarines that could stay submerged for weeks and run at twenty knots underwater, invisible to radar—remained for the most part on the drawing boards, a gleam in the eye of their architects.

In March 1945 thirty-three U-boats were lost at sea. Forward troops of the U.S. First Army established a bridgehead on the Rhine, and by the end of the month divisions of the First, Third, and Ninth Armies, the British Second Army, and the

Canadian First Army had all crossed into Germany. In April fifty-three U-boats were lost, while several divisions of the Red Army pulled up to the outskirts of Berlin, forcing the government into concrete bunkers. Refugees appeared in the west, many of them ethnic Germans. Wolfgang Lüth's parents, August and Elfriede, and his sister Vera had managed to leave Posen on 20 January, just days ahead of the Russians. They traveled separately from Posen to Frankfurt on the Oder, Elfriede in a car, Vera on the bus, and August on a truck, and then together by train via Berlin to Neustadt, where they were permitted to move into the navy housing complex.[16]

Total verloren. Completely lost. No sane military officer could believe otherwise, not even Lüth. But perhaps, against all the evidence, he still did. Karl Peter writes in his autobiography of an event that took place in late 1944 during the Ardennes offensive, the Battle of the Bulge. "In December, shortly before Christmas, one last ray of hope illuminated our daily routine. After the initial success of the . . . offensive, Wolfgang Lüth assembled the midshipmen of the Marineschule under the beech trees, and there in the snow, by the light of signal flares, he made a captivating speech which inspired everyone who heard it. We were given our hope again. I now ask myself whether or not Lüth himself believed what he said to us so sincerely. I think he did."[17]

Again the ceremony, well arranged, delivered with stirring effect in a setting that called to mind the ritual gatherings of the early Reich. Here was Lüth, able to inspire men, to provide hope where there had been despair and inspiration in the face of reality. Evidently, he was at his best that night. But reality overcomes inspiration, and in the end even this faint hope was fleeting. In February 1945, with the offensive flattened and German troops driven back even farther into the Fatherland, "some of the midshipmen had been detailed to the Army, the rest remained at the school to prepare for the final battle. Several of them fell in the last weeks of the war."[18]

By springtime the German front was so close to Flensburg that the main Marinekriegsschule building had been made into a hospital. The Reich was crumbling, its cities in ruins, its borders pierced, all shreds of honor lost, the remnants of pride languishing. In his concrete bunker, Hitler fought imaginary battles with imaginary armies while his own army was shattered and in retreat. In a last lucid moment he drew up his will. In it he named a successor. The heir to the whirlwind was Karl Dönitz.

On 30 April Hitler died in his bunker, shot by his own hand. Dönitz was on the fly when it happened. He had evacuated High Command headquarters on 20 April. When he became Führer he was in Plön. On 2 May he arrived in Flensburg, moving his entire government into the *Sportschule* (gymnasium) of the Marinekriegsschule and himself into the commandant's house with Lüth, his wife, their four children, and Lüth's brother Joachim.

It was from the Sporthalle that he issued his famous last order to the U-boats. "My U-boat men," he told them, "you have fought like lions." The war at sea could simply not continue, he explained; it was useless slaughter. All of his men could take immeasurable pride in themselves; they had fought well and without complaint; they could lay down their arms with honor. All U-boats at sea were to sail into the nearest Allied port and surrender.

Most of the U-boats came in; a few did not. Some captains wanted to go on fighting. Many scuttled their boats in the bays and inlets of northern Germany. Two boats went to Argentina (the second, U-977, arrived amid excited speculation that Hitler was on board).

One officer, Hermann Rasch, led an entire flotilla of midget submarines into Flensburg Harbor on 6 May. He reported to Lüth, the most senior man he could find, to announce that his boats were ready to fight to the death. According to Jean Noli in *The Admiral's Wolfpack,* Lüth called Rasch a pirate and told him to "get the hell out of here."[19] A startling outburst from the man who rejected any and all profanity as unbefitting an officer, but then, Lüth had been listening to a prolonged rain of Allied bombs when Rasch walked in, he had had a bad day with Dönitz, and Rasch was chewing on a huge cigar—the kind Lüth liked but could no longer find.[20]

Germany surrendered unconditionally to the combined Allied powers on 8 May 1945. By then the country was in a state of chaos: The two fronts dissolved in places, and bands of soldiers from both sides roamed at will. Refugees flooded out of Soviet-occupied eastern Germany by the thousands, eventually by the millions. The area around Flensburg was no better: Prisoners from a local Reich work camp had escaped, reportedly bent on indiscriminate revenge.

Flensburg was in the British area of occupation. British forces, fearing the threat to the general welfare, allowed Lüth as area commander to post armed German sentries around the perimeter of the Marinekriegsschule. He took the sentries from Dönitz's Guard Battalion, a unit formed for the purpose of protecting the government. The unit was composed of submarine crewmen and commanded by Korvettenkapitän Peter Cremer. "Ask once for the password," Lüth said in written orders, "and then shoot."[21]

Karl Peter spoke to Lüth on the afternoon of Sunday, 13 May. "We met in the passageway of the school outside my classroom," he wrote. "Lüth stood before me pale, with hollow cheeks and sunken eyes from lack of sleep, but still prepared to help as was his nature."[22] For the second time in a year, Peter had come to ask Lüth for assistance in housing. A British officer had ordered him and his family out of their quarters in order to billet troops. Lüth, despite his own concerns, took the time to find him and five other displaced families a place to sleep that night (Peter's old rooms stood empty for the next eleven months).[23]

Peter describes a man who had been awake for days. As his country collapsed around him, Lüth had to cater to the needs of the Dönitz government in the Sportschule keep his own command of the Marinekriegsschule in order, and care for a family of six. He may have had other things on his mind as well. It is possible that by then he had been shown the evil side of National Socialism — the concentration camps, the gas chambers, the corpses stacked for cremation — and that it had sickened his heart.

After this exchange Lüth and Peter went their separate ways. There was too much to do and too little time to talk.

But the story is not over. Not yet.

It is after midnight in Flensburg, windy, rainy, cold. The sentries are pacing back and forth along the Marinekriegsschule perimeter. They are wet and sleepy, and jittery because of the order to shoot to kill. They are scared by strange noises in the dark.

The sentry at the far northeastern corner, Matthias Gottlob, is a boy of eighteen. He is really too young for this kind of duty, but Karl Franz, the sergeant of the guard, has posted him anyway. Gottlob, more nervous than the others, is standing on the main thoroughfare between the Marinekriegsschule itself and the Sportschule: the Black Path, it is called. He must stop and challenge some of the most senior officers of the Wehrmacht as they walk between the two buildings. He cannot see far up the path because of the darkness and the woods, where rifle and pistol fire can be heard. It is a week after the armistice and Gottlob is within earshot of Reich headquarters, yet men are still being shot at.

Gottlob paces back and forth, his boots crunching on the wet cinder of the Black Path. It is 0030, and so far nothing much has happened. Good, he thinks, so much the better for me. Then he hears footsteps. "Halt!" he shouts down the path as he has been directed to do. "*Wer da?*" Who is there?

The footsteps stop. Nobody answers him, but the wind is rustling the leaves in the trees and Gottlob may not have heard the answer. He takes his rifle in his hands and calls again. "Wer da?" Still no answer, no footsteps either. The stranger has stopped in his tracks.

Now the sentry is genuinely frightened. He has to shoot, has to. In his short career, nobody has ever failed to answer a challenge. If only, *if only* this man would come forward a few yards so that Gottlob could see him . . .

He points the rifle down the path, leveling it from his hips so that he cannot aim. "WER DA?" he screams. No answer. Gottlob shoots once, wildly. Then hears the muffled sound of a man falling.

The wind shrieks in his head as he approaches the figure. Seconds, minutes, later, someone is talking in his ear. "What has happened here?" Franz says. "Gottlob, what have you done?"

"I shot someone."

Franz cannot see. He peers at the body on the ground, which is wrapped in a leather bridge coat and white scarf. A naval officer, Gottlob says to himself automatically. A senior man, one of ours.

The awful truth dawns on the sentry. He bends over the body, flat on its back looking up at the trees.

"It is the commandant," Franz says. "It is Wolfgang Lüth."

13

AFTERWARD

"I didn't aim . . ." Gottlob struggled with his words. "I didn't mean to hit him. I didn't know . . ." Franz and the other guards just stood there as the sentry, near collapse, tried once again to explain how it happened.

Stretcher bearers had taken Lüth back to the Sportschule, where a doctor was now examining him. The bullet had hit him in the forehead; he was killed on the spot.

At 0055 the doctor pronounced Lüth dead and directed that he be taken to the morgue. Dönitz's adjutant, Walter Lüdde-Neurath, was awakened at the commandant's house just after 0100. He decided to tell Joachim Lüth first, then waited downstairs while Joachim told Ilse. At 0300, the three of them left the house for the long silent walk to the morgue.

A sentry led them into the building. Ilse entered the room where her husband lay, Joachim on one side of her, Lüdde-Neurath on the other. They stepped back to let her look at her husband's body. She stood there for some time and finally, after a long and painful wait, touched his hand. "I'd like to go now," was all she said. As she left, a shroud was pulled over the body.[1]

Karl Dönitz convened a board of enquiry into Lüth's death at 0930. He had to do this quickly, since both German and Allied authorities were suspicious of what had happened. Questions would have to be asked, responsibility fixed, blame cast, for rumors were beginning to spread.

The first reaction after word got out was disbelief. Impossible, people said, that a man like Wolfgang Lüth, who had survived the war untouched, could die so suddenly and in such a way. After the disbelief came the suspicion; if it *were* true, then it could not have been an accident. Some regarded the incident as a suicide. Several senior officers had already accepted this as the only honorable response to surrender. Others speculated about a premeditated killing by die-hard Kriegsmarine personnel or the British. Rumor followed rumor, each more fantastic than the last.

The *Flensburger Nachrichten* ran a typical report: "A Hero Is Shot from Behind: The Mysterious Death of Kapitän Lüth — Accident or Murder?" It was filed within hours of the shooting, before all of the facts had been released, and the reporter was driven to speculations that border on the ludicrous. "The possibility that a contract was put out on the Kapitän cannot be ruled out," he stated in all seriousness.[2] The story cited inconsistencies in the initial reports of the shooting — differences in time, weather, distance. Confusion after such an event is always to be expected, but the reporter would not allow the suggestion of foul play to rest.[3]

The hastily convened board of enquiry had to investigate all of the possibilities, however extraordinary they seemed. Was it a conspiracy? A simple murder? A suicide?

The board's findings were based on the interrogation of Matthias Gottlob, the only man who was at the scene. The enquiry was as much an investigation of him as it was of the shooting. Gottlob was questioned at the Sportschule twice that morning, first alone, by Dönitz, then by the board. His answers were consistent.

The probable sequence of events narrated here follows Gottlob's account, the recollections of others in the vicinity, fairly reliable published sources, and supplementary information from various government agencies. Even so, it must remain an educated guess. Nobody was standing next to Lüth on the Black Path that night.[4]

Meteorological data is unavailable from the Flensburg weather station for May 1945, but data from the Danish stations at Sonderborg, to the east of Flensburg, and Tonder, to the west, indicate that a cold front passed over the Jutland Peninsula during the night of 13 May. High winds and intermittent showers accompanied the front.

In spite of the inclement weather, Dönitz's provisional government conducted business at headquarters until late Sunday evening, 13 May. Lüth remained at the Sportschule until 0015, when he left for his own quarters. The commandant's house where he was staying lay inside the perimeter. To reenter, Lüth would have to cross through one of his own guard posts.

Between the Sportschule and the main Marinekriegsschule complex was a small wooded area. There in May 1945, according to Peter Cremer, "there were nightly shootings, short bursts from a machine gun, and hand grenades were occasionally thrown—every kind of dangerous mischief was practiced."[5] It was exactly this kind of mischief that had forced Lüth to issue the order to challenge once and then shoot. Lüth was fully aware of the procedures to be followed in approaching a sentry post. It should have been no surprise when, after emerging from the wood at the northeast corner of the perimeter, he was challenged.

Gottlob testified that he heard footsteps and saw someone; he did not know who it was. He said that he challenged Lüth three times. Lüth was exhausted, and he had a lot on his mind. Perhaps he never heard the challenge, or perhaps it never "registered." But Lüth was trained to notice small things and to pay attention to warning signals. He must have heard his sentry's voice, for he stopped.

Lüth would ordinarily have replied with the correct password. His reply may have been drowned out by the wind in the trees or the rain on the pavement, or Gottlob, nervous as he was, may not have heard what Lüth said. Whatever the reason, his failure to make himself known to Gottlob doomed Lüth. After the third challenge, made in violation of Lüth's own orders for a single challenge, Gottlob fired one shot from the hip. He said he had meant to fire into the air.

Had Lüth heard Gottlob and purposefully failed to reply? This would clearly have been suicide. It seems unlikely, and not only because there were better ways to kill yourself. Lüth had a wife and four young children whom he loved deeply. Could he have left them to an uncertain fate? Nobody who knew him thought him capable of such an act. Moreover, few men in Germany had emerged from the war in such an enviable position: He had survived; he was young; he was a genuine hero, highly decorated and well placed; and apparently, he was not on anyone's list for prosecution as a war criminal. He had every reason to live, none to die. The theory of suicide was rejected.

It was clearly a tragic accident. There was nobody to blame. Dönitz assured Matthias Gottlob that he had only done his duty. Absolved, dismissed, the boy left headquarters for awful obscurity.

Three weeks after Hitler's death, and just eight days after the end of the war, on Wednesday, 16 May, Wolfgang Lüth was given a Nazi burial. He would have enjoyed his own funeral. The ceremony was orthodox, a ritual of the Third Reich in each and every detail, from the swastika on his casket to the guns over his grave, and it was properly executed. Allied authorities had granted Dönitz special permission. This was unusual, in view of their simultaneous efforts to erase every vestige of the Nazi regime. It might be worth noting that permission was not granted until the board handed its report over. Conceivably, whoever made the decision based it on whether or not Lüth died by his own hand.

On the morning of the sixteenth, Lüth's casket lay in the dark and hushed memorial hall of the Marinekriegsschule. A Reich battle ensign covered him. Six U-Bootwaffe officers, each wearing the Knight's Cross, guarded him. "Wolfgang Lüth, we now take leave of you," said Dönitz in his eulogy. "It is not mine to describe your family's loss; we, your comrades, have lost a great warrior, a true and noble friend, and I a beloved member of the old guard of my U-Bootwaffe, to which my entire heart once belonged and belongs still. . . ."[6]

Lüth's death was hard on Dönitz. He knew as he spoke that here, at last, was the end of the life he had known for over forty years. His deeds were now being weighed in the balance. As for Germany, he knew not what to expect other than shame and hardship. "Wolfgang Lüth, you will provide the coming generations of Germany—in spite of hard and bitter times today—a brilliant example to follow. You will never be forgotten; rather you will live forever in our hearts."[7]

The funeral procession left the Marinekriegsschule at 1000 under leaden skies. The caisson carrying Lüth's casket was preceded by a cushion laid with his decorations: the Spanish Cross, the Italian War Cross, the Knight's Cross. The officers who had earlier guarded the casket now marched beside it.* Behind the caisson walked a somber Dönitz, his staff, many of the senior Wehrmacht officers stationed in the Flensburg area, Ilse Lüth and her family, and a straggle of civilians. The cortege passed through the south courtyard of the Marinekriegsschule between rows of gray-uniformed German soldiers. It filed into the Kelmstrasse via the main gate, and finally to a little cemetery in the churchyard at Adelby. There Wolfgang Lüth was buried with full honors and three volleys from a squad of German riflemen.

"In retrospect," wrote Peter Cremer, "it can be said that with this last great display the Reich and the Navy were sym-

---

*Nobody seems to know who they were. Ernst Bauer was definitely one of the six. He cannot recall who the other five were, but he thinks that one of them might have been Waldemar Mehl (letter to the author, 16 March 1987). Peter Cremer, Heinrich Liebe, Günther Kühnke, Georg Lassen, and Hans Witt, all Knight's Cross holders, are also likely to have been there.

The funeral procession for Wolfgang Lüth, shot to death by his own sentry two days before. The six officers of the honor guard are barely visible beside the casket, but Karl Dönitz can be seen behind it, and Ilse Lüth follows him.

bolically carried to the grave."[8] In the epilogue to his memoirs, Karl Dönitz referred to Lüth as a symbol of the Kriegsmarine and, by implication, of Germany itself.

> On 14 May 1945, a few days after our surrender had brought the war to an end, Captain Wolfgang Lüth, one of the most successful of our U-boat captains and one of only two men in the Navy to be awarded the highest honor for valor, the Knight's Cross of the Iron Cross with Oak Leaves, Swords, and Diamonds, lost his life as the result of a tragic accident in Mürwik. Those of us naval officers who were in Flensburg took leave of him as he lay in his coffin in the courtyard of the Naval College. It was a symbolic act.
>
> In the precincts of this historic place, in which the cadets of the Imperial Navy and the navies of the Reich, who since 1919 had been trained in Mürwik, had paraded under their instructors on so many solemn occasions, we paid our last tribute, at the end of a war and on the threshold of an uncertain and sinister future, not to Lüth alone, but also the Navy we had all loved so well.[9]

To know Lüth you must know his men, and to end his story it is necessary to end theirs.

Of the crews of U-9 and U-138 there is little trace. Lüth commanded them for too short a time and too early in the war. They transferred to other boats; many were lost, the rest were scattered by the fortunes of war. Many of the crew of U-43, some Lüth's former men, went down with her in 1943.

Lüth's radioman in two boats, Herbert Krutschkowski, was present at the funeral of his captain. By a strange twist of fate, his last assignment in the Kriegsmarine was as a midshipman in Mürwik. Gottfried König was also in northern Germany, having scuttled his last boat in the Kiel estuary. Kruse and König were two of the few lucky ones at home in Germany when the war ended in May 1945.

Kurt Freiwald had come out from "behind a green desk" at BdU to relieve Lüth in U-181. Freiwald was a good man, but he was no Wolfgang Lüth, and he suffered for it in whispered comparisons: "Lüth would have done this," "Lüth would not have done that," "He can't handle her as well as Lüth," and so on and so on, week after week.[10] He had the boat for one patrol, a luckless undertaking that ended in capture and exile for him and his crew. Josef Dick described it:

> In March of 1944 we left Bordeaux and in August we arrived in Penang. Later we went to Singapore for dry-dock in order to remove the bottles of mercury from the keel. Perhaps you have heard that the boats bound for Southeast Asia carried mercury in steel flasks for the Japanese. After Singapore we went to Batavia [Jakarta] on Java. In mid-October we left for home but two men had to be left behind because of sickness. In four of our tanks we carried rubber instead of fuel. In the torpedo tubes there were boxes of opium (we had only two torpedoes) and under the deckplates were boxes of valuable ore and other things. The boat was very low in the water.
>
> We had to turn back south of Capetown because of a leak in the diesel tanks; 30 cbm of fuel were lost and there was no longer enough to get home. We went back into the Singapore yards in mid-January and while we were there the war ended for us. The boats were turned over to the Japanese. We were

glad to be free of them, even though half of each crew had to stay on board. The others were taken with trucks by the Japanese to Batu-Baha, which was about 80 miles north of Singapore in Malaysia [probably *Batu Pahat*, on the southwest coast of the Malay Peninsula]. But when the Japanese had to surrender we were brought back to Singapore and given to the English as 'surrendered personal.'

With the English we gutted the two boats and they were later scuttled about sixty miles outside Singapore; we were not there at the time. We then worked for a while at the British base at Selatar and on board British ships. In July 1946 we were brought back to England and arrived in Liverpool. We were to have been shipped from Hull to Bremerhaven, but the ship had already departed and we were told we would have to stay in camps until the next one.[11]

The Japanese refitted U-181 and gave her a new designation, I-501. But in August Japan surrendered, and in February 1946 the boat was scuttled in the South China Sea. Under the Rising Sun, she had never fired a shot in anger.

The ship for which Josef Dick and his fellow crew members would have to wait did not leave Great Britain for two years. They were interned for the rest of their stay, "just like the Nazis or the SS," complained Josef Grobelny.[12] Walter Schmidt was sent to the Lake District, where he went to work on the farm of a local MP. Dick was shuttled from Derbyshire to Newtown, on to Rhyl, in Wales, then to Shrewsbury, and finally to St. Edwards near Harwich.

Lothar Engel was more fortunate, perhaps. He left U-181 with Lüth and became medical officer for the Sixth U-Flotilla in St. Nazaire. There he became known for his extensive collection of American jazz records. At the time of the Normandy invasions he was working in the hospital at La Baule, and when the war ended he became a prisoner of the French. With that, Engel's luck ended. His stay in French camps was miserable, a cause of bitterness for the rest of his life.

Theodor Petersen, who left U-181 in January 1943, eventually commanded two of his own boats, U-612 and U-874. The only luck he had was to live. He surrendered U-874 in Londonderry at the end of the war, whereupon he and his entire crew were interned. He ended up in Northumberland with Kurt Freiwald.

Petersen was more circumspect about his fate than Grobelny. He even saw an element of beauty in his depressing surroundings:

> POW-Camp 18 was in Northumberland on the Tyne somewhere between Newcastle and Carlisle. In the vicinity of our camp was a beautiful little castle called Featherstone Park, where the Royal Family was supposed to have spent some time during the war. The nearest large town and railway station was Haltwhistle, also very pretty on the way to Newcastle. I can still see the huts in the camp, and the barbed wire, which at first kept us captive, but which we were finally allowed to take down ourselves. . . . It was beautiful along the Tyne, with wild strawberries and rhododendron, and there were deer in the river sometimes.[13]

The war was not over for some of these men until 1948, three years after arriving in England. Josef Dick remembered the day he turned up on his parents' doorstep, Saturday, 3 July. It was not the doorstep of his memory; his parents had been bombed out of their house three times.[14] It was not the same world either. In 1948, the western Allies had agreed to form an independent Germany, the Soviet Union had blockaded Berlin, and the Berlin Airlift was under way.

By 1948, the war was in the past. What of the future?

Wolfgang Lüth and Theodor Petersen had once discussed the future. Maybe they were in the tower of Lüth's huge U-cruiser on a muggy night. "You know," Lüth said, "after Germany wins the war I think I would like to become a district magistrate in one of the new eastern provinces. . . ."[15] It was a wish for a restful life; a magistrate was nothing more than a country squire. It was also an impossible one, of course. If Wolfgang Lüth had lived, if he had passed through the rigorous denazification process, more likely he would have waited until the new *Bundesmarine,* the navy of the Federal Republic of Germany, was formed and rejoined.

Many of his wartime peers did just that—Otto Kretschmer and Erich Topp, for example. Kretschmer eventually rose to the rank of Flottillenadmiral, Topp to Konteradmiral, and both men held NATO flag positions before retiring. Theodor Petersen joined the Bundesmarine and eventually retired as a Fregattenkapitän to live in Kiel with his wife, Consuela, and collect stamps. In one of many letters to the author, he sent the certificate given him when U-181 crossed the equator in 1942. "You may keep it," he wrote. "I have no use for it and my sons want nothing to do with these things."[16]

Herbert Krutschkowski changed his name to Kruse after the war. He settled in Frankfurt, where he worked in a local bank until his retirement. Walter Schmidt moved to Bad Camberg, not far from Frankfurt, where he remained active in the dwindling community of ex-U-boat sailors. Lothar Engel went to Cologne after being released from prison in 1948, then to Lippstadt in Westphalia, where he opened a practice in homeopathic medicine and lived with his wife, also a doctor, and their two daughters until his death. Josef Dick became an engineer for the railway, a *Lok-Führer* like his father before him. He retired in Cologne in 1980.

Heinz Schulz went to live in Marne, a suburb of Hamburg. Upon retiring after thirty years as a production supervisor in a factory, he became an expert of some renown on the preparation of herring. Gottfried König became a headmaster. Otto Giese moved to Florida.

The war broke the spirit of Franz Persch, the Poisoned Dwarf. When it began, he wrote, "we were proud of our Germany . . . we were prepared to die for her. . . ." And now? "I am an old man, over seventy years. I draw my pension, I have a nice house at the edge of the woods, my wife and I enjoy watching the rabbits play at the garden gate and the deer in the fields. And Germany, the divided Germany? The foreigners and the strange soldiers? My pride for this country has gone forever."[17]

In 1984 Kruse and Schmidt organized a reunion in Bad Camberg for the men of U-181. About forty of them came to renew old friendships and reminisce about U-181 and her captain. Some of these men hadn't met since 1945. "Recognizing one another wasn't easy," said Kruse mournfully. "Time changes everything"[18] — a fact painfully emphasized when they watched the old wartime newsreels of U-181 returning to Bordeaux in 1943. Taped from the West German television program "Forty Years Later," it featured among other things the banquet, the bearded crewmen being shaven by the base barber, and Lüth receiving his Diamonds from Hitler. The reunion was such a success that it turned into a regular affair.

Donald Crawford, the only survivor the author could locate from any of the ships Wolfgang Lüth sank, became a businessman in Staffordshire, England. He retained great respect for Lüth and his crew and believed that Lüth saved his life by radioing the *Clan Macarthur*'s last position to Mauritius.

After the war ended, the Marinekriegsschule became a hospital and then a school for teachers. In 1956 the first postwar class of officer candidates moved in, and by 1959 the entire compound, again called the Marineschule-Mürwik, was placed under *Bundesmarine* control. In 1985 the Marineschule published a brochure to commemorate its seventy-fifth anniversary; it began with the document signed by Wilhelm II in 1910 to open the school and ended with a description of the latest addition to its many facilities: a computerized bridge simulator built by Krupp Atlas and put to use in late 1986.

Elsewhere on the Marineschule grounds is the Wolfgang Lüth memorial. It stands, or rather lies, along the old Black Path under a large oak tree and only a few yards from where Matthias Gottlob shot Wolfgang Lüth to death. It is a rock — rough, unfinished, discolored, a large boulder taken from the side of the Mürwik-Glucksburg Autostrasse. In an unpublished monograph written when he himself was commandant of the Marineschule, Karl Peter tells how he and his wife found the boulder in 1957 and had it hauled by a construction company into town, where a local stonemason inscribed it at cost.[19]

It was dedicated on Memorial Day, 17 November 1957, in the presence of Ilse Lüth, her family, friends, Lüth's fellow officers, and the midshipmen of the Bundesmarine. Both Otto Schuhart, the man who sank HMS *Courageous* in 1939, and the new commandant, Flotillenadmiral von Wangenheim, spoke in brief, elegant terms at the dedication. Schuhart addressed the question of why Lüth had to die as he did, under friendly fire, after surviving a murderous undersea war against incredible odds. It was an insoluble puzzle of nature. "We human beings are always trying to find sense in that which is incomprehensible to us," he said. "There is no answer in this case. Perhaps the real meaning of [Lüth's] death here should be this: that it is our duty, those of us left behind, to remember even more all of those whom this great war took from us."[20]

He finished by asking a question of his own, a question, he told the gathering, that the stone itself would ask over and over again: Lüth is dead, and many like him; dare you now live for others as nobly, as fully, as unselfishly as those who died for you?

And here the story of Wolfgang Lüth ends. Not in death or defeat, but in remembrance and hope for the future. For whether it is appropriate to ask this question about a man such as Lüth (many readers will think it is not), Otto Schuhart challenged others to live as Lüth should have lived — as he lived in the minds of his family, his friends, his men, as he lived at his very best.

NOTES

Introduction

1. Introduction to Heinz Schaeffer, *U-Boat 977* (New York: W. W. Norton, 1952).
2. Richard Compton-Hall, *The Undersea War, 1939–45* (Poole, Dorset: Blandford Press, 1982), 12.

Chapter One

1. Sources for this account of the sinking of the French sailing ship *Notre Dame du Chatelet* in May 1941 were Wolfgang Lüth and Claus Korth, *Boot Greift Wieder An* (Berlin: Erich Klinghammer, 1944), the deck log of U-43, and the recollections of U-43's crew.
2. Wolfgang Lüth, curriculum vitae accompanying application for membership in the *Reichsschrifttumskammer* (Reich Authors Guild), 22 June 1942.

3. Vera Lüth, telephone interview, October 1986; supporting information courtesy of Franz Hahn, former director, WGAZ, Marineschule-Mürwik.
4. Theodor Petersen, interview, 24 July 1984.
5. Jürgen Oesten, letter to author, 10 April 1987.
6. Vera Lüth, interview.
7. Lohmann, "Die Ausbildung des Marineoffiziers" ("The Training of a Naval Officer"), WGAZ inventory no. 14718, Marineschule-Mürwik, 1942, 22.
8. Ibid., 29.
9. Ernst Bauer, letter to author, 15 April 1987.
10. Bodo Herzog, *Ritter der Tiefe/Graue Wölfe* (Knights of the Deep/Gray Wolves) (Munich: Verlag Welsermühl, 1976), 278.
11. Karl Dönitz, cited in Douglas Botting, *The U-Boats* (New York: Time-Life, 1976), 69.

Chapter Two

1. Otto Weddigen, cited in Charles Horne, ed., *The Great Events of the Great War* (New York: National Alumni, 1923), 296.
2. Sources for this account of Weddigen's action were *The War on the Sea,* Harper's Pictorial Library of the World War, vol. 4 (New York: Harper, 1920), and Botting, *The U-Boats,* 20.
3. Petersen, letter to author, 16 January 1987.
4. Lüth, *Boot Greift Wieder An,* 22.
5. Peter Padfield, *Dönitz: The Last Führer* (New York: Harper and Row, 1984), 181.
6. Lüth, *Boot Greift Wieder An,* 29.
7. The best source for tonnage figures is Jürgen Rohwer, *Axis Submarine Successes* (Annapolis: Naval Institute Press, 1983).
8. Wolfgang Lüth, "Menschenführung auf einem Unterseeboot" ("Problems of Leadership on a Submarine"), lecture given 17 December 1943 in Weimar, Germany. Translated by the Office of Naval Intelligence, Navy Department, Washington, D.C., document no. 11746, 1947.

Chapter Three

1. Edwin Hoyt, *The Sea Wolves* (New York: Avon, 1987), photograph opposite page 91.
2. Karl Dönitz, *Ten Years and Twenty Days* (New York: World, 1959).
3. Padfield, *Dönitz.*
4. Dönitz, *Ten Years,* 79.

5. Ibid., 89.
6. Petersen, interview.
7. Lüth, *Boot Greift Wieder An,* 147.
8. Heinz Schaeffer, *U-Boat 977* (New York: W. W. Norton, 1952), 72.
9. Herbert Werner, *Iron Coffins* (New York: Holt, Rinehart and Winston, 1969), 247. Passages from Werner are used advisedly; at least two reviewers were unimpressed with his interpretation of the facts.
10. Lothar-Gunther Buchheim, *The Boat* (New York: Knopf, 1975), 169.
11. Peter Cremer, *U-Boat Commander* (Annapolis: Naval Institute Press, 1984), 157.
12. Wolfgang Frank, *The Sea Wolves* (New York: Holt, Rinehart and Winston, 1955), 50.

Chapter Four

1. Petersen, letter to author, 12 December 1983.
2. Petersen, interview.
3. The paragraphs dealing with operations by U-138 in the period 21–22 September 1940 were constructed using accounts in *Boot Greift Wieder An,* the deck logs of U-138, and the records of the British Admiralty, 1940–41, Public Records Office, ADM 199.
4. "Second Officer's Report on Sinking of *New Sevilla,*" 27 September 1940, PRO, ADM 199/23.
5. "*New Sevilla*"; "Report of Attack on Convoy OB 216," commanding officer, HMS *Arabis,* 27 September 1940, PRO, ADM 199/23; "Report of Proceeding, HMS *Vanquisher,*" 26 September 1940, PRO, ADM 199/23.
6. "Report of Flag Officer in Charge, Belfast," 24 September 1940, PRO, ADM 199/142.
7. "Report of Attack [*Arabis*]."
8. "Flag Officer in Charge, Belfast."
9. Ibid.
10. Petersen, interview.
11. Lüth, *Boot Greift Wieder An,* 254.
12. Dönitz, *Ten Years,* 108.
13. Petersen, letter to author, 7 October 1986.
14. Donald McIntyre, *U-Boat Killer* (Annapolis: Naval Institute Press, 1976), 41.
15. Ibid.
16. Otto Kretschmer, letter to author, 15 October 1986.

17. The paragraphs dealing with operations by U-138 in the period 14–15 October 1940 were constructed using accounts in *Boot Greift Wieder An*, the deck logs of U-137 and U-138, and Admiralty record ADM 199/141.
18. "Particulars of Attack on Merchant Vessels by Enemy Submarines (*Bonheur*)," undated, PRO, ADM 199/141.
19. Lüth, *Boot Greift Wieder An*, 254.

Chapter Five

1. Karl Alman, *Ritter der Sieben Meere* (Knights of the Seven Seas) (Rastatt: Erich Papel, 1963), photograph opposite page 193.
2. Cremer, *U-Boat Commander*, 83.
3. Petersen, letter to author, 3 March 1987.
4. Lothar Engel, interview, 21 December 1983.
5. Petersen, letter to author, 3 March 1987.
6. Walter Pfeiffer, letter to author, 18 May 1984.
7. Ibid.
8. Engel, interview.
9. Lüth, *Boot Greift Wieder An*, 255.
10. Ibid., 256.
11. "Analysis of Attacks by U-boats on HMS *Forfar* and Convoys HX 90 and OB 251," 27 January 1941, PRO, ADM 199/1489.
12. Lüth, *Boot Greift Wieder An*, 260.
13. Petersen, letter to author, 7 October 1986.
14. Ibid.
15. Petersen, letter to author, 12 December 1983.
16. Ibid., 10 April 1986.
17. Ibid., 12 December 1983.

Chapter Six

1. Petersen, letter to author, 12 December 1983, and interview.
2. Ibid.
3. Ibid.
4. Ibid.
5. Jürgen Rohwer, letter to Paul Wilderson, Naval Institute Press, 15 January 1990.
6. Dönitz, *Ten Years*, 190.
7. Nicholas Monsarrat, *The Cruel Sea* (New York: Knopf, 1959), 130.
8. Petersen, letter to author, 4 March 1987.
9. Dönitz, *Ten Years*, 168.

11. Lüth, "Problems."
12. Ibid.
13. Harald Busch, *U-Boats at War* (New York: Ballantine, 1982), 160.
14. Engel, interview.
15. Petersen, letter to author, 20 March 1988.
16. Engel, interview.
17. Kruse, interview.

Chapter Nine

1. Kruse, interview.
2. Turner, *The Southern Oceans,* 197. This account of the November 1942 attack on U-181 was constructed using Turner, the deck log of U-181, and the recollections of her crew.
3. Kruse, interview.
4. Josef Grobelny, letter to author, 15 March 1984.
5. Engel, interview.
6. Lüth, "Problems."
7. Ibid.
8. Buchheim, *The Boat,* 143. Buchheim is perhaps better on style than substance. Said a publisher in Germany when asked for Buchheim's address, "I can only warn you about Herr Buchheim! The man is not well thought of in U-boat circles! He considers himself the sole purveyor of the truth and he likes to advertise it. He tends to oversimplify the facts to match his own experiences and his politically colored viewpoints. I do not consider him a suitable correspondent for historians. Anyway, I do not know his address."
9. Padfield, *Dönitz,* 146.
10. Turner, *The Southern Oceans,* 198.
11. "Lüth could speak English," wrote Lothar Engel. "All naval officers could speak English. We all had to learn it at the Gymnasium, and it was a required subject at the Marineschule" (letter to author, undated). "As far as I know," wrote Theodor Petersen, "Lüth could not speak English. He attended a Gymnasium in Riga where Greek and Latin were taught, and Latvian as well . . . [but] when there was an opportunity to speak English he would call on me" (letter to author, 29 April 1986).
12. Cited in Richard Compton-Hall, *The Undersea War,* 51.
13. Petersen, letter to author, 20 March 1988.
14. Turner, *The Southern Oceans,* 198.

15. John M. Waters, *Bloody Winter* (Annapolis: Naval Institute Press, 1984).
16. Lüth, "Problems."

Chapter Ten

1. Schmidt, interview.
2. Information about the city of Bordeaux was provided by several members of U-181's crew. The author has not verified the existence of any particular establishment listed.
3. Cited in Stanislaw Mikolajczyk, *The Rape of Poland* (New York: McGraw Hill, 1948), 15.
4. Engel, interview.
5. Petersen, letter to author, 31 March 1987.
6. U-181's newspaper.
7. Engel, interview.
8. Ibid.
9. Persch, letter to author, 2 December 1985.
10. Ibid.
11. Engel, interview.
12. U-181's newspaper.
13. Ibid.
14. Schmidt, interview.
15. Donald McIntyre quoting Captain Roskill's official history in *The Naval War Against Hitler* (New York: Scribner's, 1971), 317.
16. Ibid., 329.
17. Dönitz, cited in Turner, *The Southern Oceans,* 239.
18. Kenneth Poolman, *The Sea Hunters* (London: Arms and Armour, 1982), 96.

Chapter Eleven

1. Dick, interview, 19 December 1983.
2. Persch, letter to author, 22 January 1986.
3. Ibid.
4. Ibid.
5. Engel, interview.
6. Lüth, "Problems."
7. Turner, *The Southern Oceans,* 228.
8. Donald Crawford. Mr. Crawford gave the author a thorough account of the *Clan Macarthur*'s sinking in a letter dated 16 February 1984. He also provided a copy of a letter he had written on

4 May 1982 to Charles Guillois, president, Association Amicale des Forces Navales Françaises Libres, in which he described the days he and his shipmates spent in the water after the sinking. Both letters are used extensively with Mr. Crawford's permission.

9. Ibid.
10. Ibid.
11. Ibid.
12. Ibid.
13. Ibid.
14. Ibid.
15. Ibid.
16. Turner, *The Southern Oceans*, 236.
17. Jochen Brennecke, *Haie in Paradies: Der Deutschen U-Boot Krieg in Asien Gewässern, 1943–1945* (Sharks in Paradise: the German U-Boat War in Asian Waters, 1943–1945) (Herford, West Germany: Koehlers, 1967), 127–28.
18. Engel, letter to author, 19 September 1983.
19. Schmidt, interview.

Chapter Twelve

1. Newspapers used include the *Geraer Zeitung*, the *Ludenscheider General-Anzeiger*, the *Deutsche Allgemeine Zeitung*, and the *Bremer Nachrichten*.
2. Schmidt, interview; Otto Giese, letter to author, 13 January 1985.
3. *Deutsche Allgemeine Zeitung*, 2 November 1943.
4. Harry Pross, ed., *Querschnitt durch "Das Reich"* (Selections from "Das Reich") (Munich: Hans Dieter Muller, 1964), 170.
5. Ibid.
6. Herbert Sprang, "Lüth und Seine Unteroffiziere!" ("Lüth and His Petty Officers!") *Signal*(?), (1943). (The article was given to the author in the form of a poorly made photocopy, which lacked page headings and dates.)
7. This clipping is unidentified and undated. It is probably from a local Neustadt newspaper.
8. Giese, letter to author, 13 January 1985.
9. Ibid.
10. Petersen, interview.
11. Ibid.
12. Werner, 247.
13. Gottfried König, letter to author, 18 May 1985.
14. Petersen, letter to author, 12 December 1983.

15. Karl Peter, letter to author, 4 August 1982.
16. Vera Lüth, letter to author, 12 April 1987.
17. Karl Peter, *Acht Glas: Ende der Wache* (Eight Bells: End of the Watch) (Stuttgart: Preussischer Militär-Verlag, 1988), 158.
18. Ibid.
19. Jean Noli, *The Admiral's Wolfpack* (New York: Doubleday, 1974), 382.
20. Ibid.
21. Peter, "Kapitän zur See Wolfgang Lüth," manuscript, 1971, 2.
22. Ibid.
23. Ibid.

Chapter Thirteen

1. These paragraphs were written using descriptive information from Hans Herlin, "Verdammter Atlantik" ("Damned Atlantic"), *Stern* (13 December 1958): 50. The article is about events in Flensburg and northern Germany in the last weeks of the war. Lüth's death is given special treatment. It has been written in narrative form and some parts are probably speculative, but there is no reason to doubt its overall accuracy.
2. *Flensburger Nachrichten,* 14 May 1945.
3. Ibid.
4. Valuable information for this account of Wolfgang Lüth's fatal shooting was provided by the Marineschule-Mürwik, the City of Flensburg, and the Danish Meteorological Office.
5. Cremer, *U-Boat Commander,* 475.
6. Dönitz, "Bei der Trauerfeier für Kapitän zur See Wolfgang Lüth" ("At the Memorial Service for Captain Wolfgang Lüth"), eulogy delivered 16 May 1945 at the Marineschule-Mürwik.
7. Ibid.
8. Cremer, *U-Boat Commander,* 475.
9. Dönitz, *Ten Years,* 475.
10. Brennecke, *Haie in Paradies,* 132.
11. Dick, letter to author, 24 September 1983.
12. Grobelny, letter to author, 6 February 1984.
13. Petersen, letter to author, 29 April 1986.
14. Dick, letter to author, 24 September 1983.
15. Petersen, letter to author, 2 December 1986.
16. Ibid., letter to author, 1 March 1984.
17. Persch, letter to author, 26 February 1986.
18. Kruse, letter to author, undated (September 1984).

19. Peter, "Lüth," 2.
20. Otto Schuhart, "Wörter am Gedenkstein" ("Words at the Memorial"), remarks made at the dedication of the Wolfgang Lüth Memorial, Marineschule-Mürwik, 17 November 1957.

BIBLIOGRAPHY

Published Sources

Alman, Karl. *Ritter der Sieben Meer* (Knights of the Seven Seas). Berlin: Erich Papel Verlag, 1963.

Botting, Douglas, *The U-Boats.* New York: Time-Life, 1979.

Brennecke, Jochen. *Haie in Paradies: der Deutschen U-Boot Krieg in Asien Gewässern, 1943–1945* (Sharks in Paradise: The German U-Boat War in Asian Waters). Herford, West Germany: Koehlers Verlag, 1967.

Buchheim, Lothar-Günther. *The Boat.* New York: Knopf, 1975. Reprint. New York: Bantam, 1982.

Busch, Harald. *U-Boats at War.* New York: Ballantine, 1982.

Chesneau, Roger, ed. *Conway's All the World's Fighting Ships, 1922–1946.* New York: Mayflower, 1980.

Churchill, Winston S. *The World Crisis,* vol. 1. New York: Scribner's, 1951.

Compton-Hall, Richard. *The Undersea War, 1939–1945.* Poole, Dorset; Blandford, 1982.

Cremer, Peter. *U-Boat Commander.* Annapolis: Naval Institute Press, 1984. Reprint. New York: Jove, 1986.

Dönitz, Karl. *Ten Years and Twenty Days.* New York: World, 1959.

Frank, Wolfgang. *The Sea Wolves.* New York: Holt, Rinehart and Winston, 1955. Reprint. New York: Ballantine, 1981.

Gasaway, E. B. *Grey Wolf, Grey Sea.* New York: Ballantine, 1970.

Gordon, Arthur. "The Day the *Astral* Vanished." U.S. Naval Institute Proceedings (October 1965): 76–83.

Herlin, Hans. "Verdammter Atlantik" ("Damned Atlantic"). *Stern* (13 December 1958): 50–57. (Article is continued in following issue.)

Herzog, Bodo, and Schomaekers, Gunter. *Ritter der Tiefe/Graue Wölfe* (Knights of the Deep/Grey Wolves). Munich: Verlag Welsermuhl, 1976.

Horne, Charles F., ed. *The Great Events of the Great War.* New York: National Alumni, 1923.

Hoyt, Edwin. *The Sea Wolves.* New York: Avon, 1987.

———. *U-Boats: A Pictorial History.* New York: McGraw-Hill, 1987.

Kennedy, Ludovic. *Pursuit.* New York: Viking, 1974.

Lüth, Wolfgang, and Korth, Claus. *Boot Greift Wieder An: Ritterkreuzträger Erzählen* (Boat Will Attack Again: Tales of the Knight's Cross). Berlin: Erich Klinghammer Verlag, 1944.

McIntyre, Donald. *The Naval War Against Hitler.* New York: Scribner's, 1971.

———. *U-Boat Killer.* Annapolis: Naval Institute Press, 1976.

Mikolajczyk, Stanislaw. *The Rape of Poland.* New York: McGraw Hill, 1948.

Monsarrat, Nicholas. *The Cruel Sea.* New York: Knopf, 1959.

Noli, Jean. *The Admiral's Wolfpack.* New York: Doubleday, 1974.

Oliver, Edward F. "Overdue—Presumed Lost." U.S. Naval Institute *Proceedings* (March 1961): 98–105.

Padfield, Peter. *Dönitz, the Last Führer.* New York: Harper and Row, 1984.

Peter, Karl. *Acht Glas: Ende der Wache (Erinnerungen eines Seeoffiziers der Crew 38)* (Eight Bells: End of the Watch [Remembrances of a Naval Officer of Crew 38]). Stuttgart: Preussischer Militar-Verlag, 1988.

Poolman, Kenneth. *The Sea Hunters: Escort Carriers v. U-Boats, 1941–1945.* London: Arms and Armour, 1982.

Pross, Harry, ed. *Querschnitt durch "Das Reich"* (Selections from "Das Reich"). Munich: Hans Dieter Muller, 1964.

Rohwer, Jürgen. *Axis Submarine Successes, 1939–1945.* Annapolis: Naval Institute Press, 1983.

Rössler, Eberhard. *The U-Boat: The Evolution and Technical History of German Submarines.* Annapolis: Naval Institute Press, 1981.

Schaeffer, Heinz. *U-Boat 977.* New York: W. W. Norton, 1952. Reprint. New York: Bantam, 1982.

Sprang, Herbert. "Lüth und Seine Unteroffiziere!" ("Luth and His Petty Officers.") *Signal* (?) (1943).

Turner, L. C. F., et al. *War in the Southern Oceans.* Cape Town: Oxford University Press, 1961.

The War on the Sea. Harper's Pictorial Library of the World War, vol. 4. New York: Harper and Bros., 1920.

Waters, John M., Jr. *Bloody Winter.* Princeton: Van Nostrand, 1967. Revised edition. Annapolis: Naval Institute Press, 1984.

Werner, Herbert. *Iron Coffins.* New York: Holt, Rinehart and Winston, 1975.

Unpublished Sources

Berlin. Berlin Document Center. Application of Wolfgang Lüth for membership in the *Reichsschrifttumskammer* (Reich Authors Guild), June 1942.

Bordzeitung (newspaper) of U-181, 1942–43.

"Crew-Rede bei der Trauerfeier für Kapitän z.S. Wolfg. Lüth" ("Address on Behalf of the Crew at the Memorial Service for Captain Wolfgang Lüth"). Eulogy delivered 16 May 1945 at the Marinekriegsschule-Mürwik.

Dönitz, Karl. "Bei der Trauerfeier für Kapitän zur See Wolfgang Lüth" ("At the Memorial Service for Captain Wolfgang Lüth"). Eulogy delivered 16 May 1945 at the Marinekriegsschule-Mürwik.

Lohmann, Vizeadmiral. "Die Ausbildung des Marineoffiziers" ("The Training of a Naval Officer"). WGAZ inventory no. 14718. Flensburg: Marineschule-Mürwik, 1942.

London. Public Records Office. Admiralty Records. ADM 199.

Lüth, Wolfgang. "Menschenführung auf einem Unterseeboot" ("Problems of Leadership on a Submarine"). Lecture presented

17 December 1943 in Weimar. Trans. Office of Naval Intelligence, Navy Department, Doc. no. 11746, 1947.

Peter, Karl. "Kapitän zur See Wolfgang Lüth." Flensburg: Marineschule-Mürwik, 1971.

Schuhart, Otto. Remarks during the dedication of the Wolfgang Lüth Memorial at the Marineschule-Mürwik, 17 November 1957.

Washington. National Archives. German Naval Records of World War Two. Microfilm Publication T-1022. "War Diaries of U-9, U-138, U-43 and U-181." Files PG 30006, 30128, 30040, 30168.

Correspondence and Interviews

Personal Interviews
Vera Lüth, Palo Alto, California, March 1984.
Donald Crawford, Stafford, United Kingdom, October 1986.
Josef Dick, Cologne, Federal Republic of Germany (FRG), December 1983.
Lothar Engel, Lippstadt i.W., FRG, December 1983.
Herbert Kruse, Frankfurt/Maintal, FRG, December 1983.
Theodor Petersen, Kiel, FRG, July 1984.
Walter Schmidt, Bad Camberg, FRG, December 1983.

Correspondence between July 1982 and October 1989
Ernst Bauer, Jürgen Bialuch, Gus Britton, Donald Crawford, Josef Dick, Lothar Engel, Otto Giese, James Goldrick, Josef Grobelny, Franz Hahn, Franz Hawran, Bodo Herzog, Karl Kaiser, Gottfried König, Otto Kretschmer, Herbert Kruse, Johannes Limbach, Vera Lüth, Ilse Lüth, Burkard von Müllenheim-Rechberg, Jürgen Osten, Franz Persch, Karl Peter, Theodor Petersen, Walter Pfeiffer, Jürgen Rohwer, Eberhard Schmidt, Walter Schmidt, Heinz Schulz, Jack Sweetman, Erich Topp.

INDEX

The **Naval Institute Press** is the book-publishing arm of the U.S. Naval Institute, a private, nonprofit, membership society for sea service professionals and others who share an interest in naval and maritime affairs. Established in 1873 at the U.S. Naval Academy in Annapolis, Maryland, where its offices remain today, the Naval Institute has members worldwide.

Members of the Naval Institute support the education programs of the society and receive the influential monthly magazine *Proceedings* and discounts on fine nautical prints and on ship and aircraft photos. They also have access to the transcripts of the Institute's Oral History Program and get discounted admission to any of the Institute-sponsored seminars offered around the country.

The Naval Institute also publishes *Naval History* magazine. This colorful bimonthly is filled with entertaining and thought-provoking articles, first-person reminiscences, and dramatic art and photography. Members receive a discount on Naval History subscriptions.

The Naval Institute's book-publishing program, begun in 1898 with basic guides to naval practices, has broadened its scope to include books of more general interest. Now the Naval Institute Press publishes about one hundred titles each year, ranging from how-to books on boating and navigation to battle histories, biographies, ship and aircraft guides, and novels. Institute members receive significant discounts on the Press's more than eight hundred books in print.

Full-time students are eligible for special half-price membership rates. Life memberships are also available.

For a free catalog describing Naval Institute Press books currently available, and for further information about subscribing to *Naval History* magazine or about joining the U.S. Naval Institute, please write to:

Membership Department
U.S. Naval Institute
291 Wood Road
Annapolis, MD 21402-5034
Telephone: (800) 233-8764
Fax: (410) 269-7940
Web address: www.navalinstitute.org